THE CRAFT OF DIPLOMACY

ALSO BY DOUGLAS BUSK:

The Delectable Mountain, 1946

The Fountain of the Sun, 1957

The Curse of Tongues, 1965

DOUGLAS BUSK

THE CRAFT OF

DIPLOMACY

Mechanics and Development of
National Representation Overseas

PALL MALL PRESS

LONDON

Published by the Pall Mall Press Ltd.
77-79 Charlotte Street, London, W1

© *Sir Douglas Busk 1967*

FIRST PUBLISHED 1967

MADE AND PRINTED IN GREAT BRITAIN BY
THE GARDEN CITY PRESS LIMITED
LETCHWORTH, HERTFORDSHIRE

DEDICATION

This book is dedicated to erstwhile senior colleagues in Her Britannic Majesty's Diplomatic Service, and in particular to the memory of Moley Sargent.

They were not only honoured in their own country; in many continents they earned personal affection and deep respect for their integrity, steadfastness and the humour with which they lightened the burden. They will be remembered as much for their wise and patient guidance of those privileged to serve with them.

May others lead as they once led.

O.G.S. R.G.V. P.B.N. J.B. R.H.H.
H.K.H. G.G.K. W.H.C. H.S.B.

ACKNOWLEDGEMENTS

This book could never have been attempted, let alone completed, without the generous support of many past and present members of Her Majesty's Diplomatic Service, for which I am most grateful. In particular, the Administration and Personnel Departments of the Service have been unsparing in help, as has been the Foreign Office Library. At their request, I have not mentioned the names of individuals, but I must make an exception for Mr K. M. Thomas of the Library, who in the last two years has written scores of letters dealing with abstruse points.

I am indebted to friends in other government departments—particularly in the Commonwealth Relations and Colonial Offices, Armed Services, Ministry of Labour, Overseas Development Ministry, British Council and British National Export Council—who have supplied many of the facts and figures; but they bear no responsibility for the interpretation I put on them or for the general ideas I have felt entitled to express. For these I have relied much on my own notes, collected over many years, but collated only after retirement.

For France, I am grateful to the Administration Department at the Quai d'Orsay. Diplomatic colleagues of other nationalities have also helped. For the United States, my first thanks must go to a friend of forty years' standing, J. E. Johnson (now President of the Carnegie Endowment), who furnished much essential material, particularly the *Foreign Affairs Personnel Studies* (FAPS), and to John Harr, a specialist in diplomatic administration, who gave invaluable advice on American practices. I am also grateful to Messrs Charles Thayer and Ellis Briggs for permission to quote so largely from their books. To Senator Henry M. Jackson (editor of *The Secretary of State and the Ambassador*) and to Vincent M. Barnett, Jr (editor of *The Representation of the United States Abroad*) all students of the practice of diplomacy are indebted; without their research and wise counsel my own book would have been sadly incomplete.

The Controller of Her Majesty's Stationery Office authorized quotations from the report of the Plowden Committee, as did the Clarendon Press for Heatley's standard work, and Professor Max Beloff, Sir William Hayter and Mr D. C. Watt for their essays. To them also I owe a debt.

D.B.

CONTENTS

NOTE ON WORKS CITED

A list of the more important works quoted, and valuable for further reading, will be found in the Select Bibliography. In order to shorten references to sources in the text, I generally refer to these only by abbreviations, e.g., Plowden, DSR, TWFM, FAPS, etc. Full titles and details of date, publisher and year of publication are set out in the Select Bibliography.

Some publications of lesser importance, not mentioned in the Select Bibliography, are fully described at their first noting in the References.

FOREWORD

THOUGH IT can be tedious for those who wish to plunge straight into the subject without climbing through a hedge of prefatory verbiage, it is desirable to set out what this book is *not* about, because there is still, despite the efforts of writers in many tongues, considerable confusion about 'diplomacy'.

'Diplomacy' is often used to cover the foreign policy of countries great and small. In fact policy is not diplomacy. Policy is decided by the governments of states, and no diplomat has much say in it; yet he may try to influence the views of the policy-makers—in Downing Street, the White House, the Palais Schaumburg or with greater trepidation in Colombey and down-right risk in the Kremlin. The first thing, then, that this book is *not* about is the foreign policy of the United Kingdom or of any other state.

This brings us to the second popular usage of the word diplomacy: conducting relations with foreign powers on the basis of a policy decided at high level in the home country; keeping your headquarters properly informed of events and negotiating in accordance with instructions received from them. This is a fair definition of the art—for it is fair to use this term—of putting yourself up against other people often of different culture in a strange environment and trying by entirely peaceful means to influence their thinking, to live in comity with them and to reach agreement in matters often highly abstruse and fraught with prejudice or preconception.

The art of diplomacy is, however, another thing this book is

ix

really not about. It is true that it is nigh impossible to write of diplomacy at all without dealing with the art. Indeed, I have in many places alluded to it, but my main purpose has been different.

Let us take examples from other spheres. Most of us have flown, but few have any idea how a jet engine works. There are many admirable books on naval warfare. It is possible to study the events leading to Trafalgar or Midway and the course of the battles. The strategy and tactics are clearly set out and illustrated with charts and pictures. The number and weight of guns are described and notes given about the leading officers on both sides. In most readers, however, and perhaps in some historians, there subsists a more or less complete ignorance of the mechanics. To many of us a barnacle is indistinguishable from a binnacle. That need not prevent us from comprehending in general terms how the battles were fought and why.

So it is with diplomacy. There are books on international relations and on the art of Ambassadors and Foreign Ministers, but what makes Embassies tick? How are the machines put together? This can be called the craft of diplomacy. It is not to be rated as high as the art—clearly an efficient Embassy can be as crippled by an incompetent Ambassador as a superb army by a poor general. Nevertheless, the craft and the mechanics *are* important, because without an adequate machine even the wisest Ambassador is sore put to it, and without well-trained troops even the best general can only contrive. To switch the metaphor: the pianist must have his instrument before he can make music; what he does with it is up to him, but if it is badly tuned the result is excruciating even under the most skilled fingers.

The instruments, the Diplomatic Services of numerous countries, are composed of human beings who, if they are to give their best, must be encouraged and trusted. John Stuart Mill once wrote: 'A State which dwarfs its men that they may be more docile instruments in its hands even for beneficial purposes will find that with small men no great things can really be accomplished.' It is of men and women that I write and of the machinery they handle so devotedly.

Others, in many lands, worry about this problem. As only one example I will quote Barnett:

> One of the vital problems facing American policy makers, and crying for comprehension by the American public, is the conduct of our overseas public business. . . . Especially the need to evolve methods for assuring long-range continuity and consistency in that policy. . . . There can be no more important problem than that of how to organize these farflung activities. It is immediately clear that the role of the expert in overseas representation is becoming more and more important.[1]

A comparative study of diplomatic methods and mechanics as employed by the Services of other countries merits exploration in depth. I hope the reader will be content with allusions here and there to the practices of other nations. He will assuredly understand that detailed comparison is rendered difficult by the very wide variation in the overseas representation of other countries.

The last thing this book is *not* about is the organization of the Foreign Office,[2] Commonwealth Relations Office,* or other government departments, such as the new Overseas Development Ministry, closely connected with foreign affairs. The picture presented is thus incomplete. Missions and Consulates are the servants of their headquarters, reflecting abroad the instructions they receive from home, but to have included the London organization would have doubled the size of this book. Moreover, while the newly integrated Service overseas is settling down, a state of flux prevails in Whitehall.

At intervals in the past the craft of diplomacy has been described, often by authors admirably equipped for their task, to whom I have referred *passim*; but organizations and methods change. For instance, when Nicolson wrote before the Second World War

---

* Since its absorption of the Colonial Office in August 1966, the joint Department is to be called the 'Commonwealth Office'. Throughout this book I have adhered to the older nomenclatures.

there were in the British Service no Information Sections and no Diplomatic Wireless; no United Nations existed and there were far fewer independent countries. The craft, as he described it, is therefore out of date, but the art remains the same. Human beings do not change essentially, though they adapt themselves with praiseworthy flexibility to new conditions. It seems also an appropriate moment, after the adoption of the report of the Plowden Committee, to set out again something of the mechanics of diplomacy overseas. No better introduction can be found than in the Plowden Report §§ 7–36 and 167–77, and these precepts are basic throughout the world.

About once every twenty years, owing to wars or domestic failure to realize the magnitude of its task, the British Diplomatic Service almost grinds to a halt. Such a point had been reached by 1962; the Service was saved by the Plowden recommendations. This new charter was at once insidiously eroded, in a fashion all too familiar, by unpublished directives that rendered the task of constructive planners infinitely more difficult. Further inroads may be expected in a period of persistent financial difficulty; nevertheless, full advantage has been taken of the Plowden Report.

The United States Foreign Service has been subject to more frequent convulsion. Mosher in his introduction to FAPS 3 comments: 'In fact since World War II, transition seems to have become a permanent condition in the conduct and the administration of foreign affairs. Transition can breed unsettlement; it often obscures or raises disagreement about goals, directions and values.'[3] Briggs as usual does not mince words: 'Foreign Affairs would prosper if the 1960s could become known as the decade in which the American Foreign Service was *not* reorganized.'[4] It would be fairer to say that the United States Foreign Service has been subject to much examination by outsiders, not all of whose recommendations are approved in the Service; that there has been relative lack of interest on the part of Congress, which leads to failure to implement essential reforms—in marked contrast with the rapid acceptance of the Plowden Report by Parliament; and that now a consensus is emerging that changes should be gradual and based on closer co-operation among politicians, other outsiders and diplomats.

There can often be a disastrous gap between the responsibilities of a country and its professional competence. This is one of the worries about the Soviet Union and Red China. The Westerner simply does not know whether their men on the spot have the courage to report honestly and, if they do, whether their reports are heeded. Even in the West there are qualms. Policies dictated, apparently often without consultation with professionals best equipped to warn and advise, inspire no confidence. When it comes to Asiatic and African governments, there is little basis on which the ordinary person can judge how they reach a decision. All this uncertainty is worsened when allies are closely involved, yet kept in ignorance or consulted only secretively behind the backs of the (often) efficient and highly qualified professionals—military, diplomatic or other—whose counsel should at least be sought. To by-pass or ignore such advice, in any field of human activity, is dangerous and can be fatal.

I hope none will conclude, because I had the honour to be a member of HBM Diplomatic Service, that I am maintaining that it is the only Service in the world. All who have worked abroad are acutely aware of deficiencies; all have noted with admiration the competence of other nations. In particular some of the smaller countries not only have devised efficient machinery, but may well claim to receive from their headquarters instructions on policy at once clearer and more consistent than those issued to British and American Embassies. There is, however, one common denominator, a regret in all Diplomatic Services that their tasks and difficulties are not fully understood in the home country either by the public, by the press or by those in power. Bearing in mind Voltaire's *l'art d'ennuyer c'est de tout dire* I have tried to be brief. What follows can only be a compendium of the craft and mechanics of diplomacy.

If this book removes a few misconceptions, I shall be content; if it helps those in developing countries who face the problems of establishing their own Services, I shall feel that the labour was more than worthwhile. I have written primarily, but not entirely, of *one* Diplomatic Service, but the mechanics are of general application to all.

I

A DICTIONARY WITH DIGRESSIONS

EVERY CRAFT has its own jargon, its technical phrases, and diplomacy is no exception. Before we can begin to understand its machinery we must have in mind the names and meaning of the various cogs and wheels. Both Satow, at length, and Nicolson, more concisely, give glossaries of diplomatic terms. These cover, however, rather the practice of diplomacy than the mechanics; moreover they are in some respects out of date. In what follows I deal very briefly and at some risk of oversimplification with the terms more often used in the diplomatic life of today. Amplification is often given in the main body of the book, particularly of the terms and abbreviations most frequent in American practice.

The word diplomacy is comparatively modern in English—not to be found, for instance, in Dr Johnson's dictionary. It derives from the Greek word *diploma*, a document 'twice folded'. Diplomacy is defined in the Concise Oxford Dictionary as 'the management of or skill in managing international relations'. So far so good, but dictionaries are apt to continue that 'diplomatic' means 'uncandid', 'deceitful'. The compilers thus fall into the trap set for them by a Provost of Eton who had served James I as a secret agent and later as Ambassador. With his tongue in his cheek, Sir Henry Wotton once described an Ambassador as 'an honest man who is sent to lie abroad for the good of his country'. This pejorative description has endured, because few realized 'the hinge upon which the conceit was to turn'. ('Lie abroad' meant 'sojourn in foreign parts', often on a very hard bed.) But Sir Henry's 'merriment', as he termed it to his royal master in self-defence, has left an ineradicable atmosphere of duplicity about diplomats, to which he himself contributes, for his remark was originally written in Latin, which does not permit the play in words. The joke recoiled on him and there is no publicity for his later advice, given after much experience, that 'an Ambassador to be service-able to his country should always speak the truth'. The much maligned Machiavelli wrote excellent instructions for Ambassa-dors, which can profitably be read today.[1]

The influence of diplomacy is frequently over-rated. 'Its morals can never be markedly superior to those of the governments whose tool it is . . . the great bulk of criticism ostensibly aimed at "diplomacy" turns out, when analysed, to relate to particular foreign policies for which the diplomatist, who did not devise them, cannot reasonably be blamed.'[2]

The first word in our dictionary is therefore DIPLOMATIST or DIPLOMAT. The latter was for long held to be a solecism by many authorities, but in his splendid revision of Fowler's *Modern English Usage* Sir Ernest Gowers has written: 'The shorter forma-tion, standard in U.S., is increasingly used in Britain.' *The Times* (London) holds out obstinately against the times, and there may be others with this particular foible—it was a 'basilisk word', as H. L. Mencken would have called it, to Nicolson—but the *New York Times* accepts diplomat.

Diplomats of all ranks form the DIPLOMATIC CORPS in a foreign capital. It is not only impolite to pronounce these words 'diplomatic corpse', but wrong, for it is remarkably lively. The head of it is called the DOYEN, or, if you wish to be very English, the DEAN OF THE DIPLOMATIC BODY. In most predomi-nantly Catholic countries the representative of the Holy See, usually a NUNCIO, is *ex-officio* the Doyen. Elsewhere, in London or Washington for instance, the Doyen is the Ambassador who has served longest at that particular post. The Doyen has a dual character. He is at one and the same time the diplomatic representative of the state by which he is accredited and in whose name he speaks on matters affecting that state's national interests; and he is also the acknowledged leader and spokesman of all the diplomatic representatives at the capital where he resides on matters of common interest. He may thus speak for all in matters concerned with diplomatic privileges; he may arrange hospitality in the name of the Corps to prominent local personages; he may even find himself under the necessity of protesting to the local government about some outrage that has been inflicted on an Embassy or member of its staff—speaking in the name not only of that Embassy, but as a mark of solidarity on behalf of the whole Corps.

The Corps is composed of MISSIONS, more fully called DIPLOMATIC MISSIONS. These consist of EMBASSIES, LEGATIONS and HIGH COMMISSIONS. The latter designation is applied to the diplomatic representatives exchanged between the countries of the British Commonwealth. For example, there is a Canadian High Commissioner in London, but a Canadian Ambassador in Washington, and the same man might well be transferred from one post to the other. Relations with Commonwealth countries (and, by exception, with Ireland) are dealt with by the Commonwealth Relations Office, not the Foreign Office. Other countries—for instance France—have High Commissioners, but these are important administrative officers, not diplomats accredited to foreign powers.

The earliest Ambassadors were on special missions and not permanently resident in foreign capitals. Queen Elizabeth II and other Heads of States still send representatives with the temporary rank of Ambassador to represent them at the coronation of a monarch or the inauguration of a new president. Such a Special Ambassador will take precedence over the resident Ambassador. The first Ambassadors permanently resident in foreign capitals were probably those exchanged by Italian states in the fifteenth century. 'The status of these early Ambassadors was high', writes

Ashton-Gwatkin, 'but their reputation was low because they were regarded as liars and spies'.[3] Efforts were made to prevent the local inhabitants from consorting with them, and in Turkey they were even held *incomunicado*—a practice Communist countries endeavour to continue today.

Career Diplomatic SERVICES were only established in the nineteenth century. In the early days of the Republic, American diplomacy was of accepted brilliance; there followed a long period of isolation, rendered possible by the *Pax Britannica;* and later the emergence at the turn of the last century of the United States as a world power. Awareness of diplomatic needs arose and the United States Foreign Service can be said to date from the Rogers Act of 1924.[4] Many smaller countries can still hardly be said to have proper Diplomatic Services. Indeed it is not unusual for persons embarrassing to the regime to be despatched abroad in order to get rid of them. *The Times* of January 8, 1966 reported that a Latin American president had in one day nominated to the Embassies of his country: the minister of the Armed Forces, the commander-in-chief of the Air Force, ditto Army, and the leader of a political party. The *Sunday Times* next day said that in all thirty-four prominent personalities had thus been assigned to diplomatic posts abroad. Such radical solutions are no doubt beneficial at home, but they show little regard for the efficiency of Missions overseas.

During the last half century a great change has taken place, not only in the total number of Missions (there are now far many more independent countries), but in the composition of the Diplomatic Corps. Between 1822 and 1870 the number of foreign Embassies in London varied from two to six. In 1914 there were nine (representing Austro-Hungary, Italy, France, Germany, Japan, Russia, Turkey, Spain and the United States), and forty-seven Legations. In eleven of the latter countries, the United Kingdom was represented by a Chargé d'Affaires, Consul-General or Minister Resident (a grade that has now disappeared from the diplomatic vocabulary). It seems odd today that it was only in 1893 that the Legations in London and Washington were raised to Embassies. This was the first United States Embassy any-where; previously all had been Legations.

Following the First World War, it was recognized that the qualities displayed by Belgium as an outstanding ally had earned the tribute of the conduct of diplomatic relations at Embassy level, and Ambassadors were accordingly exchanged between London and Brussels in 1919. A similar recognition of close ties of friendship, commercial interest and so forth led to a like result with other countries, so that the number of Embassies in London had risen at the outbreak of the Second World War to sixteen. The general trend (termed by some 'diplomatic inflation') was greatly accelerated after 1945 under the pressure of national aspirations and other factors, such as recognition of the sovereign equality of states in the United Nations Charter. Thus, at present, diplomatic representation throughout the world at any other than ambassadorial level has become the exception rather than the rule. It follows that the designation of Minister, as applied to a Head of Mission, though still recognized, is approaching extinc-tion.

Such depreciation of the ambassadorial currency, once so rare and highly prized, was deplored by the traditionally minded among the older states. The trend was long resisted in London, but eventually Downing Street found it impossible to withstand a movement of world-wide momentum. The American govern-ment, under the influence of Sumner Welles, ran amok in raising Legations to Embassies, despite protests from the Foreign Service. When Ellis Briggs was appointed American Ambassador to Santo Domingo, Dean Acheson (later Secretary of State) asked pointedly how he liked being a 'Shambassador'. Switzerland was the last bastion of the old tradition to fall, and it was not until 1957 that that country's constitutional inhibitions against the appointment of Ambassadors abroad were finally overcome and Ambassadors were exchanged.

As a result of the general yearning for promotion, the number of Embassies in London rose in the years 1939–66 from sixteen to ninety-six, and the United Kingdom now maintains only one

Legation abroad, in the Vatican. Other countries have gone through the same tribulations and been forced to much the same conclusions. (The history of United States diplomatic representation is well set out by Thayer.[5]) There are also twenty-five British High Commissions in Commonwealth territories. Thus in 1966 Britain was represented in 118 independent countries, compared with fifty-six in 1914. There is an apparent discrepancy between the former figure and the membership of the United Nations, 122. This organization does not, however, include China (mainland), Germany or Switzerland; but it does include White Russia and the Ukraine as states separate from Russia (Moscow). Furthermore, at any given moment there may be countries that have broken off diplomatic relations with Britain— Egypt, Guatemala and Guinea are some examples at the time of writing.

In addition the United Kingdom, like other member states, maintains at the New York headquarters of the United Nations a permanent representative with the rank of Ambassador, assisted by a numerous staff. There are other such permanent Delegations: at the United Nations Geneva Office, to NATO, OECD, EEC, Council of Europe, Disarmament Conference and EFTA. The Political Resident in the Persian Gulf, stationed at Bahrein, is also of ambassadorial rank. In yet other international organizations, such as SEATO and CENTO, Britain is represented at lower level on the permanent secretariats.

In all cases but one, British representation is reciprocal, the exception being the Holy See. Though the United Kingdom maintains a Legation in the Vatican, the Pope has no diplomatic representative in Britain. The 'Apostolic Delegate for Great Britain, Gibraltar and Bermuda', based on London, has no claim to diplomatic status or privileges, though he receives unofficial courtesies. This anomaly has a historical basis. The attempts to invade England by continental powers from the reign of Elizabeth I induced a distrust of Papists. This is still nurtured today, particularly by Nonconformists in Britain, and, until recently, received back-handed support from the Vatican. At the coronations of King George VI and of the present Queen, Papal delegations were not allowed by Rome to enter the Abbey and were accommodated in a special tribune opposite the west door. Wiser counsels now prevail. The Cardinal Archbishop of Westminster and the Apostolic Delegate both attended the funeral in St Paul's Cathedral of Sir Winston Churchill, at which 113 countries were represented (exceptions were China and Mongolia).

The United States is also not represented at the Vatican, nor is a Papal representative received in Washington. For a brief period President Franklin Roosevelt was able to appoint a 'Personal Representative', who was accorded ambassadorial status by the Holy See. Perhaps now that the United States has had its first Catholic President and there is greater liberalism in Rome, there may be some rethinking. Some non-Catholic countries, such as India, accord full diplomatic status to the Papal representative, but by agreement he does not move up the file of Ambassadors, so he can never become Doyen. He is then called a PRO-NUNCIO, i.e. he is of Nuncio (ambassadorial) rank but without insistence from the Vatican that he must be the Dean of the Ambassadors. The junior rank of INTERNUNCIO corresponds with that of Minister.

The head of an Embassy is an AMBASSADOR, of a Legation a MINISTER and of a High Commission a HIGH COMMISSIONER. The officer who acts for either of the first two in his absence is entitled CHARGÉ D'AFFAIRES whatever his rank. Strictly speaking, the words *ad interim* ('for the time being') should be added, but rarely are, save in the most official documents. The officer who acts for a High Commissioner is an ACTING HIGH COMMISSIONER. It can also happen that a country is more or less permanently represented in a foreign capital by a Chargé d'Affaires. This indicates that relations between the two states are not held to be sufficiently cordial to justify the exchange of Heads of Missions. Chargé d'Affaires of this kind are not *ad interim* and are accredited to governments and not to Heads of States. At the moment there is a British Chargé d'Affaires in Pekin. In this case it is the Chinese government that refuses to exchange Ambassadors. They describe their relations with Britain as 'semi-diplomatic' and have a similar arrangement with the Dutch.

In general little purpose is served by withdrawing an Ambassador and substituting a Chargé d'Affaires in an important country; it merely makes it more difficult to exert influence.

The Ambassador's name is submitted to the Head of State of the country to which it is intended to post him. This approval bears the technical name AGRÉMENT—another of the French terms that have passed into English. It is happily rare that agrément is refused for a British Ambassador, but one case caused acute personal embarrassment to the officer in charge of the Embassy at the time, through whom the request passed. The Foreign Office was outraged at a refusal and the Chargé d'Affaires was instructed to protest vigorously; the foreign government stood its ground, however. There have also been cases where a foreign potentate has refused an agrément for an Ambassador on the ground that he had served in the country before under a different regime. An agrément is only required for a Head of Mission. Members of his staff are appointed without reference to the foreign government. It would, however, be possible for a government to object if they learned that a shady character had been selected for service in their country.

The agrément having been granted, the appointment is publicly announced. Grave embarrassment can be caused if there is an earlier leakage. The ambassadorial nominee is now free to receive the congratulations and commiserations of his friends. He will also be plunged into briefing by experts and contact with innumerable organizations interested in the country to which he has been accredited. In Britain he and his wife, before departure to his new post, will have the honour of being received by the Sovereign at a ceremony dignified by the ancient title 'Kissing Hands'. Heads of States of other countries do not always receive Ambassadors privately before they take up their appointments; the Sovereigns of England wish to make or renew acquaintance with the more senior of their representatives abroad. This occasion is most stimulating because of the penetrating interest of the Monarch. In the United States an Ambassador's appointment is not finalized until he has been approved by the Senate. This can be a more rigorous interview.

Soon after arrival at his new post, the Ambassador hands to the Minister for Foreign Affairs a copy of his LETTER OF CREDENCE. This is a message from one Head of State to another introducing an Ambassador. An audience having been arranged, the Ambassador presents the original to the Head of State personally, together with the LETTER OF RECALL of his predecessor, which states that he has been transferred to other duties.

The procedure in the case of Consular Officers is different, except that their friends are equally astounded by the idea of their departing to places untraceable in the family atlas. No formal approval for the appointment of a Consul is sought; he is merely notified to the foreign government, which, on presentation of his Royal Commission, gives its EXEQUATUR (meaning in Latin 'let him perform') entitling him to carry out his duties. Theoretically the foreign government could refuse in the case of a notorious ne'er-do-well, but British Consuls do not include such individuals among their number.

Missions are called in British parlance 'Her Majesty's' or 'Her Britannic Majesty's Embassy', and the Ambassador is entitled to the same initials HM or HBM, because, in addition to the normal Royal Commission issued to all officers in the Service, he holds a special one from the Queen appointing him the Crown's representative in the particular country. A Chargé d'Affaires may *not* use these initials; he is the 'British Chargé d'Affaires' because he represents, not the Queen, but his government. Ambassadors and Ministers, but no one else in the Diplomatic Corps, are styled 'Excellency', or in Spanish, 'Most Excellent'—*Excelentísimo*. This 'foolish title', as Nicolson calls it, is also accorded in British usage to Governors General of Dominions and Governors of Colonies. In French, German and some other tongues the word is

9

feminine, which can cause linguistic confusion. Its justification is the convenient abbreviation 'HE' used when referring to these personalities, the collective noun for whom is 'a stick'. (This derives from the wartime airmen's practice of dropping 'a stick of HE', meaning a dollop of high explosive bombs, on those they disliked.) In the United States an Ambassador (among other notabilities) is styled 'the Honorable'. In France a retired Ambassador retains his title and is always addressed as *'Monsieur l'Ambassadeur'*.

Strictly speaking, a British Ambassador's wife should not be called 'Her Excellency'. The correct form of address is 'His Excellency the British Ambassador and Lady X', not 'Their Excellencies the British Ambassador and Lady X'. In Viceregal days in Delhi the protocol was extremely strict. After a formal dinner, when the Vicereine swept out with the ladies, leaving the gentlemen to their port, she curtseyed to her husband, followed by the others—unless they were unversed in the prodigious formality of the British Raj, in which case they were no doubt blacklisted. Now it is often the practice to refer to an Ambassador's wife as 'Her Excellency', and certainly no junior officer is wise to jib at this until he has studied the local form. At one British Embassy, the Ambassador's wife was remarkably tiresome and always insisted that any entertainment given in the compound should be described as 'By courtesy of Their Excellencies . . .'. She was perhaps not unreasonably infuriated when one day, owing to a most unfortunate typing error, it was announced in the Embassy bulletin that by excellence of Their Courtesies a tennis tournament would be held. The staff was very apologetic. In contrast, at least one lady in the British Service insists that she only be referred to as 'the wife of the Ambassador'. This modesty may well become a standard practice in English, but not in French, where *'Madame l'Ambassadrice'* is of more ancient standing than our 'Ambassadress'.

☆

Diplomatic jargon has retained many French turns of phrase and terms derived from the period up to 1914, when French was the 'diplomatic' language, having taken in civilized usage the place of Latin as a *lingua franca*. In the eighteenth and nineteenth centuries much correspondence between Ministries for Foreign Affairs and their own Ambassadors was conducted in French rather than in the native tongue, which was often regarded as plebeian. In Tsarist Russia, for instance, it may be doubted whether such statesmen as Pozzo di Borgo (a Corsican), Capo d'Istria (a Greek) or Nesselrode (a German) spoke Russian with accuracy. English is now taking over as a secondary or auxiliary language throughout the world. This tongue, in all its forms, is fortunately very flexible and absorptive; it does not shudder when faced with acquisitions. Chargé d'Affaires is one example used in English, though some countries retain their own versions, e.g. the Spanish *Encargado de Negocios,* the German *Geschäftsträger* or the Italian *Incaricato d'Affari.* The Russian *Poverennyi b Delakh* is the oddest in literal translation; it means 'lawyer in affairs'.

The best debunking of the overprevalent habit of using French phrases was once made to me by a sardonic British Embassy clerk. Referring to a rather feeble line that the Ambassador was instructed by the Foreign Office to follow, he remarked: 'It is what diplomats call a *pis aller.*' Quite deliberately he pronounced it 'piss alley'—not a bad name for that particular policy.

On the first of January 1801, the British Sovereign renounced the title of 'King of France', having belatedly realized that, even in the absence of a French King, he was unlikely to make good his ancient claim. It was decreed that thenceforth all communications to foreign governments should be in English. In fact, for the sake of convenience and efficiency, British Embassies continued to use French to people who understood it better than English. Until the Second World War many British Embassies even held a cypher in French, so that they could telegraph confidentially the actual text of a communication from the local Ministry for Foreign Affairs and thus avoid any possible misunderstanding about translation.

In lesser known languages it was a helpful custom to write in

English, but attach an 'unofficial translation' into, say, Arabic, Persian or Chinese, so that there was no delay in comprehension at the Ministry for Foreign Affairs. Reza Shah once tried to insist that the Ambassador sign the Persian rather than the English version, but this demand was firmly resisted. Today all official communications from British Embassies to foreign governments are written in English. The local language may, however, often be used for semi-official or routine matters. In the Foreign Office itself communications in French are treated as if in English. If written in other languages, the translators may be called on and delay ensues. The French, German, Russian, Spanish, Portuguese and some Latin American Embassies usually write in their own tongues and the Portuguese and Brazilians add unofficial English translations. If the Pope has cause to address an official letter to the Queen, he does so in Latin, but even this does not fox the Foreign Office translators.

☆

In the British Diplomatic Service the ranks succeeding Ambassador are MINISTER (either the Head of Mission at the sole Legation in the Vatican, in which case he is 'HM Minister', or the No. 2 of a big Embassy, in which case he is 'the British Minister'). The COUNSELLOR is No. 2 at a medium-sized Mission. In the United States the word is spelled Counselor. In France they have *Conseiller*, in Germany *Botschaftsrat*, in Italy *Consigliere*, in Spain *Consejero* and in the Soviet Union, hardly surprisingly, *Sovietnik*.

There follow the FIRST SECRETARY, No. 2 at a small Mission; the SECOND SECRETARY, No. 2 at the smallest Missions; and the THIRD SECRETARY. Such officers, Consuls and others over a certain grade will be granted Royal Commissions on appointment. In British usage they often bear in brackets after their rank an indication of their special functions, e.g. 'Minister (Commercial)', 'Counsellor (Information)', 'First Secretary (Administration)'.

After the Second World War, the rank 'Attaché' faded out for career members of the British Diplomatic Service, though it was retained for specialist officers attached or seconded to Embassies (see below page 20, and also chapter III, page 121). In foreign Services diplomatic Attachés are frequent. The rank 'JUNIOR ATTACHÉ' has now been created in the British Service to cover some officers junior to Third Secretaries.

Officers holding these ranks form the 'diplomatic staff' of a Mission and their names will be included in the Diplomatic List compiled by the authorities of the state in which they reside. Individually they are termed 'diplomatic agents' and they qualify for privileged treatment in the matter of exemption from taxation, immunity from the jurisdiction of the local courts and inviolability of person and residence, prescribed in the Vienna Convention on Diplomatic Relations. This Convention—a codification of the law and practice relating to the conduct of diplomatic relations generally—was drawn up in 1961 by an international conference held under United Nations auspices and attended by the representatives of eighty-one states.[6] Fifty-four states have become parties to it and have thus undertaken to abide by the rules contained in it. The United Kingdom ratified the Convention in September 1964, following the passage through Parliament of the Diplomatic Privileges Act giving the force of law to those provisions of the Convention which have a direct bearing on the domestic law of the United Kingdom. The Soviet Union has also ratified, but the United States has not yet done so, difficulties of legislation in the various states of the Union doubtless being the reason. The later Vienna Consular Convention of 1963, though signed by the United Kingdom and United States, was not ratified by them; the Soviet Union did not even sign it.

Exemption from local taxation is not such a boon as the innocent might suppose. Diplomats of organized countries, such as Britain and the United States, pay full taxes as if resident in their own countries. From a purely personal point of view they might (if they had the choice, which they do not) opt for exemption from these—which are high and rigorously exacted—in favour of paying taxation on the same basis as the locals; which often means in practice not at all.

The history and practice of DIPLOMATIC IMMUNITY is fascinating. By far the most readable exposition is in Thayer.[7] The immunity of the diplomatic agent from the jurisdiction of local courts ensures that legal process, civil or criminal, may not be instituted against him (except in accordance with the provisions of the Vienna Convention) unless his Ambassador, acting on instructions from his government, waives his diplomatic immunity. One can, however, think of many countries in which it would not be wise to rely too heavily on the niceties of international comity in regard to such matters as detention or assault. Should the Ambassador refuse to surrender the officer, the only remedy open to the host government is to declare the offender *persona non grata* and insist on his immediate departure.

Immunity extends to the residence and office of a Mission. This raises the curious right of asylum, which is not dealt with in the Vienna Convention. The local police (or violent mobs) may not, or at any rate should not, penetrate diplomatic premises and anyone may therefore seek refuge. In Arabia until very recently, escaping slaves would flee to British Consuls or Agents, who manumitted them and saw that they were safely conveyed out of the country. No doubt an Ambassador would hand over a common criminal, but—particularly in Latin American countries— 'failed politicians' (i.e. those ejected by a revolution, or those who have failed in an attempt to eject the group in power) frequently seek asylum, with their wives, children and innumerable followers. By Latin American custom this is never refused and a small Embassy may find itself encumbered with several hundred unwelcome guests for months, while negotiations proceed for permission for them to leave the country under safe conduct. Countries outside the American continent do not formally recognize this *automatic* right of asylum. Mercifully, therefore, fugitives rarely hurl themselves on British Ambassadors. Cases have been known, but the runaway can usually be eased out tactfully by the discreet back door, with which any good Embassy is provided, before the police arrive and camp in front. One United States Embassy has been saddled with a Cardinal 'asylee' for no less than ten years, and one's heart bleeds for all concerned.

It is probable that the British Embassy in Persia will always hold the record for asylum. In 1906 agitation for a constitution against the then Shah reached boiling point. It did not occur to the Persians to stage a bloody revolution; they wished, however, to register a protest. By Persian custom this could be done by taking refuge in a mosque, a foreign Embassy or in the Shah's stables. The origin of this was the desire to grasp the tail of the Shah's horse, thus arresting his progress and giving time for the presentation of a petition. (In Ethiopia a petitioner will still run beside the car or horse of a great man and beat his head with a stone, carried in his hand, in order to show that, if the VIP would only stop, the claimant would bump his forehead on the earth in sign of humility.) The British Embassy compound in Tehran is commodious, and at least 12,000 Persians entered and camped there. They were fed from outside by their relatives, but fortunately they left after three weeks before the problem of sanitation had become insuperable. *The Times* reported in its issue of September 10, 1906, that remarkable discipline and order had been maintained by the refugees, who did little or no damage. The Persian word for this right of asylum is *bast*, deriving from a verb meaning to tie. In the same way, medieval petitioners clasped the knees of the mighty; militant suffragettes, though far from seeking asylum, used to chain themselves to railings in England before the First World War, and later fellow-travelling enthusiasts handcuffed themselves to the door handles of the American Embassy in London. Diplomats still have much to endure, but the *bast-i-buzurg*, the great asylum of Tehran, is not likely to be surpassed.

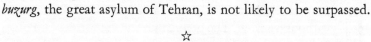

A government may demand the withdrawal of a foreign Ambassador for political and not personal reasons, i.e. because of displeasure with the policy of his government. The Mission then remains in the hands of a Chargé d'Affaires. This is not such an extreme step as the BREAKING OFF or RUPTURE OF DIPLOMATIC RELATIONS, which normally involves the departure of the entire Missions from both capitals, though sometimes only the Ambassador or High Commissioner and some others are forced to leave. If the whole Mission is withdrawn, some friendly government is asked to take over Baratarian interests in Ruritania, while another or the same one does the like for Ruritanian interests in Barataria. Even then, Consular Officers without diplomatic status may be allowed to remain, or they too may have to be withdrawn. Such a complete severance of relations will require tortuous and delicate manoeuvres when the time comes to reknit them. Meanwhile years may pass and the welfare of contiguous areas be affected.* The unexpectedness of such decisions is at the least inconvenient and can be heart-breaking to the personnel involved. How, in twenty-four hours or even in one week, can you settle your affairs? How safeguard the treasured belongings you must leave behind? How find a home for your child's pet animal? How sell the car you borrowed money to buy? Such personnel problems loom darkly behind the headlines announcing a rupture of relations. When ultimately they are resumed the previous Ambassador, in British practice, very rarely returns to that post.

One must hope that the diplomat will seldom have to deliver or receive a declaration of war, since this signifies the negation of all his efforts. A declaration of war can be made by country A through its Ambassador in country B, or to the Ambassador of B in country A, or more usually both.

I once had the experience of being thrust inadequately into this limelight. When the Japanese attacked the Western allies in 1941, they did so—as against the Chinese in 1899 and the Russians in 1904—without warning. The population and authorities of Tokyo were not informed until many hours later; life continued with a sort of subdued normality. When we in the Embassy learnt that our fears—for which we had made advance preparations—had been realized, the Ambassador (who had had an interview with

* An example is the rupture of diplomatic relations by Guatemala with the United Kingdom, which closely affects British Honduras and Mexico. Venezuela had a similar dispute with British Guiana (now Guyana), but wisely did not break off relations.

16

the Minister for Foreign Affairs an hour before, at which the subject of war was not mentioned) went out to consult his American colleague, followed by the Counsellor on a mission to rescue the wife of a member of the staff who was being held by the Japanese equivalent of the Gestapo. Shortly afterwards the courtyard filled up with police, and an impeccably dressed person in a top hat was ushered into the Chancery. In the absence of HE and the Counsellor, it fell to me to receive him in shirtsleeves and begrimed by burning documents. He announced that he had come to declare war. I explained that my seniors were absent and insisted that he must wait until they returned. I said I absolutely refused to be declared war upon. He persisted and produced an ideographic document. With not unreasonable petulance I countered that, having only been a week in the country, I could not read the Japanese script and that for all I knew it might be a grocery bill. This offensive description of an Imperial Rescript jolted the emissary, but he agreed that it would be reasonable for a Japanese speaker on the staff to translate it. I asked that this be done with the minimum of speed. Meanwhile Paul Gore Booth spun time out by delivering an admirable homily on the disastrous fate that would undoubtedly afflict any nation guilty of such a flagrant act of treachery. He regretted that the worst side of the Japanese character had now triumphed.

At the time we were all very angry, but two years later we were able to enjoy the funny side of war. The Turkish National Day falls in October and every year an official party is given to which, amongst others, the Diplomatic Corps is bidden. Clad in their most splendiferous garb and clanking with decorations, representatives of the Western, Neutral and Axis powers attended. The tactful Turks arranged segregation for the few minutes' wait before each Ambassador was received by the President. An urbane official at the top of the stairs motioned the Westerners into a room on the right and the 'Axles' into one on the left: the Neutrals obligingly stood in the hall between, popping briefly into the rooms on either side to demonstrate their impartiality. In the autumn of 1943 the Italians had decided to change sides, but this slipped the memory of the busy official. Automatically he ushered them into the Axis room; instantly the German Ambassador and all his staff burst out to protest in the central corridor. The Italians were extracted and introduced into the other room; more clamorously the Greek Ambassador and all his staff erupted similarly. The Italians withdrew to the neutral centre; the Greeks and Germans, after exchanging scowls, retreated to their own rooms muttering darkly.

Nowadays wars can rage without any formal declaration under various aliases, such as 'confrontation'. These lamentable events lie beyond the scope of normal diplomacy.

☆

All members of the British Diplomatic Service accept the liability to serve overseas as well as in the Foreign Office. Members of the British Diplomatic Service abroad are technically described as UK BASED, to distinguish them from the large number of LOCALLY ENGAGED personnel. The latter serve on different terms, and may or may not be British subjects. Officers who are UK based include those attached or seconded from other services. Those who are members of the Diplomatic Service are known as CAREER OFFICERS (a fairly modern translation of the French *Officier de Carrière*) to distinguish them from those locally or temporarily engaged.

The organization of the Foreign Office and the Commonwealth Relations Office in London is not dealt with in this book; but it should be noted that, in the Foreign Office itself, officers of the rank of Ambassador are called ASSISTANT UNDER SEC-RETARIES or DEPUTY UNDER SECRETARIES, though there are quite a few junior Embassies the heads of which are actually Counsellors in official grading and who revert to that rank when returning to the Foreign Office. The head of the whole Service is called the PERMANENT UNDER SECRETARY, to distinguish him from the PARLIAMENTARY UNDER SECRETARIES who are political appointees with seats in the House of Lords or House of Commons. The Permanent Under Secretary is often more colloquially known as the Head of the Office. Apart from his onerous responsibilities in matters of policy, he has a paternal role to all at home and abroad. A strong case can be made out for the appointment of an additional senior Deputy Under Secretary to act as No. 2 to the Permanent Under Secretary and relieve him of some of the burden.

In the United States, the Secretary of State and the two Under Secretaries of State are political appointments, as may be some of the Deputy Under Secretaries and Assistant Secretaries below them. There is in Washington no officer corresponding to the British Permanent Under Secretary.

Though the British Service overseas is now unified and known (whether in Commonwealth or foreign countries) as the Diplomatic Service, control at home is divided. The complexity of having a Foreign Office and a Commonwealth Relations Office in London is discussed later on (see chapter IX). One passing difficulty arises from the liability, already noted, of all members of the Diplomatic Service to serve overseas as well as at home. Some of the staff of the Commonwealth Relations Office, upon amalgamation in 1965, regarded themselves as members of the Home Civil Service with no obligation to serve abroad. They had to be offered the option of undertaking foreign service or transferring to another home department. The same applied to members of the Colonial Office staff in London now being incorporated into the CRO.

☆

The central hub of a Mission is called the CHANCERY, presided over by an officer who, in the British Service, is known as the HEAD OF CHANCERY. This is a function, not a rank. In a large Embassy, the Head of Chancery will be a Counsellor, in smaller ones, a First or Second Secretary.

In addition to the Chancery, but really included in it, an Embassy will have REGISTRIES (in which work ARCHIVISTS), TYPISTRIES, CYPHER ROOMS and, sometimes, a wireless room manned by members of the DIPLOMATIC WIRELESS

SERVICE. Senior Ambassadors will enjoy the services of PRIVATE SECRETARIES (usually Third Secretaries), while junior Ambassadors and Counsellors will have PERSONAL ASSISTANTS. These are experienced shorthand typists who, although they do not figure on the Diplomatic List, can reach a high rank, corresponding to Third or even Second Secretaries. The immunities of these junior personnel are prescribed in the Vienna Convention on a more restricted scale than those of diplomatic agents. It is only proper that they should be accorded a certain measure of protection and some privileges by the host government for, without their stout underpinning, the glittering structure of a Mission would collapse.

On the staff of a Mission also serve officers, not members of the Diplomatic Service, who belong to other departments of government or, in some cases, to business, industrial and academic spheres. In an increasingly complex world the need for such specialists is obvious. Some countries, such as the United States, employ them in large numbers; the German Service employs twice as many as the British. In the British Service a clear distinction is made between 'attached' and 'seconded' officers. SERVICE ATTACHÉS (NAVAL, MILITARY and AIR) are now the only officers in the British Service who are attached and not seconded. The distinction is that their conditions of service (pay, leave, etc.) are those of their own Service and not of the Diplomatic Service. SECONDED OFFICERS, on the other hand, are engaged on Diplomatic Service terms for their period of duty in a Mission. They come mostly from branches of the Civil Service: the Ministry of Labour, for instance, or the Ministries of Power, and of Agriculture. These officers bear such titles as 'Counsellor (Labour)', or 'First Secretary (Petroleum)', or 'Second Secretary (Agriculture)'. Both attached and seconded officers are often accredited to more than one Embassy.

Consular Officers are divided into CONSULS-GENERAL, CONSULS, VICE-CONSULS and PRO-CONSULS. The first named are usually equivalent to Counsellors, but they may, in very important posts (such as New York and Paris), correspond in grade to Ambassadors. Consuls and Vice-Consuls correspond to First and Second Secretaries respectively. Pro-Consuls are locally engaged personnel. They need not be British subjects.

The total number of British consular posts in 1914 was 843, in 1924 it fell to 772, and by 1966 it was only 350, to which should be added 151 posts staffed by non-career officers. This decrease is partly accounted for by the raising of many consular posts to embassy status when new countries become independent; and partly by the closing of many posts of slight importance for reasons of economy. Like Embassies, Consulates differ enormously in size. In 1914 the staff on the Diplomatic List in the British Embassy in Washington was 8, including 2 Service Attachés. Today it is 75, including 6 Service Attachés and 10 Seconded Officers. The total Diplomatic Service staff of the British Embassy in Washington is now 79 UK based and 190 locally engaged personnel a total of 269. At Stockholm, a medium-sized Embassy, the total staff is 59, of whom 26 are UK based and 33 locally engaged. One of the smallest Embassies, that in Tananarive, has a staff of 10—3 UK based and the rest locally engaged. The Ambassador to Madagascar is a Counsellor in grade. In contrast, the staff of the Consulate-General in New York consists of 11 UK based and 37 locally engaged personnel, making 48 all told. The Consul-General in New York is an Ambassador in grade. I give no figures for the Staffs of High Commissions, sometimes very ample, because these are under review since the integration of the Foreign and Commonwealth Services.

The head of a consular post in the British Service, like an Ambassador, holds a special Royal Commission from the Queen and is thereby entitled to be called 'Her Britannic Majesty's' or 'Her Majesty's' Consul-General or Consul. Other Consular Officers use the word 'British' before their rank. Unlike officers on the Diplomatic List at an Embassy, Consular Officers in all Services enjoy no extraterritorial rights, though in most countries they receive, as a matter of courtesy, certain privileges—such as the free import of their belongings on first arrival. These concessions apply only to career officers who are nationals of the country they represent. The governments of major powers seek to improve conditions for their Consular Officers by signing Consular Conventions with one another to regulate such matters.

In our 'dictionary' mention must also be made of the DIPLOMATIC COURIERS—known in Britain as *Queen's* (or *King's*) *Messengers*—who travel the world conveying the DIPLOMATIC BAGS from their respective Foreign Ministries to posts abroad and vice versa. It should also be noted that CHAPLAINS are attached to twenty-one British Missions and are granted diplomatic status. In four cases, a contribution to the stipend is made by HMG. Quite a few British Embassies have Anglican churches attached to them.

The different 'ranks' referred to are those currently used and normally accepted in equivalent form all over the world. Nevertheless, every Foreign or Diplomatic Service must have its own internal arrangements. It is exceedingly difficult to arrange a single series of grades beginning from I (which might be for newly joined Registry Clerks) and progressing up to, say, XXI for the most senior Ambassadors. Widely differing educational backgrounds and duties prevent this. Every country therefore works out its own system. The British grading is based on two 'streams' that overlap in the centre range. It is set out in Appendix A.

Throughout this book, when I use the word 'Officer' I usually mean one who is on the Diplomatic List, bearing such a title as 'Counsellor' or 'Secretary'. It must, however, never be forgotten that a good Personal Assistant, well-versed in diplomatic practice and perhaps speaking the local language; a Head Chancery Guard who has found his way round; or a clerk in the Commercial Secretariat who has intimate contacts in local business circles—these are all more valuable than a newly joined Third Secretary. Similarly, good platoon sergeants or petty officers of long service outweigh any number of junior lieutenants. Even if the Secretary has just acquired First Class Honours at Oxbridge in

Pure Metaphysics or Impure Astrology, he does well to remember this.

The word PROTOCOL looms large in diplomatic life. It is not to be found in the original Fowler but does appear in Gowers' revision of *Modern English Usage*, where he writes:

> Protocol has travelled a long way from its original meaning of the first leaf glued on to a manuscript. As a term of diplomacy it is now used in two very different senses. One is for an agreement that supplements, amends, or qualifies an existing treaty, or deals with some temporary aspect of it. The other is for the ceremonial etiquette observed in diplomacy. The second is the sense in which it is popularly understood; the word seldom appears in the newspapers except in connexion with some delicate procedural question in diplomatic relations.[8]

I had served for nigh on thirty years in the Diplomatic Service and been frequently enmeshed in protocol before it occurred to me to seek the derivation of the word, which, as Sir Ernest has now revealed to a wider public, is delightfully appropriate. Protocol comes from two Greek words meaning 'first glue'. Everyone in any Service frequently feels gummed like an insect on fly-paper by the primeval glue of protocol, but it is not really as bad as all that. There must be rules of procedure and a technical language in any Service, business undertaking, academic institution, trade union—or indeed family. An internationally accepted code to which all subscribe is immensely helpful to members of the group and to others prepared to submit to it while they are living in that environment. It would be fairer to say that protocol does more to glue people together than it does to gum up the works.

It is true that one is apt to remember the glaring cases of friction rather than the emollient side of protocol. Some individuals—alas, indeed, whole nations—seem to dote on minutiae and take offence with astounding violence if their susceptibilities are so much as breathed on. Not long ago a British Ambassador gave his first dinner in a notoriously touchy European country. As the meal progressed he noticed that one of the guests, a national of the country, addressed no word to either of his neighbours at table and only replied to their remarks in monosyllables. When the party moved to the drawing room for coffee, the Ambassador asked a member of his staff to enquire of the guest if he were feeling unwell. He was, but his malady was a profound sulk, because he reckoned that he had been wrongly placed at table. The Ambassador was new to the country; what would you have done? What *he* did was to take the guest aside, express regret that an error appeared to have been made and say firmly that there were only two courses open to him: he could leave at once, or remain and behave courteously. The guest stayed. Thereafter before every formal party the Ambassador asked the Protocol Department of the Ministry for Foreign Affairs to arrange the seating. He let this be known, and if there were any complaints Protocol took the rap.

Wariness is required in Scandinavia, where it is often the custom to place the guest of honour on the left of the host and hostess. This would not matter were it not that he is expected to rise when dessert is served and express in a few well-chosen phrases the thanks of all the guests for the meal. An American or Briton seated on the left of his hostess naturally assumes that it is up to the man on her right to make the speech. He only realizes that something is wrong when he becomes aware of concentrated glances, pregnant with anticipation, directed at him from all round the table by guests who dare not place a spoon in the ice-cream until he has done his duty.

Two other formalities prevalent in some countries merit mention. The first is a passion for signing the book that every Ambassador is expected to keep in his front hall. People sign because they want to attract his attention; they sign when they come to a meal; they often sign again next day to show their appreciation and leave a bunch of flowers. Allied with this is card-dropping, and every member of any Diplomatic Service is wise to equip himself with a large stock. We once found this habit useful in an oriental country where the suspicious monarch would allow no one to leave the city without a pass, the particulars of which had to be copied laboriously into a book by a semi-literate gendarme. As a result of protests by the Diplomatic Corps, it was agreed that it would suffice to hand over a visiting card. As this was printed in the Latin and not in the local script, the gendarme could not read it. The drain on one's stock of cards became very heavy and I am proud of inventing the solution of using cards dropped on us by others. This worked to the satisfaction of the British Embassy staff for months, but the gaff was blown by an alert official in the Ministry for Foreign Affairs, who spotted that the Afghan Ambassador, who happened to be out of the country, had apparently left the city one day by two different gates simultaneously.

Any recruit to any Diplomatic Service is wise to have his photograph taken in passport size, order lots of copies and buy the negative. In the course of his service he will need literally scores of such photos in different countries for various essential identity cards, driving licences, etc., with which his note-case will be burdened. No one will ever actually compare the photo with his face, so unless he grows a beard—and perhaps even then—one negative will see him through his career.

Punctuality is another point to bear in mind under protocol. Finns, for example, are apt to arrive five minutes or more early for any party, while you are still upstairs searching for your cuff-links. Swedes walk up and down outside your house in droves, glancing at their wrist watches, and at the appointed hour make a concerted rush for the door. Latin Americans and Africans arrive anything up to an hour and a half late, or fail to turn up at all (and do not bother to ring up to say they are not coming). A buffet meal with no fixed seating is a useful remedy for this sort of rudeness.

We once witnessed a successful counter-attack on this slipshod behaviour. When one President gave an official dinner to the Duke of Edinburgh during his tour of Latin America, he was acutely aware of the failings of his countrymen. All guests were therefore warned that, after a round of drinks, he would take the Prince in to dinner at 8 p.m. precisely and that when all had entered the doors would be locked. His compatriots simply did not believe this, and about eighty of us found ourselves seated at a table laid for a hundred and twenty. We shuffled up to close the ranks and an excellent dinner was enjoyed. When we emerged it was not entirely disagreeable to observe the disconsolate faces of the unfed Cabinet Ministers and other VIPs waiting outside in the hope that sooner or later they would be admitted to the feast.

As another example of situations requiring finesse, over-generous gifts by foreigners should be noted. They present a grave problem to the recipient. In Tsarist days the Russians were a most generous folk, only too apt to offer you valuables from among their possessions. There was, however, a useful phrase to avoid embarrassment: 'This is mine', you said. 'Please keep it here for me.' On one of his jaunts to the Middle East, Churchill, his family and members of his entourage were presented with gifts of fabulous value by Ibn Saud; these they handed over to HM Treasury. Also during the last war, the British Ambassador at Jedda woke up one morning to find an 8-cylinder Packard limousine parked outside his door as a present from His Saudi Majesty. Sir Hugh Stonehewer-Bird was well versed in the right techniques. He accepted the car and reminded the Foreign Office that he had for some years been asking for a private car to be sent to him; for this he was prepared to pay £x, which was all he could afford. As a return present to Ibn Saud was required, Sir Hugh asked that his £x be spent on a movie projector and stock of allied war films. This swap was approved and the gift duly presented to the King.

Protocol and etiquette, though much mocked, have their uses. They can be a valuable lubricant for the machinery of diplomacy. A good *Chef de Protocole*, working cannily with the Doyen of the Diplomatic Corps, will iron out many ruffles and smooth the asperities of life. A bad one will drown in very little water and try to drag you under too. In general there is nothing 'right' or 'wrong' about local customs; there are merely differences. Anglo-

Saxons tend to be unceremonious in ordinary life, but British official ceremonies are unparalleled. Many a foreigner attaches more importance to protocol than we do in Britain or North America; but, if you are living in his country, it is uncouth not to make some effort to conform. Guidance on matters of protocol is provided by the Foreign Office to all members of the Service and attached personnel.

Precedence is sometimes a sore problem, particularly to the petty-minded. There must be inter-Service rules governing such matters. In British practice it is laid down that a Consul-General ranks with but after an air vice-marshal (who himself ranks with but after a major-general, and he with but after a rear-admiral); a Consul with but after a group captain of the Royal Air Force, and a Vice-Consul with but after a squadron leader. Inside the Diplomatic Service, a Counsellor equates a Consul-General and a First Secretary a Consul. In American practice there is no 'Senior Service', and precedence among the staff at an Embassy is arranged by simple rule of thumb: the higher your salary the higher your place at table or elsewhere.

A British Ambassador, or a Minister who is a Head of Mission, is the Queen's personal representative and while in the foreign country officially outranks any other British subject, even Cabinet Ministers—though it would be usual for him to yield precedence to the Prime Minister or Foreign Secretary, and he would invariably do so to a member of the Royal Family having the title of 'Royal Highness'.

In this 'dictionary' the main technical terms have now been set out. I have dealt almost entirely with 'people', most of whom do not figure in the Concise Oxford Dictionary (Head of Mission, Head of Chancery, Service Attaché, etc.). I have included some 'things' (e.g. agrément) not mentioned in the diplomatic sense in the standard dictionaries. I have not added many other 'things' in fairly common use since they are defined in dictionaries (e.g. détente, aide-mémoire).

II

THE HEAD OF MISSION

THE DIPLOMATIC Officer whose duties we must first examine is the Ambassador. He is selected by the Head of State as a personal representative. In the United Kingdom he is appointed by the Queen, acting on the advice of the Secretary of State for Foreign Affairs for the time being. If, as is almost invariably the case in Britain, the Ambassador is a member of the Service, the Secretary of State in turn is advised by the Permanent Under Secretary and a board of senior officials. The procedure is the same for British High Commissioners appointed to Commonwealth countries, except that in this case it is the Secretary of State for Commonwealth Relations who advises the Queen.

Shrewd eyes have recently been cast on the role of United States Ambassadors.[1] Some of the observations made in American studies in this field are not applicable to other Diplomatic Services, but they should be borne in mind by *everyone* engaged in diplomatic representation and administration.

An Ambassador is officially styled 'Ambassador Extraordinary and Plenipotentiary', but he is wise not to be too conceited about this. As for the 'plenipotentiary'—which literally means 'full-powered'—he is, in fact, pretty feeble. If an Ambassador is to sign a treaty in the name of his government, he requires an additional document (known as 'Full Powers' or, in French *'Pleins Pouvoirs'*). This always arrives at the last moment. He thus has it embarrassingly demonstrated to him in the most public fashion that neither government trusts him an inch. High Commissioners are not Plenipotentiaries.

On arrival at his new post, the Ambassador presents his Letters of Credence to the Head of State at a formal audience. It is important that public recognition should thus be given to the status of an Ambassador as a personal representative of his own Head of State. The Ambassador should feel entitled to direct access to him, be he Emperor, King or President. This is a privilege not to be abused, but in moments of crisis it may have vital significance—particularly in countries where the Head of State is also, constitutionally or in practice, head of the government. One British Ambassador, untrammelled by regulations, recently showed the draft of his annual economic report to the President of the small African republic to which he was accredited. No eyebrows were raised at the Foreign Office, because the predictions in the report proved sound, and the Service values men who go straight to the top instead of wasting time at lower levels.

Audiences vary in formality in different countries. I have presented credentials in a lounge suit; a morning suit is quite frequent; but usually full uniform is worn by a British Ambassador and his staff attending the ceremony. The full blue uniform of the old type was something of a trial, as the coat with all its gold embellishment weighed about as much as a fur coat and was equally hot. A simpler uniform has now been designed for the British Diplomatic Service. There is also a light-weight white tropical uniform, to which some countries object, even in a temperature of over 100°F, on the ground that they are being treated as 'colonials'. Many countries have no diplomatic uniform and it is then often the custom for the Ambassador and his staff to wear full evening dress, which looks extremely odd in the morning, except on waiters. Some Africans and Asians wear their national costume on ceremonial occasions; this is both comfortable and colourful. Attempts have been made to design uniforms or at least badges to be worn on official occasions by women officers. They have failed in the British and, as far as I know, in all Diplomatic Services employing women. The British regulations merely hint that in certain circumstances a grant towards the cost of additional formal clothing may be made.[2]

Whatever his costume, the Ambassador may have to inspect a guard of honour with a band, which will endeavour to render the national anthems of the two countries. A serious crisis was once averted in a British colony, where the bishop by chance ascertained twenty-four hours beforehand that the local band was proposing to greet a Soviet envoy with the Tsarist hymn. Fortunately his Lordship was a fine musician and, by sitting up all night, was able to orchestrate the *Internationale* for them.

Only after an Ambassador has presented his credentials—and there is often a delay of some weeks before the ceremony is arranged—can he perform his official functions. Until then the Chargé d'Affaires remains responsible for the post as far as the foreign government is concerned. After the ceremony the Ambassador will inform his government and write formally to his diplomatic colleagues announcing that he has now entered officially on his duties. He may expect in British practice to occupy his post for at least three years and often much longer in important posts. In the American Service transfers are more frequent; this has given rise to complaint.[3]

The poor man cannot, however, settle down comfortably in his Embassy and get on with his job—which may include learning or brushing up his knowledge of the local language. He is now faced by diplomatic custom with the time-consuming rigmarole of calls. He will wish to make the acquaintance of various cabinet ministers and other notabilities; by diplomatic etiquette he should call on every other Head of Mission, and his wife on their wives. Moreover, these calls must in due course be returned. When it is remembered that in a major capital there are well over a hundred foreign representatives, the magnitude of the task becomes clear. It is also not necessarily constructive. The system will, for instance, involve a call by the Baratarian Ambassador, whose only means of communication is a deteriorated form of Spanish, on his Ruritanian colleague, who adds a few traces of Russian to his unknown native language. In London, at any rate, the futility is recognized and compulsory calling is falling into desuetude. The wise Ambassador at least tries to insist that he and his wife call and receive their calls together, thus halving the number of visits; yet even a hundred hours can involve an impressive car mileage. There is, moreover, no end to the task. It is like painting the Forth Bridge; by the time you get to the end you must start again at the beginning, for Heads of Missions are constantly being transferred and the new ones demand their calls. I never personally served as ambassador in a post with more than fifty diplomatic colleagues, but even then the task of keeping up with the rust on the bridge was formidable. Only too frequently one encounters colleagues who have nothing whatever to do and find calling an agreeable way of passing the time (a round of calls for them is the equivalent of a round of golf in Britain or the United States). For the busy Ambassador there is only one solution short of complete abolition of the practice; he and his wife would make their joint calls but without any separate return calls. Instead, the newcomers would give a reception to all the older established colleagues on whom they had dutifully called, thus polishing off the return visits in one go. As far as I know, this device has never been tried out, but it should certainly be possible for a tactful Doyen, supported by a few senior Ambassadors, to gain acceptance for it.

Almost as time-consuming are the parties given by Ambassadors on their National Days (with the British, the Queen's Birthday) which all their colleagues expect to attend. It is entirely reasonable that an Ambassador should give a party to his own nationals; a case can be argued for prominent local personages; but to include all the Diplomatic Corps is preposterous. The wise Swiss throughout the world confine invitations to Swiss; the Americans invite foreigners and diplomats, but not their own folk (this is a recent ruling, an economy measure); the British indulge all, even if it means giving two parties on one day owing to restrictions of space. Plowden comments wistfully: 'Some reduction in the extent of National Day celebrations is desirable. . . . This is not something which could be achieved by unilateral action.'[4] I disagree with the last phrase; the British should follow the Swiss model. Even then, discrimination and much consequent heartburning or even vituperation will be involved in capitals where the British colony is so large that it is impossible, owing to lack of space, to include them all. Similar difficulties face some American, Spanish and Italian Ambassadors in posts with enormous expatriate colonies. As a final warning: so long as these parties continue, the hosts will be wise to remove all portable objects of value from any room to which guests may gain access and lock the doors of the rest. It is unwise to put too much faith in honesty, even at the most distinguished capitals and in the most affluent society.

Ambassadors are not only occasionally shot at, but also shot over. The former sport is indulged in by foreign terrorists; our residence was once machine-gunned by unamiable desperadoes. The shooting over is highly ceremonial and occurs when a British Ambassador calls officially on one of HM ships and sometimes when he visits a foreign warship. On such an occasion he is entitled to a salute of nineteen guns. Needless to say, the Royal Navy manages this ceremony to perfection. They use a special saluting gun which, while it makes an impressive bang, does not split your eardrums, and they are careful to fire it outboard and not across the quay. 'We have no desire, Sir, to blow your hat off', said one Captain to me (but he artfully rigged an awning so low that it enmeshed the spike on my old fashioned helmet; I was forced to descend the gangplank in a simian crouch).

The scale of British salutes is clearly laid down in the *Queen's Regulation* and *Admiralty Instructions*, which are for the most part internationally accepted. It may seem surprising that Prime Ministers (of Britain or Commonwealth countries) are entitled to none; nor are High Commissioners, though they perform much the same function as Ambassadors. Governors General of Dominions receive the Royal Salute of twenty-one guns. An Ambassador is entitled to nineteen guns, a Minister to seventeen (though the chances of the sole British Minister receiving a salute from a Vatican warship seem remote), a Chargé d'Affaires or Consul General thirteen, and a Consul seven; at the bottom of the British scale the Political Agent at Abu Dhabi—a more important place than one might suppose—receives five.

Her Majesty's Consul in a South American post, a lady, was highly gratified to be shot over by the Royal Navy. The Ambassador was less pleased because he received a complaint from the Harbour Master who had particularly asked that no salutes be fired lest the local inhabitants assume that their navy had mutinied again. A foreign potentate once ordered a sixty-two gun salute, imitating the number fired on occasions at the Tower of London. On this memorable occasion the guns were twenty-five pounders, the loudest available, sited on top of a hill. They fired without warning straight down one of the main avenues of the city. Even with blank the blast was considerable. Many car windscreens were shattered, shocked drivers ran off the road or collided with vehicles racing down the hill to avoid the detonations. Mules, horses and donkeys panicked, throwing their riders or bolting with carts. Pedestrians flung themselves into ditches, presumably uttering fervent prayers for the long life of the monarch, who meanwhile read a speech in his native tongue that lasted for two and a half hours.

Ambassadors have the right to fly the flag of their country over their official Residences and the Embassy Offices. There are local customs about this. In some countries it is flown every day, in others on local and national holidays. It may be flown half-mast as a sign of mourning, national or international. Most countries do not have ambassadorial flags differing from the ordinary national ones, but American Ambassadors have been known to fly on their cars, in addition to Old Glory, an ambassadorial flag (dark blue with thirteen white stars) that is a sort of miniature of the Presidential Flag (dark blue with a white star for every State in the Union). In the British Diplomatic Service there is an ambassadorial flag of special design, incorporating the Royal Arms in the centre of the Union Jack. This is flown over the Ambassador's Residence or Office and on cars, boats and ships (or from aircraft on landing, though I have not seen this done). On a vehicle the flag is personal to the Ambassador; the worst sort of Ambassadress has been known to sack the chauffeur when he properly removed it after the Ambassador had quitted the car.

British Consular Officers are entitled to fly their own special flag —a Tudor Crown in the centre of the Union Jack.

At last we have finished with a mere outline of ceremonial (there are many other complexities) and can get down to business.

☆

The Ambassador is the Head of Mission and, as that title implies, he is the boss—maybe of a very small Embassy or of a large one but still the boss. In his office should be inscribed, as in President Truman's, the motto: 'The Buck Stops Here.' This ambassadorial leadership may seem a truism, but it is well to stress that he should control the whole Embassy machine, including attached organizations. Divided control of foreign policy is disastrous; weak leadership of an Embassy as deplorable on its own scale. American comment is emphatic. Barnett remarks on the difficulties of co-ordination under the vast American system.[5] He also recommends 'a considerable degree of unified supervision, co-ordination and control'.[6] Jackson observes: 'To a degree, the primacy of the Ambassador is a polite fiction . . . nevertheless a strong Ambassador can pull a team together.'[7] The best illustration is provided by the letter the late President Kennedy thought it necessary to write to all United States Ambassadors in May 1961, setting forth clearly their authority and responsibilities. It is quoted in Jackson.[8]

No Ambassador can be expected to drown himself in detail and know everything that is going on, but he must maintain general guidance. He can adopt as motto a phrase written in his diary by Robert Hooke, the great contemporary of Wren and Newton: 'Spent most of my time considering all matters'—for the Ambassador holds the ultimate responsibility to his country. This is not the case with all foreign Embassies. In some Services, Military Missions or even Service Attachés pursue lines divergent from the rest of the Embassy; sections devoted to economic aid, though clamouring for the protection of diplomatic status, will blithely go their own way to the general confusion; and groups charged with cultural and information work will endeavour, sometimes successfully, to follow courses flatly contrary to the over-all Mission policy. Such behaviour makes nonsense of the reputation of the country concerned and should never be tolerated.

A 'small' Ambassador will have little share in shaping the main lines of the foreign policy of his government; even 'big' Ambassadors can only influence the grand strategy. However, 'big' and 'small' are entrusted with tactics and it is not only their right but their duty to express their views. Any government that does not consult its Ambassadors and give them reasonable freedom of action should have its collective head examined; the 'theirs not to reason why' mentality at both or either end can only lead to disaster.

An excellent American Ambassador was once accused by a particularly fatuous Foreign Service Inspector of being 'the worst Ambassador after the one in London for querying his instructions'. 'So what?' replied my friend tersely. An Ambassador is failing in his duty if he does not draw attention to instructions that appear to him either unclear or from the local point of view dangerous. He must never flinch from telling his government unpalatable truths. He may be over-ruled for good reason; then he can only resign, or carry out his instructions loyally, even if they order him to charge into, as it were, 'the valley of death'. It is rare, if foreign affairs and diplomacy are being well conducted, for an Ambassador to be given such limited discretion that he cannot make any manoeuvres during the 'charge'. It is thus often possible to swerve at the last moment and take in the flank the guns that volley and thunder down the obvious but fatal route of approach. Talleyrand once wrote: 'To engage, or at least to persist, in a struggle in which you may find everybody interested on the other side is a mistake, and nowadays all political mistakes are dangerous.' Governments must possess in high degree the *sens du practicable*; and, risking unpopularity if necessary, Ambassadors must tell them what they can get away with.

Governments vary much in the extent to which they heed their Heads of Missions. Long-established states tend to be resigned to the odd things that can happen thousands of miles away. They have

35

the commonsense to appoint a good representative in the trouble spot and accord him a considerable measure of confidence—at least until he has been proved demonstrably wrong. Such governments may also profit more from experience. 'It is easy to be wise after the event. It is also wise', as Sir Norman Angell once wrote. Newer states, like totalitarian regimes, are apt to be more rigid; they tie the hands of their representatives to such an extent that the change in position of a comma almost becomes a *casus belli*. This inflexibility is in part due to the fears of the government of the new state that, owing to lack of highly trained manpower, their representatives may not be able to resist the cunning of their opponents; while the representatives themselves, harried and homesick in a strange atmosphere, fear that they may be recalled and dismissed to ignoble poverty. Finally, there is often a marked reluctance of the ambitious to leave the fount of power.

It inevitably takes much time to build up *esprit de corps*, but without it and a properly established Diplomatic Service, the state and its ministers will soon be frustrated. There are, alas, far too many long established countries that have no Diplomatic Service or civil servants as these are understood in Europe and North America. Ambassadors and Consuls are appointed on the basis of nepotism or to remove a potential trouble-maker from the home country. When appointed they are given no instructions, or they ignore them. Frequently they are not even paid, and lead precarious and nefarious lives. No credit can redound to a state that so orders its affairs.

A Latin American Ambassador in a Middle East post—about the most engaging rogue I ever met—once complained to me that his pay was years in arrears. I asked how he circumvented this tiresome difficulty. He explained blandly that there were 'various devices'. For instance, he had a brother in a minor position at home who had much to do with visiting foreigners engaged in business with his government. The brother persuaded the government that he should give a slap-up party to these visitors at a cost of $1,000. 'But he no give de barty,' concluded the Ambassador, digging me in the ribs triumphantly. I have often wondered what a British Ambassador would do in the same position. He would probably not rise to the repartee of a Spanish general to King Ferdinand the Seventh, who reproached him for appearing at Court in summer uniform, although it was midwinter. General Castaños, the victor of Bailén, replied that seasons were a matter of opinion; as far as he was concerned it was summer, because only two days before he had drawn his pay for July.

The servants of a well-organized country are better off. They are paid regularly, if not as much as they would like, and their masters at home realize their difficulties, listen to them, give them freedom of action and do not expect the impossible. An Ambassaador thus sustained can get on with his work no matter how vile the political or meteorological climate.

☆

In many ways it is a remarkably humdrum job. The Head of Mission has to read far too many papers and write as economically as he can. He must, either directly or through his staff, keep in touch with feeling and events in the country in which he is stationed, not only in the capital but in the provinces. He should be acquainted with the prominent personalities in all walks of life. He should not model himself on one foreign Ambassador in London who recently, in reply to an invitation from the Prime Minister (Mr Harold Wilson), wrote that he was happy to accept Mr Patrick Gordon Walker's kind invitation—and this six months after Mr Gordon Walker had been replaced as Secretary of State for Foreign Affairs by Mr Michael Stewart.

On the other hand, every Ambassador has to display considerable ingenuity to avoid the spongers who long for an invitation to the Embassy. Often they are the idle rich who infest every capital, or self-important tourists eager for a free meal during a world cruise. A Head of Mission soon discovers who are the wiser among his diplomatic colleagues, and there can be much reciprocal profit from contact with them. Many of the rest will be valueless and sometimes a social incubus.

Complaints are often made that Embassies are not in contact with the 'right' people and cannot therefore report accurately on the local situation. There are certain limitations on a Head of Mission. He is accredited to the government in power, and in the less liberal countries it would be indiscreet for him to be in frequent converse with opposition leaders whose policies are anathema to the ruling party. To take a slightly extreme case, if any Ambassadors in Cuba under the Batista regime had visited Castro in the Sierra Maestra, the Cuban government would have demanded their recall. Sometimes it may be possible for a junior member of the Embassy staff to make such contacts, but even this can be perilous.

Personal contact with worthwhile individuals is a fascinating part of all life, but particularly of diplomatic life, since it involves dealing with people of so many different races, religions and languages. It is usually conceded that the art of speaking—the gift of the gab—is of vital importance. In medieval times Ambassadors often bore the title 'Orator'. Less mention is made of the art of listening, yet this should bear great weight. Remember Bacon: 'He that questioneth much shall learn much, and content much; but especially if he apply his questions to the skill of the persons whom he asketh; for he shall give them occasion to please themselves in speaking, and himself shall continually gather knowledge. But let his questions not be troublesome, for that is fit for a poser; and let him be sure to leave other men their turns to speak.'

Needless to say, a Head of Mission will include leaders of his own colony among those with whom he is in close touch. Many of them will have long been resident in the country and there is vast experience on which the newcomer can draw. The value of such support of the national interest is stressed in TWFM.[9]

Intimate contacts with the nationals of the country give the Ambassador the opportunity to carry out another of his duties: explaining to the local government the views of his own cabinet on international affairs. It is on this build-up of confidence between an Ambassador and the Head of State to whom he is accredited that good relations depend. A competent Ambassador will feel rather than know how others will react in any given circumstances and can warn his own government. The necessity for this contact explains to some extent the prevalence of cocktail parties and other entertainments, in which diplomats are often accused of overindulging. To anyone not mentally deformed they are a crashing bore, but they do provide occasions for the 'bridge-work' in which Ambassadors should be as adept as highway engineers or dentists. Social gatherings give the opportunity to raise official matters in an apparently fortuitous manner, for it is often desirable not to exaggerate the importance of a tricky subject by arranging a special interview to discuss it. I can recall many occasions when I was particularly keen to mention something to a certain official, but felt it wiser to wait until I had other subjects I could plausibly discuss. Then at the end of the talk, when rising to take leave, one could say casually, 'Oh, by the way, what about . . . ?'

Lord d'Abernon, the first British Ambassador to Germany after the 1914–18 war, was a master of the art of contact.[10] He was not what we should now call a 'career officer', but he had the highest qualities as an economist, diplomat and linguist. Like all Ambassadors, he often received telegrams from Whitehall couched in somewhat the following terms:

You should approach the German Government about . . . and urge them to act as follows. . . . You should explain our reasons which are. . . . If the German Government feel they cannot accept, you are authorized to offer the following alternatives. . . . In no circumstances however can His Majesty's Government agree to. . . .

On receipt of such a telegram, d'Abernon would cogitate profoundly and then draft a reply reading something like this:

I took action today on your telegram. As was to be expected, the Secretary of State could not agree to your first proposal because. . . . He did not seem at all keen on your second suggestion, which obviously conflicts with his undertakings given in the Reichstag. I therefore enquired what he would think of the following idea. . . . I made it plain that I was speaking for myself and could not be sure that you would approve. His first reactions were favourable. If you too agreed, he would consult his cabinet colleagues. I should be grateful for early instructions.

Only after completing his draft would d'Abernon telephone for an appointment at the Ministry for Foreign Affairs. When he returned from his interview he would sometimes amend it, but often would merely say to his private secretary: 'You can send off that telegram.' His knowledge of the facts was so sound and of German thinking so intuitive, that he could gauge reactions in advance and prepare alternative and acceptable proposals.

At least one other Head of Mission developed a similar practice. Quaroni relates that, when Italian Ambassador in Moscow, he used to test his knowledge of correct Communist dialectic by writing an account of a conversation with some Soviet panjan-drum *before* it took place. Only very rarely did he have to make any important alterations afterwards.[11]

An Ambassador must not only be able to sort out, with the aid of his staff, the intricate local jigsaw puzzle, but present the resulting picture to his government in such manner that it is comprehensible to them at a distance. Unless they readily grasp the pattern, he cannot hope that they will approve the line he proposes to take. This is not easy for either Ambassador or Foreign Office. 'Nations are like men', wrote de Tocqueville; 'they love that which flatters their passions more than that which serves their interests.' The Ambassador will therefore often have to tell his government that Ruritanian intentions are such and such. He knows that his own Secretary of State will regard this course as sheer lunacy (which indeed it probably is), but the fact remains that this is going to be Ruritanian policy, until perhaps they have burnt their fingers. It is hardly for the British, who can be pretty unpredictable in foreign eyes, to cast the first stone, so it serves no useful purpose to moan, 'what fools these

Ruritanians be', and send ludicrously impractical instructions to the Embassy.

☆

It might appear from the foregoing that an Ambassador's main duty was to interpret to his government the views of the country in which he is posted; even more to act as its advocate. Interpretation is certainly necessary to promote international comity and prediction should be essayed, but advocacy should be left to the other government—after all, it has its own Ambassadors. This distinction is particularly important when we consider another of the Ambassador's vital roles—that of negotiator. After having interpreted the situation to his own government, predicted reactions and, let us hope, received instructions that give at least a faint chance of success, it is up to him to dicker with the government to which he is accredited. More complicated still may be multilateral negotiations involving many powers— some friendly, some the reverse. An additional hazard is the newspapers' thirst for publicity, which can easily wreck a carefully planned voyage.

The arts of persuasion are needed not only in the law courts but in diplomacy, business and, indeed, in everyday life. In diplomacy always and in other spheres sometimes, the artistry required is higher because the protagonist is dealing with people whose mentality may be utterly alien. Moreover, there may well be linguistic difficulties. If a Head of Mission cannot handle the local language fluently and if the local Foreign Minister is similarly handicapped in the languages at the disposal of the Ambassador, the latter is wise to take with him some member of his staff, familiar with both the languages and the subject to be discussed. This has several advantages, which are well brought out in TWFM; there is no risk of misunderstanding on the spot; younger staff members learn, or at least should do, how to handle negotiations and are thus brought more closely into the team; Ambassador and Secretary can co-operate in drafting the report of the interview, thus ensuring accuracy.[12] Incidentally, all talks of any importance by anyone on the staff should be recorded in writing and circulated to all departments of the Mission; thus all are aware of what is passing.

The artistry required of an Ambassador differs from the legal form of advocacy in that it is better exercised privately rather than publicly. In diplomacy little is likely to be achieved by a thunderous address that might impress a large and unlettered audience or a bewildered jury. Persuasive, intimate conversation in a relaxed atmosphere is likely to achieve more. The greatest Ambassadors owe much of their renown to their gift for inducing others to agree with them; or, if disagreement becomes inevitable, to their skill in leaving no scars on amity. To some extent this art can be acquired, but the essence is probably innate and can often be descried at an early stage in an officer's career. The basis can only be absolute loyalty to instructions, preferably drafted with some flexibility. Throughout the discussions it must be borne in mind that complete agreement, entirely satisfactory to both sides, can rarely be reached. It is unproductive to strive obstinately for perfection; in this as in many other matters *le mieux est l'ennemi du bien*. Aim well, but be not disappointed if you score a magpie instead of a bull.

If eventually the negotiations are reasonably successful, public rejoicing or reference to a 'diplomatic triumph' should be deprecated. Diplomacy is an endless road with many ups and downs, unexpected twists and bifurcations. The surmounting of one skyline is not a 'triumph', merely a step forward. There are many more hills further on. Nicolson comments: 'The worst kind of diplomatists are missionaries, fanatics and lawyers, the best kind are the reasonable and humane sceptics.'[13] I fancy that when Sir Harold wrote 'missionaries', he meant 'people with a sense of mission', but having served in the same capital as a Lutheran missionary disguised as an Ambassador, I could hardly agree more. Sir Harold's objection to lawyers was that 'their argumentative faculties are too much on the alert. Negotiation should never degenerate into an argument; it should be kept always on the level of a discussion.'[14] Sir Orme Sargent, once

Permanent Under Secretary at the Foreign Office, also used to maintain that lawyers made bad diplomats and worse statesmen, because they tended to regard each crisis or event as an isolated brief—a 'case' to be won or lost and forgotten. He would quote telling examples and maintain that in foreign affairs 'winning a difficult case' was a futile objective.

The experienced Head of Mission takes as much trouble to keep in touch with the thinking at home as he does with the atmosphere in the country in which he is serving. Before leaving for his post he should endeavour to make contacts at the highest level with the sources of power at home and take care to keep these lines open by correspondence. Particular importance is attached to this by American Heads of Missions in the Washington labyrinth, as shown by their notes in TWFM.[15] Jackson also stresses this: 'The Ambassador's ability to give helpful counsel, and to get attention paid to it by policy officers in Washington, depends in great measure on seeing his country's problems in the perspective of American policy as a whole.'[16] Home policy, and above all the reasons behind it, which may conceal many tensions, is often not fully revealed in correspondence. Personal contact at regular intervals between the Head of Mission and his government is therefore most advisable. The misunderstandings that can arise are appalling. Barnett quotes the story of a man with many years service overseas, who remarked: 'In the field we look upon Washington as the enemy.' The rejoinder from the equally experienced home-based man was: 'We think of the field as a cross we must bear up Capitol Hill several times a year.'[17]

All Diplomatic Services must ensure contact. This can take the form of a brief visit by the Ambassador to his own country at least once between his leaves, or at worst a tour in his area by a senior official from home. In the latter case it is often possible to bring together several Heads of Mission from neighbouring posts for an informal conference. This will not, however, entirely provide the essential 'home touch'. Jackson recommends visits to Washington two or three times a year by United States

Ambassadors.[18] If his recommendation is adopted, it will be surprising. The penurious British cannot hope for such frequent contact, which is often more necessary from very distant posts, of which the public has not heard, than from nearer centres of world activity.

It may at times be necessary for an Ambassador to fight desperately for the causes or courses he believes right—particularly in matters connected with the welfare of his staff. He may also find it necessary to make long and expensive efforts in his own 'free' time on leave to seek advice from and explain local conditions to non-governmental groups at home. Commerce, industry, banking, insurance, educational and academic circles, trade unions, shipping and airline magnates, telecommunication experts—all these have much to teach and can provide much help; they are not fools and will appreciate the opportunity to learn at first, or at least second, hand.

Above all, a good Ambassador, though driving himself to the limit, will remember the wisdom of self-effacement except in times of gravest crisis. 'One ought never to be obstinate, except when one ought to be', wrote Talleyrand. 'Then one should be unshakeable.' A mixture of strength and modesty will always pay in the interests of one's country. The wily Ambassador will console himself with a remark made by Sir Robert Watson Watt, who developed what is now called radar just in time to save Britain in 1940: 'There is nothing a determined man cannot accomplish, if he will allow others to take the credit.' Part of the art of diplomacy consists in persuading others (compatriot or foreign) that *they* have devised a brilliant gimmick to save the situation. One can then give it unstinted support.

A Head of Mission is wise not to appear too energetic, nor to write too much, particularly telegrams. As far as the foreign government is concerned, he is the big gun and his trigger should not be pressed at every opportunity, lest the effect of his constant discharges be reduced. The locals will, as it were, so reconstruct their mental buildings that they become salvo-proof. It is thus often preferable for a member of his staff to fire at least the initial shots with a weapon of smaller calibre that may prove as effective and less noisy than a fifteen-inch gun.

This leads us to discuss the relations between a Head of Mission and his staff. Field Marshal Wavell once quoted in a secret directive some words of Wellington. I have been unable to trace the source and similar remarks are attributed to the German General von Fritsch, who may well have read his Wellington attentively. Whatever the source, the burden is clear; there are four classes of officers: 'The clever and lazy should be placed in command; the stupid and lazy should be sent to regimental duty; the clever and industrious should serve on the staff; the stupid and industrious should be got rid of at all costs.' An Ambassador cannot choose all his staff, though he can make suggestions. He can and should, however, refuse any officer who he suspects is in the fourth category—or for any other valid reasons. Exceptionally he is justified in refusing an officer because of his name. One such was glad to be rejected for Tehran on the ground that his surname, when pronounced in Persian, meant 'dung'.

An Ambassador must be able to depend on his staff, but he should be capable of delegation—though this should never become abdication. There are few things more tiresome than a chief who keeps dogs and barks himself. The 'laziness' quoted from Wellington should never degenerate into lethargy, but too much fussing is almost worse. There are even occasions when, as Metternich once wrote: *Die Dinge machen sich von selbst, vorausgesetzt, dass man sie nicht macht*—which can be rendered, 'Leave things alone and they'll settle themselves'. To this extent he shared his opponent Talleyrand's view that the zeal of the inexperienced in times of crisis was extremely dangerous.

Few newly appointed Ambassadors, only the better Chargé d'Affaires and the rarest amateur or political diplomats avoid succumbing to the temptation to impress, in part because they suffer from the delusion that their advice is being neglected by officials at home who simply do not understand the local situation. This is a most unwise assumption; the officials in a good Ministry for Foreign Affairs know a very great deal and are probably viewing local events against a wider background.

The Head of Mission should not write a report or, above all, telegraph it until he has pondered three times whether it is necessary. He should not make recommendations in a hurry; a few more hours consultation and reflection may either lead to amendment of his views or remove the necessity to put them forward. It is better, particularly in the earlier stages of high responsibility, to be known as placid rather than hysterical; the rare accusation of not keeping your government adequately informed can easily be brushed off. Meanwhile, balance can be maintained. Kelly was assuredly right when he wrote: 'I have many times seen purely personal likes or dislikes, personal health, vanity, prejudice or just lack of time for proper consideration, decide important issues.'[19]

All telegrams and other communications emanating from an Embassy are signed by or in the name of the Ambassador, but it should be widely realized that he has not necessarily seen them all personally before despatch—he has learnt to delegate, he trusts his staff. In a moment of leisure he may call for the file of outgoing telegrams to refresh his memory and keep tabs on traffic. He may then be in for shocks, like the one inflicted on an Ambassador during the last war, when the British issued what were called 'navicerts'. These guaranteed shippers that 'clean' items of cargo would not be confiscated by the Royal Navy as contraband destined for the enemy. One happy day in Lisbon he found in the Embassy file of telegrams one to a British Consul in the Azores that read: 'You may issue navicert for one pregnant goat.' It was signed with his name.

Between the wars, a Head of Mission in the British Service was expected to sign personally all despatches. Nowadays if he cannot be available at the time the diplomatic bag to the Foreign Office is closing, because he is keeping an appointment or making an official tour, it is quite in order for his Counsellor to sign for him. In those easier times it was the custom of HM Ambassador in Brussels to spend the summer months in a villa at Ostend; his colleagues in Madrid moved to Santander or San Sebastian. In Spain the King and government also moved to the cool Atlantic, but in Belgium the Embassy remained in Brussels with the government. Before leaving for the beach, therefore, the Ambassador signed his name dozens of times in various positions —top, middle or bottom—on foolscap sheets with the Royal Arms embossed on the top. The despatches were drafted and typed by his staff in Brussels, and the final sheet was selected with the signature in the right place to allow for the number of paragraphs remaining. This artifice was known to and implicitly approved by the Secretary of State for Foreign Affairs, who could be entirely confident that at the slightest sign of real crisis the Ambassador would be back at his desk in the Embassy within the hour. Kelly records a similar practice in Buenos Aires.[26]

Even more spacious was then the custom of members of the Indian Political Service on duty as Consular Officers or Agents of the government in the Persian Gulf—which before the days of air conditioning was intolerable in summer. They closed their offices, leaving them in charge of some wretched native clerk, and moved to 'Camp', from which they wrote their reports on recent events in Bushire, Kuwait, Bahrein or Muscat. Nobody worried that the nearest 'Camp' was a thousand miles away in Karachi, but the Embassy in Tehran was once surprised to receive a report from the Gulf dated from 'Camp, Srinagar, Kashmir'. No complaint was made, because it would have been unworthy of those living in the permanent coolth of 4,000 feet to criticize any European who longed for respite from a temperature of 120°F plus 90 per cent humidity.

It is implicit that an Ambassador must not only be leader but trainer of his team. He will remember that there are no bad men, only bad officers and worse COs. When he leaves he should be able to feel that every member of the staff is happier and more competent; that all the dogs will bark more melodiously when (but only when) necessary, and that they will eye him askance if he himself barks too loudly or too often. He must keep a watchful eye on their work, encourage, suggest and never be chary of praise. If he has to prod, he will do so in such a manner as to inspire improvement, not implant a grievance. He will permit the frankest discussion in an informal atmosphere and will himself benefit much from such freedom of expression by his staff. Though they must know what is in his mind, he is wise, particularly in small Missions, to reduce portentous conferences to a minimum, for these tend to waste the time of many of the participants and may increase an undesirable sense of hierarchy. If they *must* be held daily, they should be strictly limited to half an hour, as are the Permanent Under Secretary's daily confabulations with senior officials in the Foreign Office. It is noticeable in many foreign Ministries and Embassies that one cannot make contact with any senior official between the hours of, say, 9 a.m. and 10 a.m. and sometimes until far later, because they are all 'in conference'. One wonders how on earth they manage to get through their stint when so long has been spent on talk.

'The virus of decision by committee which has clogged the wheels of government in Washington for a decade has spread to every Embassy of any size', Thayer records.[21] He continues with examples that will cause the most thick-skinned to wince with pain; and Jackson states tersely that planning discussions are not a cure-all and may be a narcotic; above all they must be flexible.[22] He also quotes the present United States Ambassador in London as testifying: 'If you want to see anybody in Defence or State, or any other Department I know of, they seem to be perpetually off in committee meetings.'[23] American Embassies have an informal organization known as the 'Country Team' consisting of the Ambassador, the Deputy Chief of Mission and other senior officials, including the heads of attached agencies and attachés. This group will meet regularly—perhaps in some cases too frequently. The practice of more casual meetings in the evening over a drink, to which the title 'Dongo' has, for good reason, been applied in some British Embassies, is preferable to many eyes.

The equipoise between the tug of too much zeal, much to be

deprecated, and the push of initiative, to be encouraged, is not easy to teach—but it must be done. The *locus classicus* of the combination of uninstructed zeal and effective initiative occurred when Lord Bryce was British Ambassador in Washington. One day the State Department rang to say that they were ready to receive him ceremonially to sign the Anglo-American Fishery Convention. Not having heard of this important international agreement, the Ambassador temporized. Hasty enquiries revealed that a junior secretary of the Embassy had for weeks been negotiating privily with the State Department on the basis of some faint indications from London. Alas, the Convention was not signed that day, and the secretary no doubt harboured a colony of fleas in his ear for many a day. Even so, most Ambassadors, if interrogated privately, would admit they preferred initiative to lethargy and utter reliability to both.

A Head of Mission must avoid the temptation to become tethered to the capital. Conditions—climatic, economic and political—may vary widely throughout the country and he should be familiar with the provincial atmosphere. Touring is always arduous; even if conditions of travel and sojourn are not rugged, the visitor is under the constant strain of meeting many new people, listening to them and trying to assess their worth— possibly in a language with which he is imperfectly acquainted. Particularly if the area has rarely or not lately been visited, careful planning is required; this is underscored in TWFM.[24] A Head of Mission is wise always to take with him a member of his staff and, after they return to hotel or camp, they will have many late and prolonged sittings together collating their views and noting down personalities and headings for a report. Such a record is indispensable for continuity. The next to make a tour in that district will know what and whom to look for and will ink further details into the picture.

☆

Apart from work in his office, his tours in the country and heavy social engagements, a Head of Mission and his wife—and also to a considerable extent senior members of the staff and their wives—are involved in countless extracurricular activities. Space does not permit a recital of all these, but it is easy to envisage their scope and variety. A Head of Mission is *ex hypothesi* an important personage, whose presence at a gathering is considered an honour, but this should not lead *him* to think he is a demigod. He should not, for instance, fall into a sulk if his entire staff do not turn up obsequiously to meet him or see him off every time he travels. They are better employed elsewhere; it is quite sufficient for one or two to be at hand on arrival or departure in case there are any important bits of news or last-minute matters to discuss. It is a pleasant custom in the British, American[25] and some other Services that, when an Ambassador and his wife attend a reception given by someone else, members of the staff should invariably drift up to greet them when they arrive and watch out unobtrusively to see if they need anything. In earlier days it was *de rigueur* that none of the staff should leave before the Ambassador, but once again it is preferable to be sensible. Some may have later engagements of their own (possibly involving serving up a meal); it should be quite enough for one or two to stay and see their Ambassador into his car. Such matters can easily be arranged in advance if the Embassy is working smoothly as a team.

The Ambassador and his wife will be flooded with invitations, often not merely to attend but to open anything from a bridge to a school, an art exhibition to a power station. Frequently these ceremonies demand a speech, sometimes even a lecture. It is only wise, therefore, for members of any Diplomatic Service to learn very early not to flinch from the sound of their own voices. When they attain higher rank they will speak easily, let us hope briefly and with a due injection of humour, in their own or if necessary the local vernacular. To cope with the latter can be something of a trial, particularly if there is a sudden call for an impromptu speech. Until fluency in the language has been attained, it is well to enquire carefully in advance if a 'few words' are likely to be required.

An Ambassador, and very much more his wife, runs something like an official hotel—as do members of the Mission's staff on a scale at least as onerous in comparison with resources. Not only meals and drinks, but accommodation must be provided. In large Embassies these demands can be very heavy. It is, for instance, safe to assume that in the course of a year the British Ambassador in Paris will give beds to the extent of 250 'house guest nights', meals to not far short of 2,000 persons, and drinks or teas to another 1,800—not counting the annual reception in honour of the Queen's Birthday, which will average 2,800. For comparison, in a very small Embassy the total would be more like: house guests 20, meals 500, drinks and teas 900 and Queen's Birthday Party 400. Even so, these are formidable figures and in the less civilized posts demand prodigious work and ingenious improvisation by host and above all hostess.

The burden of accepting hospitality can be as severe. Recently a Consul-General at what is probably the busiest British post in this respect accepted invitations on the average per month to seven lunches, seven dinners, thirteen cocktail parties and five other 'functions' (meetings, exhibitions, lectures, etc.). This works out at about one a day, on top of his *own* entertaining and office work. No wonder that one of his predecessors was said on leaving 'to have nothing left but a tired smile'.

Heavy though the burden may be, Ambassadors of any nationality would agree that the great majority of their guests give them enormous pleasure. Most are, in the nature of things, men and women of distinction in one field or another, and browsing through a visitors' book calls up a wave of happy recollection. It is nice to be well enough housed to be able to put up such charming and interesting folk and see that their requests are met. The visitors in return will often render valuable service. They can discuss important matters with authority in public or in small groups, and it may be profitable to invite them to address the Mission staff. Moreover, when they return home they will be able to some extent to act as emissaries of the Mission. As TWFM puts it: 'I think embassies have a role to play in creating a more informed attitude on the part of the American public toward their State Department and Foreign Service. It is only through actual contact with the embassies that our citizens can fully appreciate the vital role we play.'[26] Visitors of all nationalities can thus serve as interpreters at home.

Mention of houses, however, will remind some Ambassadors that not all official Residences are convenient, gracious or economical to run in an era when every penny is scrutinized by persons unacquainted with local problems. Some date from days when dozens of servants were not only easily obtainable but cheap to hire. In the world of today such a mansion can be a millstone round the neck of the incumbent, who finds himself rapidly sinking into a sea of debt, while his wife is desperately trying to run a vast house efficiently with staff inadequate in skill and numbers. In the Chancery the Head of Mission can count on a high degree of competence; his wife will be the envy of all colleagues if she finally achieves a similar level with the staff of the Residence. Many guests in smaller Embassies do not realize that it was often their hostess who had not only cooked much of the dinner, but supervised every detail. We all do this every day in our own homes, but it is a mighty achievement in more grandiose surroundings. Informality may often be the best solution; one United States Ambassador has written: 'I tell my staff "Let's not keep up with the Joneses. We don't have to. We are the Joneses".'[27]

There is sometimes a backlash of criticism, which can take two forms. If an Ambassador tries to give his guest a decent meal—opens that precious tin of pâté and decants one of his last bottles of drinkable claret, for instance—he may hear later that he is being accused by the guest after his return home of living like a millionaire. Alternatively, if a recently engaged and half-trained maid slops some soup over the visitor, the criticism takes some such form as 'they didn't even serve me a decent meal; but I bet they do to their rich foreign friends'. The same will apply to transport. If a Cadillac, Mercedes or Rolls meets some people, they will complain of ostentation, though the official car is ten years old and anyone would personally prefer a more modest and reliable vehicle; if they are met by a station wagon, they have been insulted. One has to learn to live with this.

One of the most attractive features of a diplomatic career is that wives can play a greater part than in most other professions, both behind the scenes and on many a brightly lit stage. It is one of the first duties of an Ambassadress to help wives of the staff, some of whom may have little experience of life abroad and need pilotage in social niceties. The aftermath of an invitation can be surprising. A wife once rang mine dutifully after a dinner party. 'Thank you for a lovely evening', she said, 'I did enjoy my food. I felt quite full.' We were delighted by this honest expression of appreciation. Too often it is one's lot to serve carefully chosen wines and food prepared with much concern and labour to people who gulp and swill. Another Ambassadress invited to lunch a wife who manifested hesitation on the telephone. 'Oh Lady X', she said, 'you should see my stomach.' It turned out that she was badly sunburnt. The Ambassadress advised her not to wear a girdle and the itching wife duly came. I tell these stories not in mockery—for nicer wives than those I have quoted do not exist—but to illustrate a social point. It may not matter to make such frank remarks in your own country or to your Ambassadress, but many a foreigner would take them amiss; hence the need for guidance in the conventions of expression.

While the Ambassador has been reading with selective voracity and writing frugally, listening much and talking little in his office or out visiting, he will know that his wife has been calling at the nursing home, where an archivist's wife has had a difficult confinement, having a heart-to-heart talk with a homesick typist over a cup of coffee, and visiting a committee of local ladies who are trying to improve their own world. At meetings like this she may well be accompanied by one or two Embassy wives, and others will be working with different groups. The target for wives in diplomacy, apart from their manifold household problems, is at once large and inchoate. There are some valuable reflections in TWFM[28] and further reference will be found in chapter VII(3) under Welfare.

The Ambassador and his wife will compare notes that evening. They may well be looking forward to a pleasant entertainment at their own house or elsewhere, at which they will be meeting old friends or making the acquaintance of interesting new people. The odds are, however, that in duty bound they are changing their clothes hastily for that party at the Khoon Consulate, which they feel they must attend, because he may manage a word inconspicuously with Herr Blut about the Sangre hydroelectric scheme, and she with the Krov Ambassadress about that Charity Bazaar at the Veri Insititute.

They are likely to reflect ruefully that because, for duty reasons, they are going to yet another sticky party, they will be accused of belonging to an effete and sybaritic tribe by those who have no inkling of the arts and crafts and immense burden of diplomacy. They will be strengthened by conviction that the task is worthy and by pride in seeing it well done. Yet it would only be human if sometimes they wished that they could have scrambled eggs and bacon at seven and bed at eight, with those books that have lain unread too long.

☆

It is salutary for an Ambassador to remember that, while a Mission can carry on without him (indeed it is not unknown for it to be suggested that it functions better), it would break down instantly without the Queen's Messenger who conveys the diplomatic bags, the Cypher Officer who copes with the telegrams, the Accountant, the Archivist, the Typist, the Messenger, the Telephone Operator and the rest of the key staff. A good Counsellor can instantly step into the ambassadorial shoes; an Ambassador with no such impunity into the teleprinter room. If a Head of Mission maintains this sense of proportion and humility, it will help him and his wife to realize the importance of what the Royal Navy calls a 'happy ship'.

It is true that all Heads of Missions count on support from their staffs on duty occasions. My wife and I always took the explicit line: this is not *our* house, but the Queen's; we are honoured to represent Her Majesty, but you too are hosts; make yourselves at home and above all see that the guests feel at home too; we cannot supervise everything at a large reception. It is up to you to tip the wink to the servants if more drinks, cigarettes or snacks are required. Above all, we rely on you to look after guests as you would in *your* house.

This should be a pleasant duty, but a 'happy ship' is much more than duty; ultimately it depends on the real human interest that the Ambassador and his wife take in the well-being of every member of the staff, no matter how junior, and in their wives and children—all alike exiles. If the staff of a small Embassy feel they cannot drop in without invitation at the Residence; if those at a medium-sized Embassy are not asked to intimate friendly parties; if those at a large one feel completely ignored, there is something wrong—and there is no doubt where the responsibility lies. The snooty Head of Mission may occasionally be mentioned in the world press, but he will have no standing in the hearts of men and women, where alone victories are won.

He will also be wise to remember that, even if he does hit an occasional headline—usually because he has been hit on the nose by an adroitly thrown rock—he will not go down in history, not nowadays. For the century from 1770 onwards, the student will still find in his textbooks the names of Ambassadors who influenced the course of history; Benjamin Franklin in Paris and Stratford Canning in Constantinople are clear examples. It is improbable that the school books (i.e. the general reading, not the select material of specialists) of 2066 will mention the name of any Ambassador of any nationality, active between, say, 1926 and 1966. The present-day Ambassador had better resign himself to this and meanwhile realize that, even without historical immortality, he can still be of inconspicuous service to his country and perhaps to the world. Others may reap the credit, both today and later in the books, but someone has to help and that is worth doing, modestly and happily, with the acknowledged assistance of a loyal staff. It is something if he has made sufficient impact on the country in which he is serving for his name to be remembered there with affection for a few years.

III

THE STRUCTURE OF
A MISSION

WE MUST NOW look closely at the machine that supports the Head of Mission, for without it he would be helpless.

1. THE CHANCERY

The core of an Embassy is, in British parlance, the Chancery.[1] We can begin with some language delving. A Chancellor was originally a kind of door keeper in charge of a chancel, a latticed barrier. We now only use the word chancel in church architecture for the area behind the rood screen. In German the Latin word has produced not only *Kanzel*, a pulpit, but also *Kanzler*, a Chancellor, and the office in which he works, the *Kanzlei*. The chief Minister of State of Austria and Germany in imperial times and still today has been the Chancellor. *Reichskanzler* was the correct title of the demonic house-painter Adolf Hitler, even though he preferred that of *Führer*. In most Spanish-speaking countries the *Canciller* is the Minister for Foreign Affairs, who works in the *Cancillería*. In French we find a *Chancellerie* in an Embassy, exactly as the British use Chancery for its main office, but this may be a recent importation from the English (it is not given in Larousse). A *Chancelier* in the French Diplomatic Service is a comparatively junior official, comparable with the archivist of a British Embassy (and a *Chancelière* is not only his wife but an old-fashioned foot-warmer).

The Concise Oxford Dictionary gives as one of the meanings of Chancellery: 'Position, staff, department, official residence, of a chancellor; an office attached to an embassy or consulate.' This is simply not true in England. No taxi-driver in London (by far the best-informed source), no MP, no member of the electorate has ever referred to No. 11 Downing Street, the official residence of the Chancellor of the Exchequer, as the 'Chancellery'; nor thus to his office, which is called the Treasury; nor thus to the office of a British Embassy. In British parlance the Embassy office is not a Chancellery* but a Chancery, and neither in English nor French are the operative words 'Chancery/*Chancellerie*' ever attached to a Consulate; the sooner Oxford wakes to these facts, the better.

In times past, when staffs were much smaller than today—in fact in most cases up to 1939—the Chancery formed part of the Ambassador's Residence; at the very least it was in a wing or contiguous block. Up to 1914 entirely, and until 1939 almost completely, the Chancery was the whole Embassy, with the sole addition of Service Attachés. There was only political work; such accretions as Commercial and Information Departments came later. To have the office so close was highly convenient for the Ambassador and also for his staff who, if they were working late, could drop into the Residence to consult their chief. Moreover, many of the Residences were gracious old buildings of considerable architectural merit. It was pleasant to work in such surroundings, and the feeling of being members of a family—so difficult to maintain nowadays in much larger establishments—was agreeably preserved.

Staffs of all countries in all capitals have now swollen enormously. Not only must offices be larger, but spacious areas have to be provided for parking cars, and an office is better placed

---

* Thayer (p. 113) does give this word for the central office of an American Embassy, but I think this usage has died. *The Times*, dreaming its long dreams, also still occasionally uses it in this sense.

where it is most accessible for the business purposes of visitors. In smaller cities the Ambassador and members of his staff will prefer to live in residential areas on the outskirts, where gardens are a possibility, the ears not deafened by the roar of traffic and the nose less assailed by fumes.

☆

The Chancery, then, is the hub of a Mission. The linchpin of the Chancery, without which it cannot safely revolve, is in British usage the Head of Chancery—an officer for whom there exists no equivalent title in other languages. Indeed, it has not hitherto existed in High Commissions, though Plowden has recommended the adoption of the practice.[2]

In the United States Foreign Service, the place of the Head of Chancery is to some extent taken by the Deputy Chief of Mission —a title (it is not a rank) not known in the British Service, which does, however, have Deputy High Commissioners. The DCM is the chief of staff as well as the second in command, and as the *alter ego* of the Ambassador he exercises what has been well described as 'an unclear authority over other segments of the Mission'. There has been some talk in the State Department of reinstituting the title 'Head of Chancery', but the idea has not gained momentum. Sometimes the Chief of the Political Section informally assumes the function of Head of Chancery as in the British Service. Some of the manifold responsibilities of the DCM are set out in TWFM.[3]

In British practice, the Head of Chancery is not a grade or rank and he may be a Counsellor, First or Second Secretary, depending on the size of the Embassy. He is not only what would be called in the Royal Navy the executive officer of the ship or in the army the adjutant of a battalion, but also the chief of staff to the Ambassador, though there may often be other Diplomatic Officers senior to him on the staff. In the same way the chief of staff of a general commanding an army may be a major-general, though there are lieutenant-generals senior to him, each commanding a corps in the general's army.

It is this double function of chief of staff and executive officer that throws such a burden on the Head of Chancery. In the first role he is the Ambassador's adviser on political matters and must know just as much as his chief about what is passing in the country in which he is serving. He must have at his own level the same intimate local contacts that are essential for the efficient conduct of diplomatic business. If, as is often the case in large establishments, there is senior to him on the political side in the Embassy a Counsellor or Minister, he must still have his direct day-by-day contact with the Ambassador and yet keep the other officer informed of all he needs to know. Strictly speaking, such a Counsellor or Minister is not a member of Chancery; he is off on a side line, ready to step in as Chargé d'Affaires when the Ambassador is absent, but also playing his full part by relieving both Ambassador and Head of Chancery of some of their burden. In the largest Embassies there will also be 'Commercial' and other Ministers senior to the Head of Chancery. They are heads of their departments, but show themselves unwise if they bypass the Head of Chancery in matters of general concern—which nowadays most important matters are. The Head of Chancery, like any good chief of staff, is responsible not only for political work, but for co-ordination of the manifold activities of a complicated machine.

In his second capacity as executive officer, the Head of Chancery is charged with the supervision of all the organization and day-to-day work of the Embassy. Though he may have an Administration Officer under him to deal with the details, responsibility for intricate personnel and welfare problems falls to him, mixed up with accounts, transport arrangements, teleprinter breakdowns, lack of ventilation or heating in the typistry—the whole gamut. Above all, the Head of Chancery is the prime recipient of complaints from inside or outside the Embassy. The only thing he can be utterly confident of is that, if anything goes wrong anywhere, it is his fault.

It is of historical interest to interpolate that up to 1914 it was a grave *faux pas* for a British Ambassador to enter uninvited the rooms housing the Chancery—and the invitation was rarely extended. The Ambassador summoned the Head of Chancery, discussed with him and gave his orders, but what happened then was up to the Head of Chancery, king in his own domain. All this sounds odd today, when there is more camaraderie and many an Ambassador has been known to help decypher telegrams.

A good Head of Chancery is beyond all price. The work is intensely hard but very rewarding, since it involves not only the normal political activity of diplomacy and contact with commercial and other branches, but the human touch required to form and direct a team. There are few keener satisfactions than helping to guide without friction a machine equal to all the demands of one's superiors, maintaining their peace of mind by concealing from them the artifices sometimes required in emergency, and seeing to it that—no matter what the obstacles—the letter is delivered, the telegram cyphered or the asperities smoothed. For an Ambassador there is no greater solace than a happy team in close support behind him; the knowledge that any sudden crisis will be met by an unflurried Head of Chancery, himself sustained by well-ordered and cheerful subordinates. On the other hand, there is nothing more nerve-racking than an inadequate Head of Chancery, forcing the Ambassador, instead of looking forwards and around him, to peer nervously over his shoulder with only half his mind on his real job.

Among many other qualities required by the Head of Chancery, prevision should be rated very high. The unexpected is bound to occur, but provision should have been made for it. A sudden attack of appendicitis will necessitate a rapid reallocation of duties, so that the smooth working of the machine is not interrupted. The Ambassador may be absent for the day and therefore unreachable when trouble bursts. Such tornadoes may be of local origin (the wilier would-be dictators are apt to choose Easter Saturday or some similar holiday for a putsch), or, in all Diplomatic Services, they may originate from the home end, and again Saturday afternoons are a favoured moment. The reason for this is obvious. After mulling over a problem during

61

the week, the various Foreign Offices finally despatch their instructions on Friday afternoon and leave for a restful weekend— such at least is the view of everyone serving abroad. Thus it is at the most inconvenient moment that there arrives an 'emergency' telegram instructing the Ambassador to tell the Minister of Foreign Affairs instantly that his government takes the gravest view of . . . and hopes that the Baratarian government will at once do . . ., something so improbable that the Cypher Officer checks and rechecks the telegram. Even if the telegrams are despatched in the middle of the week, all is not well, for home ministries have to deal with so many countries that they can hardly be expected to recall every local feast day. These hurricane messages tend therefore to arrive on the Feast Day of St Simon and St Jude, or the Birthday of the Prophet's Aunt—one or other of which is rightly celebrated as a whole holiday in Barataria. Or they arrive when the Minister for Foreign Affairs is absent, perhaps engaged in diversions so unorthodox that he has carefully refrained from informing his staff of his whereabouts.

If the Ambassador is away when the storm breaks, the efficient Head of Chancery will not be flummoxed, for he will have been careful to maintain cordial relations with the uncle of the Minister's chauffeur. By the time his chief returns his Head of Chancery will have ascertained an unlisted telephone number, to which a surprised Minister will reply. Happy the Ambassador who is so served; miserable is he who can never leave his post, lest the unexpected strike an inefficient subordinate.

Ambassador, Head of Chancery and all their subordinates (also the Service Attachés and Seconded Officers, who are mentioned later) may be caught out by local crises, but they have no excuse for ignorance about what is happening in a wider sphere. Daily, weekly or fortnightly they should receive by bag or telegram from home reports on the most intimate details of what is passing in the world. It may be uncomfortable or even dangerous to serve in some posts, but at least you should have the means to rasp the rust from your blade and keep it sharp and shining.

There we can leave the Head of Chancery. Under a good chief, his capacity will be enhanced and he will bear in mind the dictum quoted by Sir George Mallaby to the effect that you should always learn the job of the man above you because you never know when you may suddenly be called on to fill it.[4] The Head of Chancery realizes that he has been given the chance to show his ability with men and women of varied nationalities, languages and religions, and with intricate political, economic and military problems. He may rise to these heights, inspire confidence above and below him, and thus be assured of rapid advancement. He may not attain such standards—he should be the first to realize this himself—in which case less onerous responsibilities will fall to his lot. The conduct of diplomatic affairs is too strenuous and potentially dangerous to be entrusted to those who cannot control themselves, lead their subordinates or inspire confidence in their superiors, and of course in the foreigners among whom an Embassy dwells.

The work is now more strenuous than in the past, not merely because there is more of it, but because of the proliferation of attached departments. In the American Service this is a byword, and there is grave danger that the British Service may fall into the same error. A political Chancery should be strong enough numerically and in quality to run a Mission and, if necessary, over-rule enthusiastic but politically inexperienced attached experts, even if they are very senior in rank. Similarly it is the political departments in the Foreign Office that should have the last say, though they are now outnumbered by a swarm of 'specialist' departments and heavily staffed outlying organizations.

☆

As the Ambassador depends on his Head of Chancery, so does the latter depend on his team. In a small Mission this may consist of only one other officer and a handful of juniors; in a large one, such as the British Embassy in Washington, of a couple of dozen officers and numerous subordinate staff (not counting the Commercial Secretariat and other semi-independent departments).

In a big post the Chancery will be divided into subsections and, as no one man can keep in effective touch with every detail, the Head of Chancery will delegate much to the heads of these; as with an Ambassador, he is a menace if he keeps dogs and tries to do all their barking for them.

In a small Embassy everyone must expect to be a maid of all work. There will probably be only one typist and one archivist; when either is absent the Third Secretary will buckle down to their jobs, as well as doing the cyphering. The Pooh Bah role is, of course, very valuable experience, and Ambassadors and Heads of Chancery should encourage their juniors to play such parts. If the Labour Counsellor is on leave, someone must attend the local Trade Union Conference and he will learn much in the process. If the Air Attaché is away and an enquiry is received about the length of the airport runway and the average temperature thereon at noon in November, an efficient Third Secretary will not only acquire the information, but a lot of knowledge about personalities and politics in local airlines. In the absence, owing to a violent domestic dispute, of one of the Embassy chauffeurs I once took over his job for a couple of days, which included a most enjoyable backstage evening at a palace party, where, quite unintentionally, I learnt more about the reigning monarch from his domestics than the most expert secret agent could have acquired at great expenditure—indeed, far from disbursing money, I was remarkably well fed from the royal kitchen.

The larger Embassies will have separate sections for subordinate departments of the Chancery. These more than deserve individual mention, because it cannot be sufficiently stressed that without devoted and unpublicized service at lower levels, the whole machine would grind to a thunderous stop, no matter how much Whitehall blew off steam or the Ambassador thumped his desk, announcing loudly, 'I am badly served'—this was the actual phrase frequently used by one British Ambassador who, though he never attained fame, so trained his subordinates that many reached the highest levels.

In the largest British Embassies there will be what is known as 'the Private Office' consisting of a Private Secretary, a Personal Assistant and perhaps another typist, who attend to the needs of the Ambassador. At very busy posts the Ambassadress will also require a Social Secretary, not a member of the Service, who will perhaps be a native of the country. In the United States Foreign Service the Private Secretary is known as the Staff Aide or Assistant. The Private Office will keep the senior staff of the Embassy informed of the Ambassador's engagements, so that they can ask him to raise with Ministers or others matters of moment, on which perhaps they have failed to obtain satisfaction at their own level. It is rare for an Ambassador to keep a social engagement without having to do some business.

In all Missions there will be a Registry, where papers are filed by the archivists and where the diplomatic bags are opened and made up, and ordinary mail received and despatched. Next door will be a Typistry, the purpose of which is obvious. Here labour the girls without whose brisk fingers the Embassy machine would collapse. Ashton-Gwatkin records that the first (female) shorthand typist was engaged in the Foreign Office in 1889,[5] and a pretty stir that must have caused.

I had the good fortune to play many parts during my service. Thinking back over those pleasant years, I am sure that the brief period during which I was the only typist at a Legation under a meticulous Minister was the most exacting. Like anyone else I can 'hunt and peck' with two fingers and an occasional thumb on the space bar, but to turn out neat work was a grievous burden. There is much to be said for being forced to try your hand when young and formative at every job a Service can offer. You are unlikely thereafter either to overestimate your own importance or to underestimate the skill of others. I had been for periods cypher officer, accountant and archivist at an earlier post, but in these roles errors could easily be retrieved. If, for instance, one added up a column of figures incorrectly, one crossed out the wrong total and wrote in the right one. Not so with typing. I gave a slap-up dinner to our Miss Macintosh when she returned from a month's leave.

Nearby, too, will be the Cypher Room, which requires a large staff if telegraphic traffic is heavy. On the whole cyphering and decyphering are sheer drudgery, but there are occasional moments of excitement. Such was the incident many years ago when the cypher safe with all its precious contents fell through the floor of the lorry conveying it from the British Legation in Tehran to the summer Legation in Gulhek up in the hills. The lorry was immobilized and the safe for some hours inextricable. Fortunately the door was uppermost, so telegrams were brought to the site of the accident, where the Cypher Officer coped with them, spending the night on guard by the roadside.

Much more embarrassing was the discovery early one morning at the height of the last war that the safe containing the cyphers of another British Embassy would not open. At such a period of pressure this was a real crisis. Telegrams were pouring in and many awaited despatch. Complicated and tedious alternative methods had to be used, involving such delays that the Embassy would obviously soon be swamped by the rising flood. All efforts to manipulate the combination lock failed, so the Head of Chancery scoured the town for a powerful electric drill. When applied to the door, the bit merely skidded over the surface, doing little more than scar the paint. Explosives were ruled out by lack of experience in safe-cracking, so a letter was sent by the overnight King's Messenger to a neighbouring post in a city with a large and variegated population, asking it to send spare books and above all a competent tame burglar. For purposes of telephone calls he was to be referred to as 'Jameson'. Each morning the Head of Chancery rang up to ask after him. He was 'on a holiday', but it was hoped to trace him soon. Three days passed and then came the welcome news that Jameson was on the night train and would wear a white buttonhole as identification. The Head of Chancery met him next morning. He was a quiet little man, soberly dressed and carrying a small black bag. He was rushed to the Embassy, the problem was explained and he was shown the drill. He indicated derisively that any fool should know that, while the doors of safes were of hardened steel, the rest was usually tin. Sure enough, when half a dozen of the staff had manhandled the safe out from the wall, the drill perforated the back like putty. Jameson bored a dozen holes each touching the other, until he had made an opening about three inches square. Mercifully the books were not tightly packed and could be pushed aside. By the light of an electric torch, the back plate of the lock could then be seen and its holding screw undone with the aid of long pliers from the little black bag. Then for an hour Jameson poked skilfully at the concentric rings of the lock until they were properly aligned and the door swung open.

No fee had been fixed for Jameson and the Head of Chancery asked him for a valuation of his services. Looking, without his identifying daisy, more demure than ever, he diffidently suggested the equivalent of £3 10s. He was given a fiver and seen off on the night train to resume his interrupted 'holiday'.

The volume of telegraphic traffic round the world would stagger the normal person, if he allowed himself to worry about it. He might then fear that a sort of electric smog was building up in the atmosphere that would soon stifle all living creatures. The Department of State's *daily* contribution (in and out) is put at 400,000 words. The Foreign Office lags with 165,000 at the latest count, but the British maintain with some pride that their 1965 figure is over twice that of 1962.

When there is a sudden spate of telegrams in a small Mission— and Whitehall, which emits three times as much as it receives, may forget how meagre the staff is in some places—it is not unknown for the Ambassador and even the Honorary Chaplain to lend a hand when the normal teams are tiring late at night and strings of figures continue to arrive. This practice is not to be recommended, unless Ambassador and Chaplain have previous experience in cyphering, which is rare with the Church. At least it is better restricted to incoming rather than outgoing traffic, lest you receive a monotonous series of telegrams in reply to yours stating bleakly: 'Your No. so-and-so completely inde-cypherable. Please check and repeat.' Clearly all staff should be trained in this work early in their careers. Fortunately nowadays much cyphering is done by machine and the long hours of slavery are reduced, though they remain vivid in the minds of those who endured them in the past.

Grander establishments lead more sedate lives, but even so the Ambassador occasionally and the Head of Chancery frequently will drop in on cypher or wireless room, registry or typistry out of hours to pass the time of day or night, on Saturday afternoons and Sundays, when everyone else has gone home and only a lonely few are left working. The welcome intruder will be given a greeting more heart-warming than at many social diplomatic receptions and high level interviews.

In many parts of the world telegram traffic is both heavy and liable to interruption. Some countries therefore prefer to man their own communications network. In Britain this is known as the Diplomatic Wireless Service, representatives of which work in Embassies. Through their agile hands pass, in clear language or in cypher, messages between the Foreign Office and the Missions overseas. The highly skilled members of the DWS are technical experts, separately recruited. Those of them who serve overseas in Missions are temporary members of the Diplomatic Service. They and their wives are just as much part of the Embassy 'team' as all the rest.

☆

Attached to the Chancery there will also be an Administration Section, which will include a subsection dealing with Accounts. In a very small British Embassy with a modest staff, these roles will be doubled. The Head of Chancery will be his own Administration Officer; the archivist will also do the accounts and the typist will assist with cyphering, if she cannot trust the Ambassador with this task.

Administration can be a very heavy burden, increasing with the size of a Mission. The Administration Officer has to be a person of outstanding versatility and patience, since his duties have no boundaries. Apart from the obvious work in the Embassy itself, he will assist staff to find accommodation and this may well produce curious results. After his first month in a house in a Near Eastern post, a Secretary in the British Embassy found that his electricity bill was gigantic. Investigation disclosed three wires coming over the wall from neighbours. These he cut one evening and the district was plunged into darkness. Within minutes he was besieged by indignant callers, including a garage proprietor and a half-shaved individual with the soap still on his face, who protested that the barber must be allowed to finish the job.

The Administration Officer, with the help of volunteers, may well run a sort of shop or commissary, for which supplies are ordered in bulk from the home country or some other convenient source of supply.[6] The United States Service has not Administration but Administrative Officers and Sections. The burden on them is similar to the British but heavier owing to the much larger size of Missions. For a brief review see FAPS 3[7] and TWFM.[8]

On the subject of administration Plowden has said what many had for so long argued:

> Good management is a matter which, both at home and abroad, must not be regarded as in any way inferior to policy work. All senior staff must accept that they have a responsibility for good management. If Administrative work is regarded by senior officers as something which merits only their passing attention or if the Administration Officers are not up to their job, the effectiveness of the entire Service will be reduced.[9]

This view is not shared by all Diplomatic Services; the French, for instance, who have fewer in the 'officer grades' than the British, concentrate their efforts on the higher levels of policy and leave administration to juniors.

The Administration Officer will control inter alia the messengers. Some of these will be local. The British, known as Security Guards, form a separate branch of the Diplomatic Service;* there are about 300 of them. American Embassies throughout the world employ nearly 1,000 Marines in this role. The telephone and teleprinter operators also come under the immediate

---

* For British Diplomatic Service grades and branches see Appendix A.

supervision of the Administration Officer. So do drivers. A large Mission will have a pool of cars with local chauffeurs available to the staff for official journeys and sometimes, in places where public transport is poor or unreliable, on repayment for recreational or social purposes. The Administration Officer will check inventories and supervise official stores of stationery and the like; he may even be responsible for a 'Travel Section'. Posts like Washington and New York receive and despatch streams of visiting firemen by air, sea and train. The more important of these must be met and seen off, often at ungodly hours. These travellers include the Queen's Messengers, who convey round the world diplomatic bags that must be carefully safeguarded. Such activities will bring the Administration Officer into intimate contact with the local Customs officials. If they are obdurate he may well be involved in protracted conflicts over the importation of goods addressed to the Embassy.

In short, while the functions of an Administration Officer, who in larger Missions deserves a high status, may be said to have a beginning, there is certainly no end to them. In this vast and inchoate sphere he is as much a key man as the Head of Chancery, who will lean heavily on him if he is capable and grieve *sotto voce* if he is not.

Finally, mention must be made of the locally engaged staff, for the most part not British. Some will be menials, cleaners and the like, but many will be of considerable seniority and long service. Without them no Chancery could function, because they provide the local expertise so difficult for a newcomer to acquire. The obscure clerk who knows his way round the Customs; the translator who can produce for you a daily summary of the local press in an obscure tongue and act as interpreter; the skilled mechanic who services the electric light plant and the plumbing —all are indispensable. The British Service throughout the world employs some 8,600 locally engaged staff—loyal servants of the Crown, who may at times suffer persecution from their co-nationals because they serve a foreign power. It is the more remarkable that there have been countless examples not only of very long service, but of devotion in circumstances of strain and danger by employees, both publicly and privately paid. Some, since the Second World War, have been 'stateless persons'—a grief-shaken phrase, easy for those with established homes to forget. The United States Foreign Service is laudably solicitous about its local staff.[10]

Such, then, are some of the duties of the Chancery. From this hub many spokes radiate. Before turning to them, we will note that a Chancery only works efficiently if it is a 'happy family', not only in the office but out of hours. Single members of the staff may well be lonely and will welcome invitations to picnics or sports at weekends. Outsiders of many nationalities will be invited, so that all can share in what the country has to offer and make the most of it.

2. THE COMMERCIAL SECTION

Of all the departments of an Embassy, the Commercial Secretariat* is and must be the most closely allied to the political Chancery. Indeed, the work is largely interwoven; in British practice the staff of both are now drawn from the Diplomatic Service, whether serving in Commonwealth or foreign countries. The Commercial staff will not necessarily have done all their service in this sector, but they will have shown a bent for economics and will have received special training either in the Foreign Office or by secondment to industry, to the Board of Trade, or to a university course. For an excellent survey of the economic representation of the United States abroad, see Barnett.[11]

The Commercial Departments of British Embassies are of

---

* In this sector, differences of national practice are marked, particularly between Britain and the United States. Space does not permit full comparison; I deal primarily with the British organization, with allusions to the methods of others.

comparatively recent creation. Germany first and later the United States realized earlier than the United Kingdom the importance of this facet of diplomacy. Although a Commercial Department was established in the Foreign Office in 1866, it was only during the last two decades of the nineteenth century that Commercial Attachés were first appointed to the larger Embassies. Their work grew steadily in importance, and in the same period greater impetus was given to the commercial work performed in British Consulates, some as important as smaller Embassies. At the end of the First World War, the Department of Overseas Trade was set up, semi-independent of the Foreign Office, and the first Commercial Secretary is mentioned in the Foreign Office list of 1919. Despite the ability and devotion of many of the staff, this compromise solution was doomed to failure; integration was preferable to cleavage into too many subdepartments. The Department of Overseas Trade was abolished in 1946 and all commercial work in foreign countries was thenceforth entrusted to Diplomatic Service personnel, whose postings are cleared with the Board of Trade, to which they do most of their reporting. In Commonwealth countries an odd arrangement endured up to 1965. The High Commissions were controlled by the Commonwealth Relations Office in Whitehall, but Trade Commissioners fell under the Board of Trade. They had separate offices, sometimes even in different cities, and were on occasion inclined to make it painfully plain that they worked entirely independently and were subject to no jurisdiction by the High Commissioners, who for their part often took no interest in economic matters.

Up to 1914—and indeed between the wars—what is now called 'export promotion' was left to private enterprise, and British businessmen needed less recourse to a Mission or Consulate. Nevertheless, they noted with envy the drive and enthusiasm of other countries and requested similar facilities. Today the far greater complexity of international trade and the enormous increase in governmental controls, quotas, tariffs and so forth, have rendered such support essential. No nation can afford to ignore its overseas trade, though many seem to delight in inventing new obstructions for the free movement of goods around the world. Transportation, in earlier years also left to private and free enterprise, is also involved. Many states impose nationalistic restrictions; others devise concealed subsidies to those who 'trade foreign'; almost worst is the constant change in regulations all over the globe dictated by governmental whims.

It is thus inevitable that, faced by constantly shifting complexities, the exporter is forced to rely more for information and assistance on Embassies abroad. Much of this work is the responsibility of the economic departments in London, primarily the Board of Trade, the Ministry of Power, the Export Credits Guarantee Department and the Treasury; but the Foreign Office must have a say in these important aspects of foreign relations—indeed, as I argue in chapter VIII, probably a more effective say than at present. The Foreign Office now therefore has its own economic departments* working in liaison with the economic Ministries in Whitehall, with which must be linked the Bank of England—so long an independent body which, though now nationalized, does not hesitate to take its own line. Among other matters senior officials must now be increasingly prepared for international economic conferences. These become more complex each year, partly owing to the increase in the numbers of participants as new nations emerge and urge their own cases with pardonable enthusiasm in an international forum.

Such are the reasons why it is necessary for governments to expand highly skilled departments dealing with economic matters, and for similar sections in Missions abroad to help commercial undertakings in a highly competitive struggle for markets. For Britain, the loss of foreign investment in two world wars and a persistent balance of payments problem particularly necessitate a large expansion in export promotion at home and abroad.

☆

* Sir Victor Wellesley, once an Under Secretary in the Foreign Office, had long urged that these be set up. See his book *Diplomacy in Fetters* (Hutchinson, London 1943); also Ashton-Gwatkin *passim*.

73

Before we come to the organization of the Commercial Department of a British Embassy abroad, we should be clear about the work expected of it and of its counterparts in the Missions of other countries. This task can be briefly summarized as follows:

1. To keep the Ambassador informed on local economic conditions.

2. To interpret the local situation to the Foreign Office and economic departments in Whitehall, and to act as their spokesman with the local government on economic matters.

3. To give industrial and commercial undertakings an honest picture of local economic conditions, so that they can judge for themselves whether an export effort will be rewarding and if so to what extent.

4. To acquire for the benefit of home country exporters full knowledge of local regulations, tariffs, contacts etc.—in fact everything affecting the mechanics of trade.

5. To report, either to the Board of Trade or at the request of individual firms, on the market for particular commodities.

6. To report openings for trade or investment, such as calls for tenders, the possibility of major industrial expansion and local demands for goods from the home country.

7. To advise firms in their dealings with local governments, especially when they are trying to obtain a government contract or experiencing difficulty with local regulations.

8. To help importers from the home country to find the best agents and to report on the commercial standing of local firms.

9. To guide visiting businessmen, often in minute and personal detail and be able to introduce them to the most influential contacts.

10. In conjunction with the Information Section of the Embassy to ensure that the local business community, industry, government and press are aware of what the home country has to offer.

11. Finally and continuously to bear in mind that economics

and politics are merely two aspects of one whole. Economic advantage may have to be sacrificed to political exigency, but in the field the closest liaison must be maintained by the Commercial Section with the Chancery and other departments of the Embassy.

It is against this background that we should discuss the organization of a Commercial Secretariat in an Embassy or Consulate. With the amalgamation of the Overseas Services in Britain, a similarity of practice in High Commissions in Commonwealth countries will follow.

In a large Embassy the Commercial staff will be appropriately numerous. Barnett makes the point that in American practice the economic section will be larger than the political.[12] In the British Embassy in Washington, for instance, there is a Commercial Department headed by a Commercial Minister, with two Commercial Counsellors, three First and two Second Secretaries —a body of officials large enough to staff a medium-sized Embassy completely. In a smaller Embassy the senior officer will be a Counsellor presiding over a Commercial Section. In Embassies of medium size there will be one or at most two UK based Commercial Secretaries, and in the smallest commercial work will be performed by the Chancery. In addition to these officers on the Diplomatic List there must be supporting staff. In large Missions typists and a registry of non-confidential papers separate from that of the Chancery will be required. In smaller establishments amalgamation will be more economical. In either case common services (telephones, messengers, cars, accounts and so on) will be shared.

Commercial work involves much local experience, and this implies knowledge of the language. It is therefore highly profitable to employ locally engaged specialists who provide continuity, as they are not shifted round the world like their career colleagues. They can render invaluable service to the UK based staff in pursuing enquiries, arranging agencies for British firms and so forth. They are often known in the British Service as

Market Officers, because one of their main tasks is to study demand. Sometimes these locally engaged officers are British subjects who happen to have settled in the region, but as likely as not they will be foreigners, probably nationals of the country. These highly qualified men, often with long years of service, have been shabbily treated in the past as regards pay, pensions and other conditions of service. It is pleasant to record that they are now receiving more recognition.* It is only right that such devotion should be recognized in this and other ways, but, as usual it will be a hard struggle to extract sufficient funds. I have known a visiting tycoon spend on one lunch party half the monthly salary of an invaluable local officer, who was not invited although he had arranged it.

Commercial Officers deal with a different range of contacts from the Chancery, though overlapping is never amiss in fruitful fields. The Chancery have much to do with the Ministry of Foreign Affairs and with local politicians, the Commercial Secretariat with the Ministries of Commerce and Finance, technical Ministries (Communications, Mines, Petroleum, Public Works etc.), nationalized industries, banks and businessmen. The Ambassador will deal at the highest levels with all these, and the Head of Chancery, as his chief of staff, will direct on economic affairs one of his many eyes.

Apart from a voluminous correspondence with private concerns in Britain, Commercial Secretaries report both to the Foreign Office and directly to other government departments such as the Board of Trade and Treasury, to which their specialized reports are of particular interest. In such matters a good Commercial Officer has much latitude. The United States Department of Commerce uses computers to direct such reports advantageously. Thus a manufacturer and exporter of bicycles will not receive general pamphlets by the ton, but only those touching his own activities. It is high time that the Board of Trade adopted such methods. At the moment in Britain many laboriously compiled and valuable reports are consigned to the wastepaper basket

* See, for example, chapter VI (2) below.

because firms have not time to extract from the mass of paper what is of direct interest to them.

There is always so much paper floating around that no Ambassador will want to read every routine report by his Commercial Secretariat. One effective device is the 'float file', which ensures that all sections of an Embassy, including Attachés and Seconded Officers, are kept in the picture. The value of this is not confined to Commercial Sections, but this is a convenient point to describe how it works. At the end of each week the Archivist will collect in folders all inward and outward telegrams, letters, despatches and reports, and circulate them to all members of the staff. Many of these papers will be merely routine, some can be skimmed through for the gist, others will require careful reading. Sometimes a paper in a 'float file' will provoke pained comment from another section, which will maintain that a wrong impression has been given and that they ought to have been consulted in advance. A correction may have to be sent off, and the Head of Chancery—who is rightly blamed for everything that goes wrong in an Embassy—sighs wearily and makes a mental note to ensure that in future X does not try to work on his own, but always has a word with Y and Z before bursting into type.

It is sometimes suggested that, if the Embassy is situated at any distance from the business centre of the capital, the Commercial Section offices should be placed more conveniently for local visiting businessmen. In one or two British posts this is the practice. Although at first sight there is much to be said for it, the disadvantages are overwhelming. The Commercial Section is not an outlying limb but an integral portion of the Embassy. It is essential that it work in the closest physical as well as mental liaison. It is noteworthy that the American Embassy in London, situated in the West End, does not find it necessary to rent an office in the City for its commercial or financial officers. However, this is not to say that a Commercial Secretary should be tied to his office. More than most members of the staff he must get around the capital and the country. This can be particularly necessary in connection with foreign aid programmes, to which I refer in

77

section 4 of this chapter. In Britain such funds are administered by the Overseas Development Ministry, but schemes must be locally appraised. This work is best confided to the Commercial Section under the Ambassador's over-all eye.

In some countries commercial work abroad is still allocated not to the Diplomatic Service, but to the Ministry of Commerce, as was the British practice in the Commonwealth. Some of the older Dominions still retain the divided control and it would sometimes seem that the Departments of External Affairs and Commerce are barely on speaking terms at home. This can produce wrangling abroad that becomes even more bitter if, in addition, there is any clash of personality between the Ambassador and the Commercial Counsellor, who is paid on a different basis, reporting to another department, using a separate accounting system and even different stationery, so that the letters of the Chancery will not fit into the commercial envelopes. It may well be that the divided system will soon be recognized as non-viable.

The United States has a different method again. Every Embassy has an Economic Section and there may in addition be a Commercial Section in the more important Missions.[13] The economic officers will deal with economic reporting and policy guidance; the commercial officers with trade promotion, representing the Department of Commerce. Both sets of officers come, however, from the Department of State. In addition, the Economic Section will exercise some supervision over the specialist attachés (Petroleum, Agriculture, Labour etc.).

It is now becoming possible for Commercial Officers in the British Service to be seconded to other departments at home, but it is very rare for members of those departments to be seconded to Embassies. There is an unfortunate if comprehensible reluctance on the part of many officials to leave their well-ordered homes to face the suspect discomforts of foreign parts and, of course, the inevitable separation from children at school at home. Officers may in later life rise to deal with world economic problems in Whitehall without ever having any experience beyond their own shores. This is regrettable and every inducement should be offered to them to serve for a spell overseas on an exchange basis. In the case of the Treasury, officers may even be exercising control over broad aspects of the administration of the Diplomatic Service when, as a colleague of mine once bleakly remarked, 'their overseas experience is limited to the Isle of Wight'. The Department of State in Washington wisely does not permit such interference from those whose experience is similarly limited to Long Island.

✤

The economic departments of no government, the commercial section of no Embassy, can themselves sustain foreign trade; they can only help to nourish it. The Commercial Secretary should be familiar with the local economic and political climate, obscure though this sometimes is. He should certainly be able to suggest the best local contacts to the visitor. He will either be able to speak the local language, or, if it is very abstruse, produce reliable interpreters. These are his roles.

But, ultimately, outlets for exports must be sought and orders obtained by the representatives of firms travelling themselves to foreign parts—whether this be to sell consumer goods, semi-durables or heavy machinery; to win contracts for construction work; or to investigate the possibilities of financial investment. It is often difficult to persuade such 'commercial travellers' to visit regions unfamiliar to them. It is such reluctance that the Commercial Secretariats of Embassies try to overcome. They long for enterprise, for personal exploration. They write concise reports that are easily available in the home country to those contemplating a venture into Darkest Europe, Africa, Asia or America; they reply diligently and with exemplary patience to specific enquiries, some of which display a complete failure to do any homework and unrivalled ignorance of local conditions, such as asking a tropical post about the prospects of selling electric blankets. (This is an actual case.) All this, and more too, is the duty and indeed pleasure of an efficient Commercial Secretariat.

Its personnel are most anxious to improve and they hope for a like enthusiasm from private enterprise.

In Britain, particularly during periods when the balance of payments is adverse and the need for the country to export becomes obvious even to the layman, many expedients are suggested to induce manufacturers and merchants to make more effort overseas. These may involve principles of high policy (for instance, export subsidies in one form or another) that lie beyond the scope of a chapter on the commercial work of Embassies. Another hardy decennial is the suggestion that the staff of Commercial Secretariats are inefficient and untrained in 'business' methods. If this means that no Commercial Secretary is a master of all trades to the extent that he can discuss technical details of say, petro-chemicals and worsted yarn equally glibly, the charge must be admitted, with the amendment that few other individuals of any nationality would be able to do so either. Kelly rightly qualifies as absurd 'the claim often made that diplomatists, to be able to promote trade, must themselves be commercial men. The answer to this is not only the analogy with the barrister; there is also the vital point that a diplomatist must be impartial'[14] (between one particular trade or firm and another). Nevertheless, the accusation of inexpertness is made often enough to merit examination.

There is no doubt that British Commercial Secretariats have been grossly understaffed in the past. The Plowden Report recommended an increase of no less than 10 per cent in manpower, but it will take years not merely to recruit but, above all, train the necessary personnel, political or economic. Admitting the grave deficiency in trained manpower, it would be unwise to refuse skilled men, provided they could help. We must first agree on the level or rank at which that aid is likely to be most effective and whence it should be sought. We must have regard also to that delicate flower, the morale of any Service in any country, which withers if, after years of work, promotion appears to be blocked by an inrush of newcomers and if a general impression burgeons that the regular staff are going to be bossed about by a lot of enthusiastic outsiders.

Injections from other spheres can be useful in any Service anywhere in times of crisis, but whence are they to be recruited? Innumerable business undertakings have most efficient employees, but there would be profound reluctance to lend them elsewhere, even for only three or four years and even if the men were themselves willing. There is every reason to suppose that such a scheme would thus break down before it started. Even if they were made available on loan, is it as certain as is sometimes supposed that they would be an improvement on Commercial Officers long trained in overseas conditions? They would know their own trade, but would they be able to 'generalize'? Would they have the essential knowledge of languages? Above all, would they recognize that, despite the vital importance of economics, politics must hold the primacy in foreign relations?

There is, of course, plenty of manpower available, but nothing could be more fatal than to engage second-raters or men without the necessary experience. In 1949–50 a scheme was devised to boost British exports to the United States, where there was at least no language problem. Much trumpeted in the press at its birth, it died silently, but not before a lot of efficient Consular Officers had been driven to the verge of resignation. The solution must be to improve the quality of Commercial Officers in Embassies by giving them wider training throughout their careers, including emphasis on the unity of political and economic work. This objective can only be achieved if numbers are increased to permit more secondments to other organizations. Furthermore, the cadre of locally engaged officers should in many posts be enlarged and above all better paid.

It is not always clearly grasped that individual representation abroad by British firms is often essential, because each has its own trade secrets from the others as well as from its foreign competitors. No Commercial Secretary can in detail represent two rival firms; he can only advise both impartially in general. He is not there to sell, but to help sell. It is not unknown for British firms to express polite diffidence if it be suggested that they take a Commercial Secretary fully into their confidence. They trust him

81

against foreigners, but fear he might leak to a British competitor. American concerns, more lavishly supported and ruthless in competition, show an equal reluctance to confide in a government official—'except, of course, when they have fouled it up', as one American Commercial Counselor remarked ruefully to me; 'then it is *my* fault.' Groundless though such fears of leakage are—after all reliable lawyers or bankers do not discuss one client's affairs with another—the balance can indeed be difficult and the only effective solution must be effective individual representation abroad of undertakings in the home country, either through highly qualified resident agents or by very frequent visits by representatives from home, who must be competent technically and linguistically, and familiar with local conditions. A Commercial Secretary will spare no effort to support either or both of these, and at higher levels the Ambassador will be eager to help.

It was once suggested, in support of the separate offices set up by the British Dollar Export Council in the Americas, that they would not only be more efficient than the Commercial Secretariats of Embassies or Commercial Officers in Consulates, but be less open to the possibility of criticism on the score of leakage; firms would have more confidence in them. It was not clear why one individual should have been expected to be more close-mouthed than another and, in fact, no difference in discretion was noted. These offices were useful to the extent that they provided more skilled manpower in key centres at a time when Treasury niggardliness prevented an increase in the staffs of Commercial Secretariats, but there was inevitably some duplication (a British firm would tend to write to both and receive two almost identical answers), and the expense of separate accommodation, staff, transport and so on, was considerable. The Dollar Export Council, which later came to be called the Western Hemisphere Export Council (WHEC), with counterparts in other areas, was presided over by the late Lord Rootes with whom, shortly before his death, I had frequent consultations aimed at increasing efficiency and reducing overlap and expense. In consequence I obtained his agreement to move the WHEC office in one capital to the same floor in the building that housed the Embassy and Commercial Secretariat. Liaison became close and intimate, duplication was avoided and costs reduced. Some trade and commercial associations in the United Kingdom still attach importance to the maintenance of an organization separate from the Commercial Secretariat. If it is properly run and well integrated with the Embassy, no objections should be raised. It has the advantage that, not being official, it need not be so desperately discreet and its activities are less subject to niggling enquiry.

In 1964 a new export promotion organization was set up to take over all the work of its predecessors. This is the British National Export Council (BNEC), sponsored by the government, the Confederation of British Industries, the City and the Trade Union Congress. It incorporates a dozen area committees covering the main markets of the world and its financial resources are drawn half from private enterprise and half from matching government grants. Much of the work is done by some 200 businessmen, who voluntarily give their time. The BNEC has no exact counterpart in other countries, save perhaps in the Netherlands. Some countries (e.g. Canada and the United States) rely wholly on their official Services; others (e.g. Austria and Norway) set up independent statutory bodies financed from levies on business enterprises and on imports and exports; yet others (e.g. France) have mixed bodies, wholly state-financed, to control their diplomatic Commercial Services.

In larger world capitals there are often British and other Chambers of Commerce interested in economic relations between the home and the local country. They can exercise great influence. Leading foreigners and local representatives of their firms are members, but here too there can be lack of frankness between rivals. It is primarily when facing menaces that threaten all the members and in supplying background information to visitors that such organisms can be of great value. Commercial Secretariats will maintain the closest contact with them, as will the Embassy in general with other individuals or groups of the local colony of their nationals. The results of such co-operation will

83

always be informative and sometimes, in times of crisis, beyond price.

3   THE INFORMATION SECTION

The next department of an Embassy with which we must deal is the Information Section. The United States Information Agency (USIA) was separated from the Department of State in 1953, but it co-operates closely with the Foreign Service overseas. For information and cultural work under the American system see Barnett.[15] In British practice the Information Section is a comparatively new organ, more recent even than the Commercial Secretariat. A semi-official Information Officer was attached to the British Embassy in Paris from 1916, but the first regular officers (then called Press Attachés) were not appointed until 1927 —to the British Embassies in Paris and Berlin respectively. They were specialists, not members of the Diplomatic Service. It was their duty to advise the Ambassador on public opinion in the countries concerned, particularly as reflected in the press, and to keep in touch with both local and visiting journalists. During the Second World War this work was enormously expanded by the Ministry of Information, which was charged with responsibility for publicity at home and abroad for the British war effort and aims. In 1946 the Foreign Service (which has now once again become the Diplomatic Service) absorbed all information work affecting foreign countries.

Plowden has commented succinctly on information work:

> The Information Services must not come to regard themselves as purveyors of information as an end in itself. . . . The more closely the information effort can be related in the mind of each Information Officer to the pursuit of a conscious British interest, the greater his worth is likely to be. . . . Sometimes effective propaganda can make the vital margin of difference between the success and failure of a policy. . . . We should strive relentlessly to make our views heard. The aim should be to be selective and realistic.[16]

It is not easy in Britain to eradicate the prejudice against expenditure on propaganda, political, economic or cultural. All information work is to some extent an act of faith; it is impossible to *prove* that it effects anything—hence the scepticism. It is, however, noteworthy that all experienced observers consider it essential. The costs of it in Britain are remarkably low, particularly in comparison with those of other major powers. The overseas services of the BBC absorb some £10 million annually, the British Council (see chapter VI (3)) a like sum, and the Central Office of Information and all the overseas information work of HMG the same. About 5 per cent of the UK based staff of the Diplomatic Service are employed on this work. Few would wish to see this percentage increased; it is quality that counts.

Conclusions similar to those of Plowden are reached by an American observer with wider experience of the propaganda of the greater powers than most of us are ever likely to attain. Thayer rightly insists that propaganda is the handmaiden of diplomacy or—more vividly—the cowcatcher attached integrally to it and designed to sweep impediments from its path. Alone it has no creative force, but as an extension of the diplomatic arm it can further the country's interests.[17] The manpower employed by the USIA to cover both information and cultural work is enormous—more than 1,000 US citizens and 7,000 locally engaged employees in about 200 posts in more than 100 countries. Some of these employees have had, to outside observers, a pretty raw deal. As an agency separate from the State Department, the USIA has been forced to use the Foreign Service Reserve category for its overseas officers, instead of the career Foreign Service Officer category. Members of this organization have shown great skill and won deserved repute abroad; it is almost a compliment that their offices are the first to be attacked by foreign objectors. The latest attempt to obtain for them 'career conditions' was baulked by Congress in 1966. Analogous difficulties have been encountered by the British Council, as mentioned in chapter VI (3).

The USIA budget is about $200 million a year, which includes expenditure inside the United States. Barnett notes: 'This is a good deal less than the three companies that make most of our soap spend in a year for advertising.'[18] There has been recent complaint in Britain that two manufacturers of detergents spent £12 million annually on advertising. The BBC is not allotted as much for all its vitally needed overseas services and is threatened with reductions.

☆

It is vital for every major country that its views and policy be known throughout the world, not only to high officials in foreign governments, but to influential members of the public and press. Ambassadors inform their governments of the views of foreign governments, but they must also report on public opinion generally and at the same time disseminate the views of their own country through all the media of publicity available—the press, films, wireless and television. Exposition can often best be done privately, but it may be desirable to issue prepared statements; or the Head of Mission and senior members of his staff can express their views at press conferences or in public speeches at important gatherings; or visitors of high standing will take the opportunity of a foreign tour to set out publicly the views current at home. The objective cannot be attained without expert assistance and this is where the Information Section of an Embassy has its part to play, except in lands where fear of foreign ideas imposes tight censorship.

Lord d'Abernon mentioned that the first quality required for successful propaganda was 'perhaps self-satisfaction; the second, adequate devotion to the task and the expenditure of time and money on its accomplishment'. In his day he maintained that the French were consummate practitioners. Professor Max Beloff has recently written:

> Unless people have a high regard both for the country which is endeavouring to persuade them of the advantages of a certain course of action, and for the credibility and reliability of the institutions through which it purveys information in

support of its views, the machinery available will not be able successfully to perform its required function when a specific case arises. Successful work in the information field demands a high degree of continuity both as to the regional area of concentration and as to the substantive content of what is offered. It cannot simply be turned on and off at will.[19]

I would myself add that, without unified direction at the top (i.e. cabinet) level, efficiency cannot be attained.

The limitations of the press must be realized. Watt notes:

> Nor can it be assumed that the press represents 'public opinion' as opposed to the opinion of those in power. The serious press in Britain only really represents opinions which have been made public by the act of their ventilation in the pages of the press. The debate which precedes or accompanies the formulation of any major move in British foreign policy takes place as much in private as in public, and that part of it which appears in the serious press represents only the visible part of the iceberg.[20]

Nor is the popular press as influential as might be supposed. The foreign editor of a British daily with one of the largest circulations in the world recently has reminded me that for over a year his paper had constantly urged that Britain join the Common Market. Six months after de Gaulle had blocked this, the paper organized an opinion poll among its many millions of readers which disclosed that 54 per cent did not know what the Common Market was.

There is a considerable difference in technique between an Ambassador explaining and discussing policy with the Foreign Minister of the country to which he is accredited (i.e. in confidence and protected by a professional code) and an Information Officer doing the same to the people of the country (i.e. in a blaze of publicity and without the protection of a code). The Head of Mission may be talking with a sceptical, perhaps even hostile, Minister, but he can be reasonably frank. The Information Officer is much more likely to meet the 'loaded' question, and the deliberate distortion when his interview is published. He is an apologist, a defender of the controversial policies of his own government and he may have to be pretty tough. While he will wish to be as open as possible, he will have to tread warily through the prickly jungles of barbed questions, lest he worsen an already difficult situation. Every Secretary of State and Head of Mission knows that a good spokesman can further an intricate and important political manoeuvre and a bad one mar it. It is not too much to say that, at the highest level of danger, peace or war may depend as much on what is said—or not said—in public by a comparatively junior officer as on the anxious talks behind closed doors or over 'hot lines'. This is a great art, of which Metternich was alleged to be master: 'When he wished to make his meaning plain, no one could do so more clearly; when he wished to be reticent, no reticence could have been more charmingly eloquent.'

Thayer has some wise reflections about the relations between diplomats and journalists:

The parallels and similarities between the two professions frequently lead to fundamental misunderstandings because of the basic but less obvious differences in their objectives. Both seek to find and identify truth, but it is the journalist's task to publicize facts and the diplomat's to reconcile conflicting ones. Since publicity is often a deterrent to the reconciliation of conflicts, the diplomat attempts to conceal what the journalist strives to reveal.

Furthermore, the average ego rebels at hiding knowledge. Most people can succeed only at the expense of appearing stupid or by making their interlocutors appear stupid. A rare few can do it without giving offence or losing face. On the other hand, only a naïve journalist believes that a diplomat can or will reveal to him the whole truth. However, correspondents are occasionally naïve.[21]

The diplomat, while maintaining wariness, should realize from the outset of his career that the press is not a dragon to be feared, but an ally with whom cordial relations should be established.

Guide lines have been laid down by an American Ambassador in TWFM:

> The basic consideration in the relationship between Foreign Service Officers, including Ambassadors, and newsmen is one of attitude. Like all other people the newsman is susceptible to a friendly, forthcoming approach. I approach an appointment with a newsman with the attitude of 'What can I tell him to help him understand the issues with which he and I are both concerned?' rather than the negative one of 'What do you suppose he's after, and what do I have to hide from him?'.[22]

The only gloss on this is that the rare journalist has been known to break confidence. Such men should be shunned; they are usually well known.

A general wariness may also be necessary in some countries always and in others at times of crisis. The freedom of the press is an accepted principle in all democratic countries, but the extent of that freedom and the moment when it becomes licence can be argued. Sometimes a certain tactful close-mouthedness may be essential while delicate discussions are in progress. This balance between saying too much and being over-reticent can be very difficult for the diplomat. A good Information Officer must be relied on to say the minimum when necessary, the maximum when possible.

The officers in the Information Section of a British Mission, like their colleagues in the Commercial Secretariat, will be for the most part regular members of the Diplomatic Service—outsiders with experience of specialized techniques can still render useful service, but they can usually be better employed in a subordinate, advisory capacity. In the old Commonwealth Service, prior to amalgamation, Information Officers were not regular members of the Service and tended to be monoglot. It will take some years to build up a cadre fully equipped to fill posts in Embassies and High Commissions throughout the world.

Information Officers may be appointed to any part of the world and will not necessarily spend all their lives on this work. Like their colleagues in other branches, the best of them will rise to Head of Mission. If earlier they show promise, they will receive special training and be familiar with the mysteries of the press, television and broadcasting. Particularly close liaison will be maintained with the BBC which, whatever the constant criticism levelled at it at home, has won an enviable reputation overseas for objectivity and reliability. They will also have to be knowledgeable about films, projectors and tape recorders. The Ambassador will take pains to know important editors and correspondents, but his Information staff must be on friendly terms with less prominent but nevertheless influential men in all media of publicity, and not only in the capital but in provincial centres. They will associate closely with the Embassies of allied and friendly powers and with newspaper correspondents of all nationalities.

An army is composed of different 'arms'—infantry, tanks, artillery, engineers etc.—and so, less martially, is an Embassy. The inefficiency or absence of one 'arm' can spell defeat in diplomacy as in war. Just as the Commercial Secretariat will work in alliance with the Chancery, so will the Information Section with both. Effective diplomacy, the achievement of political ends, can only be achieved by an Ambassador with full support from his Information Officer who, as Plowden puts it, 'must be, and be seen to be, a full member of the Embassy or High Commission team'.[23] Only thus can he attain a position of intimacy and confidence with the rest of the staff at his post and, it goes without saying, with the foreigners among whom he works.

To be effective an Information Officer must have a sound knowledge of the traditions and institutions of his own country. He will often be required to explain to incredulous foreigners the working of his nation's organism—as a whole, and in the most abstruse detail. There is in foreign parts a flattering thirst for knowledge of the United Kingdom, and woe to the Information Officer so ill-advised as to say that the archiepiscopal residence of the Archbishop of Canterbury is at Canterbury. The correct answer will provoke the obvious follow-up, 'Well, if he doesn't live there, why not?'. The Information Officer must know why—from Stephen Langton onwards.

A good Information Officer must possess three qualities. In the first place, he must accept wholeheartedly that, while he is endeavouring to win respect for his country, it is futile to expect that his hosts manifest affection for or even gratitude to his homeland on a national scale. This is one of the reasons for the British practice of employing as far as possible career diplomats as Information Officers. They are less inclined to expect love and thanks; more immune to hard knocks; less disappointed if their advertising methods fail to increase sales. In short, they are not Innocents Abroad who yearn for popularity; all they can hope for is respect. These remarks apply to all members of any Diplomatic Service, but they are particularly applicable to Information Officers.

Secondly and more actively, the good Information Officer must have the necessary 'feel' to know how best to put over publicity for his country. It may be futile to try and use a certain medium for publicity on certain items. It may be necessary to work hard to induce in Ruritania any interest at all in some subject that is a burning question in London, Paris or Washington. Sometimes it is better to tell headquarters to drop the matter. If it is essential to pursue it, long hours of cajolery may be required; but, except in totalitarian countries with a muzzled press, good newspapers in any land welcome a tactful and a well-informed approach. The paper may not have the resources to gather all the news it would like. It wishes to present a truthful picture and thoughtful comment to its readers. As the Information Officer seeks no credit for himself, it is often possible for one on really intimate terms with a foreign editor or broadcaster to arrange publicity for some item without attribution, i.e. he gives the facts to his friend and leaves it to him to put them over as, when and how his experience dictates. On some occasions a journalist may be given a scoop—the right to first publicity of some important item of news. This is rare, however, for the important thing is to achieve the widest possible publicity and not to show favouritism to one particular paper.

Here again the British practice favours career diplomats. Even when they have received special training, they may well be technically less expert than professional journalists or advertising men, seconded temporarily to Missions; but it is probable that they will preserve more sense of proportion and almost certain that they will not long be allowed to believe that technical efficiency is more important than a sound knowledge of human reactions. Thayer maintains that in his wide experience it was always easier to teach the political specialist the basic techniques rather than *vice versa*. This was partly because 'salesmen of information' tended to regard their work as an independent force and not the ancillary that it actually is.

As explained in chapter VI (3) below, the British allow wide freedom in purely cultural matters. Information work, on the other hand, is an integral part of the 'policy machine'. A slightly erratic genius can work wonders in organizing an art exhibition or in teaching English, but he is unlikely to fit easily into a co-ordinated team that must be closely directed from thousands of miles away towards a general objective. The star correspondents and the brilliant slogan merchants are probably less flexible than the specialist in politics or foreign relationships; they wish to impress their own ideas. It can be dangerous to fit them into a slot where personal views must be kept under full control. They can maintain, often with complete justification, that they know their jobs better than most, but timorous foreigners prefer to seek advice from the humbler and less assertive. The really successful Information Officer—as in all walks of life—should not have to do too much proffering and nudging; people should come shyly to him.

Thirdly, the Information Officer must realize that he is working with and for policy makers at home and that his eyes should therefore be fixed on their counterparts in the country in which he is posted. He should never believe that he can attain his ends by flooding his 'parish' with pamphlets. Surprisingly, there are still people who through ignorance or indolence advocate such measures. If he cannot contact and influence the men at the top, he might as well go home; if he can, they will explain things to their countrymen at lower levels far better than he can.

The work of the Information Officer is particularly arduous. Newspapermen and broadcasters are notorious, perhaps unjustly, for the odd hours they keep. Foreign correspondents in particular —usually working singlehanded and in intense competition with others representing rival organizations—have to be alert twenty-four hours a day, seven days a week, lest there be delay in cabling some important item of news. The Information Officer must be equally available. In return he will often gratefully receive early news of impending events. After a full day in the office he may have to spend the night hours in pursuit of some key publicist, so as to ensure the appearance of an item of news or comment in a late broadcast or in tomorrow morning's paper. The strain thus imposed is considerable and wives are justified in complaining about spoilt dinners and cancelled outings. More than most of his colleagues, the Information Officer lives on the telephone. Temperamentally he must be, in modern jargon, an extrovert, 'hail-fellow-well-met' at all hours, persuasive and knowledgeable. Unless the local tongue is preposterously difficult, he will be expected to be fluent in it. Information work is emphatically not a job for the studious stay-at-homes, valuable though these may be in other sectors of diplomacy, and there is an additional burden —he is often regarded as a member of some Secret Service, spying out the land. It is assumed from his title that he is acquiring information, whereas his real job is to impart it. He must learn to laugh off such accusations.

The gentlemen of the press are not, as they themselves admit, the easiest people to deal with. They have deadlines beyond which they stray at their peril. Foreign correspondents have clocks in their heads recording press time at home no matter where they are in the world—just as airline pilots keep their wristwatches set to GMT. The press is always eager to get a story on the wire. Sometimes it is in so much of a hurry that, to the dispassionate observer more obsessed with accuracy than speed, it would seem that a half-digested report fast is considered preferable to a complete one slow—in accordance with the old slogan, invented by a sardonic correspondent, that runs: 'Don't get it right; get it written.' It is only fair to add that sometimes the press is prepared to inform itself carefully and lend its support to a good cause. Then the slogan can be rephrased in happier fashion: 'Get it righted; get it written.' It is the duty of an Information Officer to try and ensure this.

In one important respect diplomats have much to learn from journalists, who are trained to write up a story concisely in telling phrases. Diplomats tend to be far too verbose, even in telegrams. It is an education to learn how to deal with the best of the Fourth Estate. They are no fools, they welcome the 'off the record' briefing on the local situation that a competent Information Officer can give them and they have acquired a remarkable ability to sift rapidly and to absorb information from mere tones of voice —or silences. These are great gifts and it is not the fault of the individual journalist that he is hounded by a distant editor. One must even try to forgive the special correspondent who rushes away after twelve hectic hours in an interesting region, because the editor has discovered another crisis a thousand miles away, which in his opinion is of greater import to the public.

The new entrant into the Service will learn early in his career the apparent rule that to be publishable news must be bad. A classic example was the opening in 1963 of a bridge across the entrance of the Gulf of Maracaibo in Venezuela. This is the longest concrete bridge in the world, with central arches high enough to permit the largest tankers to pass under it. It is a great engineering achievement that will revolutionize the economy of the area. No organ of the British daily press noticed its opening, but they did report when a tanker collided with one of the spans some months later. This lack of sense of proportion is bewildering. All this, and more, must be patiently learnt from the press by the diplomat in search of the facts of life. So must smaller countries learn too. They are naturally resentful about the emphasis placed on damage to a bridge rather than on its construction and they cannot afford a world-wide press organization of their own to give proper publicity to events or trends of real regional importance. They yearn for fame, but they are wise to be patient with the international press; they already waste too much money on other 'prestige' items. Unless you are very rich, it is better to resign yourself to the peculiarities of newspaper publishing, and meanwhile employ cheaply in key capitals diligent Information Officers who will ensure by personal and tactful contact at high level that the world's publicity media are fully apprised of important events in your country.

Information work also provides the possibility to exchange ideas by arranging visits to the home country of groups from foreign lands. These may be of many different types—MPs, trade unionists, officers of the armed forces, prominent businessmen, educationalists or distinguished private individuals. The relevant section of the Embassy will sponsor these tours and help to select the guests, but much of the work will fall on the Information Section and on its counterpart in London, the Central Office of Information. Also concerned in Whitehall will be the Government Hospitality Fund, which looks after distinguished visitors, arranges accommodation, entertainment and so on.

Like other departments, the Information Section of a British Embassy will vary enormously in size—in fact, from nought up to platoon strength.

The smaller Missions will not be able to afford a separate Information Officer and the work will be done in the usual Pooh Bah fashion by some officer in the Chancery, who must spare time from his political reporting, commercial investigation, cyphering, typing or what have you. This can provide valuable opportunities to the novice in information work. In larger British establishments (they include some consular posts in the United States) there will be one, two or more UK based Information Officers on the staff, and in the largest you may find a 'Counsellor (Information)' and several secretaries. These will be only the visible portion of the iceberg, glittering on the Diplomatic List above the much-tossed international sea. Submerged beneath them, but far more active than the four-fifths of a real iceberg, will be a group of toilers, many locally engaged. They will include officers with wide experience of the local press and other media of publicity; translators, for London cannot be expected to produce material in all the languages of the world; typists, teleprinter, film, photostat and duplicator operators. Plowden has recommended that the Central Office of Information could lend technicians to fill some of these appointments.[24] In large Missions a reference library will be required, with a staff trained to answer the most recondite questions posed by the public or official organizations in the country concerned.

It is sometimes possible for an Information Officer to have a regional responsibility. He can reside and spend most of his time in one capital, but have under his wing neighbouring posts with a similar culture and language,* to which he pays frequent visits in support of the Missions. Such an arrangement is, for instance, particularly practicable in Latin America which, apart from the vast Portuguese speaking area of Brazil and the minute French speaking half-island of Haiti, shares the Spanish tongue (in admittedly divergent forms) from the Rio Grande down to Cape Horn. It can work equally well in the large areas of Africa where English or French is the *lingua franca*.

4. THE MISSION AND AID PROJECTS

Although richer lands for generations have been assisting the poorer, earlier efforts were largely in private hands, many directed by Christian missionaries. Only in this century did government begin to take part.†

* The distinction in British practice between Information and Cultural work is dealt with in chapter VI (3) below.

† For comments on American Aid see Jackson, pp. 174–203. The only monograph on Aid in the particular context of British foreign policy known to me is unfortunately unpublished. In general see *International Aid* by I. M. D. Little and

In Britain a Colonial Development Act of limited scope was passed in 1929. It was followed by a succession of Acts under which Britain's policy of aid to the less privileged members of the Commonwealth has since been operated. Meanwhile the Charter of the United Nations presented the obligations of wealthier countries to the underdeveloped, but in Europe the ravages of war had first to be repaired. British financial assistance on a large scale to independent Commonwealth countries started in the late 1950s; more limited help was extended to some foreign countries in the early 1960s. The administration of technical assistance to all developing countries was centralized in 1961 by the setting up of the Department of Technical Co-operation, and in 1964 the Overseas Development Ministry (ODM) was established and assumed responsibility for all economic aid, including technical assistance. For detailed information about the work and objectives of the ODM, the latest in a long series of White Papers should be consulted.[25]

The short word 'Aid' may here be preferred to all the polysyllables. It coincides with the American counterpart, the Agency for International Development (AID),[26] an imaginative title rich in possibility of achievement, provided the dangers are comprehended. In this context Aid is exclusively civilian. Military Aid is another matter. One can only hope that it be kept sparse. Not only do richer lands feel compelled to gigantic expenditure; far too many lethal weapons are scattered over the surface of the globe. 'There is something intrinsically obscene in the combination of ill-fed people and well-fed armies deploying the most modern equipment', Professor J. K. Galbraith has remarked.[27]

J. M. Clifford (Allen and Unwin, London 1965), *Two Views on Aid to Developing Countries* by Barbara Ward and Peter Bauer (Institute of Economic Affairs, London 1966), and two articles in *International Affairs*, January 1966: one by Robert Buron on considerations that should guide technical assistance (the author is French and bears in mind the difficulties of nations other than Anglo-Saxon); the other by Susan Strange, who makes a cogent plea for increasing the trade of poorer nations rather than giving them aid—a line also pursued by UNCTAD. A survey of German Aid has been produced by John White (Overseas Development Institute, London 1965). The whole subject is beginning to receive the close attention it merits and further general or specialized studies should soon be available.

There is a perilous lack of precision in much thinking about Aid; hearts are too apt to run away with heads and richer countries are under vociferous pressure. Whatever may be the situation elsewhere, the British are faced, and will continue to be faced in any foreseeable future, with a grave threat to the whole economic stability of their country, heavily in debt across the international exchanges. The extra burden of Aid is severe, only slightly behind the direct foreign exchange element in British defence expenditure.

It is wise to reflect how far it is safe to add this charity to the national load, and to ponder whether methods of disbursing it are in the best interests of both donor and recipient. If money and other assistance were more tightly controlled, the beneficiaries might also be led to evaluate more seriously their essential needs. It has been shown that on the average 40 per cent of Aid has been spent on unnecessary imports (such as tobacco, beverages, perfumery and passenger cars).[28] India is a shining exception, dispensing only 1·9 per cent of Aid received on items that could be classified as non-essential. Though the statement will fall on many emotionally blocked ears, the donor is entitled to claim a return for his generosity, if only because all but the very poorest in Western countries are heavily taxed to provide the gift. This is apt to be overlooked by the recipients, who could make an equivalent effort—in particular to think, not politically, tribally or religiously, but economically. In many of them, conditions can only be improved by local action. Who but an Indian, for instance, could touch the caste system, advocate contraception, or suggest the slaughter and sometimes the consumption of animals that drain foodstuffs from an ill-nourished population? Such far-reaching social and religious changes will require much time, but unless the goal is pursued internally much external Aid will be nugatory.*

The Aid problem burdens the Communists as heavily as the Western countries. In their role of Mrs Jellyby ('She has devoted

* The idea of self-help in addition to external Aid has been forcefully put by Jerome Caminada in an article in *The Times* (April 21, 1967). His views will doubtless be disputed; yet in all considerations of Aid, a generous heart needs to be allied to a steady brain if schemes are to be successful.

herself to an extensive variety of public subjects and is at present, until something else attracts her, devoted to the subject of Africa') both blocs have expended astronomical sums* with small return to themselves and, worse, little advantage to the recipients. In particular, the less privileged in underdeveloped areas have far too often been the last to benefit, though in countless lands they are undernourished, uninstructed and fecund. 'Where the existing administration is thoroughly inefficient, the visible results of aid are Mercedes cars, foreign travel and fancy wedding receptions.'[29] Dr Lübke, the President of the German Federal Republic, has rendered notable service on long tours in Africa and Asia by his down-to-earth criticism of prestige projects and his appeals for realism. Indiscriminate Aid is not a cure for all ills. Even in affluent societies there is disparity of personal income; it cannot be expected that all nations instantly achieve an equal standard of living.

Other aspects of Aid that cause anxiety are the brain-drain and wastefulness of some international administration. The former is complained of in Britain, but is far more serious in underdeveloped countries, where those who have acquired specialized skills— usually abroad—emigrate rather than work in unsettled conditions at home. If all Asian and African doctors, for instance, served their own countrymen, the menace of disease in those areas would be much slighter. This problem is probably as insoluble as lavish staffing at the United Nations, where every member country— including those that pay practically nothing towards the cost of the organization—insists on its quota of UN staff. Many are untrained and in practice passengers; efficiency is reduced and the expense alarming. *Per contra,* Britain and the United States benefit from the accretion of skills—a sort of reverse Lend-Lease.

These warnings uttered, what is important within the framework of this book is to examine the impact of the Aid policy, decided at cabinet level, on the work of Diplomatic Services

---

* To give one example: since 1952 the Eastern and Western blocs have *each* committed some $1,620 million to Egypt, which has also received over $200 million in international aid (cf. *The Times,* May 11, 1966).

overseas, for on Embassies, High Commissions and Consulates falls much of the administration.

☆

Western Aid in the form of grants or loans totals some £2,500 million annually. United States Aid expenditure approved in 1966 amounted to $2,158 million (£735 million), reduced and more closely supervised than in the lavish past. The British Aid programme was to be stabilized at about £225 million a year, but whether this figure can or should be maintained at a time of persistent financial crisis remains to be seen. It represents far more than the cost of all overseas services and about 0·7 per cent of the Gross National Product. Not all this is a 'debit' to the British economy; a considerable percentage is a 'credit', in the sense that it provides work for factories. This Aid is partly direct or bilateral, and partly multilateral via international organizations. Aid can be in the form of grants, or loans (with or without interest). As loans cause more resentment than grants, it would seem wise to avoid them, particularly as the chances of repayment are usually minute. Nine-tenths of French Aid is in grants and the percentage of the GNP is higher. Britain could well follow a similar course as regards grants and also concentrate more on bilateral rather than multilateral aid, since the former can be more efficiently supervised.

Basically Aid can either be technical (i.e., the provision of experts in many fields) or financial—or of course a combination of the two. Both impose a severe burden—highly qualified technicians are as precious as cash—and the strain is increased because Aid to be of any value must, once started, be continuous; except in the form of capital grants it cannot be switched on and off and it demands careful long term planning in co-operation with the governments concerned. Financial Aid may be 'free' (the recipient can spend the money as desired) or 'tied' (the money must be expended in the donor country).

The United States Agency for International Development (AID) employs, at home and abroad, a staff of 15,262.[30] This total includes non-US citizens engaged overseas. Aid is administered in Whitehall by the newly formed Overseas Development Ministry, which already boasts a staff of 1,500 in London. This seems a large number—already more than half the combined staff of the Foreign and Commonwealth Relations Offices. It is maintained in justification that the Aid programme has increased six-fold in Britain in the last few years and that technical (as opposed to financial) assistance demands far more detailed supervision.

A few Diplomatic Service personnel are seconded to the Ministry and it is hoped to extend this practice, but, as usual, the obstacle is shortage of trained manpower. Meanwhile the Ministry is largely staffed by officers from the, now vanishing, Colonial Office and from the dwindling Colonial Civil Service. Specialized training is desirable and it is hoped that the new Institute of Development Studies now being established on the same campus as the University of Sussex will act as a centre for research. The Institute's objectives and problems have been well summarized by Paul Streeten.[31] He stresses the need to make Aid more effective by increased knowledge of technical and local conditions and their intricate inter-relation. This is a profitable task, but much local education will also be required, for those undertaking to assist less developed countries are in effect often trying to influence the course of social change, without which aid will be ineffective. This is an enormously complicated undertaking.

What is of more concern to us is supervision overseas. It is now part of the duty of a Head of Mission to interest himself in the problems of Aid in his area. In forming a judgement he will rely much on the expert advice of his Commercial Counsellor, who is best able to weigh up the economic strength and weakness of the putative recipient country. Thus apprised of detail and bearing in mind the political factors that often prevail over strictly economic (or economical) planning, the Ambassador or High Commissioner will be able to suggest to his own government how the effort can most fruitfully be directed; he may well even suggest that the country in which he is serving is undeserving for one reason or another of such help. There are warnings:

'Indonesia is strewn with the debris and the rusting scrap metal of all the technical and economic aid programmes of the world—a gloomy illustration of the futility, not to say the harmfulness, of giving assistance to regimes dedicated to retrogression.'[32] Sukarno's Indonesia is probably the worst example, but there are countless others and the cumulative wastage throughout the world is heart-breaking. An Ambassador might also well suggest that his own country hold back, leaving it to another more familiar with the region or with special interests in it to furnish the help. There is a tendency for potential recipients to play one donor off against another. This results in waste and should be resisted.

Assuming that Aid is granted, there arises the question of supervision on which Plowden recommends 'technical assistance work overseas should be regarded as an integral part of the tasks of the new Service. Wherever possible technical assistance staffs should be regular members of the Service,* though there is scope for secondments'.[33] There can be no doubt that the Commercial Sections of Missions—and, if necessary, Consulates—are best qualified for this work, under the over-all control of the Ambassador or High Commissioner. It is essential that one man or section—Jackson urges the importance of this in the United States Service[34]—should handle all aspects of Aid and that it should not be split up between, say, 'technical' and 'financial'. One difficulty here presents itself because the British Council, both at home and abroad, is well placed to advise on the technical or personnel side. The Commercial Departments of Missions must therefore collaborate closely with overseas representatives of the British Council, to which the Overseas Development Ministry is now a very substantial contributor, particularly in developing countries. The ODM, for instance, supports some 3,000 students in the United Kingdom, additional to those offered grants by the British Council.

The broad task of a Mission will be to suggest possible avenues

* Little and Clifford (*op. cit.*, page 336) disagree; they would like to see vast staffs of experts attached to Missions.

for Aid to the relevant agency of government at home, and to vet proposals put forward by the local government. Then, when schemes are approved, to supervise and assist throughout their duration. In some regions there may be several schemes running at once and many scattered experts requiring help from the Embassy or a Consular Officer in the provinces. In other posts demands on the Mission may be slighter; yet it remains important for all members of the Service overseas to be fully familiar with this recent additional responsibility. To avoid unnecessary proliferation of staff, special officers should be seconded to Missions only if these tasks are of considerable magnitude. There is nothing particularly esoteric about the work; commonsense, general local knowledge and a long political view are what is needed. American Embassies are frequently burdened by an immense tail of experts, despite the fervent pleas of Ambassadors that their swollen staffs be reduced. Tours by administrators from the home agency concerned (e.g., in Britain the ODM) will suffice to keep posts up to date on policy and visits by experts in the most recondite subjects will often be required.

There is a particular satisfaction in helping to see through such schemes to a successful conclusion. Only rarely can one hope to watch the steel mill rise or the power station in operation, but there are minor and no less valuable achievements. To cross the vitally needed bridge, to talk with students who have been well trained, gives a palpable satisfaction.

Yet, as he surveys the Aid scheme, the experienced Head of Mission will reflect on human nature. He will remind his government that they must expect no gratitude, recalling to them the French play *Le Voyage de Monsieur Perrichon*, the moral of which is that you can expect less thanks from the man whose life you save than if you arrange for him to save yours. He will leave wise books on the bedside tables of visiting delegations in the hope that they will read the marked passages before they drop off to sleep. One of these should be: 'International love is a fiction the search for which has frequently ended in embittered frustration, particularly among Americans whose passion for popularity is seldom understood and practically never requited by our neigh-bours.'[35] Human dignity is affronted by charity; nations, no matter how needy, feel just the same. Maturity of mind is required to realize that even pity can be an affront.

The Ambassador will also urge with all the emphasis at his command that the administration of the Aid be in the hands of as few expatriates as possible. The munificence of some countries has been turned against them owing to the ill-feeling aroused locally by the hordes of overenthusiastic individuals exported to administer it. Refrain from publicity and ostentation; attach the minimum political strings and seek no credit; endeavour to ensure that the objects of Aid are well chosen locally and of potential benefit to donor as well as recipient; do not attempt to impose a foreign way of life, but improve the local way; these are the prerequisites for successful Aid. Parliaments and Congresses, journalists and publics often render such wise courses impossible. They clamour for recognition and thanks; they are outraged if the recipients not merely display ingratitude, but continue to pursue policies unwelcome to the benefactor.

This problem will be with us for decades. Some of the implica-tions have best been put by Guizot: 'All powers, especially new ones, need a touch of grandeur in their activities and on their banners. Good order and the regular protection of private interests —this daily bread of nations—does not suffice them long. These are the necessary conditions for government; they are not the sole need of humanity.' Every donor does well to bear this in mind if he feels indignation rising within him over the way in which his gift is being dispensed. 'It does not suffice to feed the hungry', said His Holiness Pope Paul VI during the first Papal visit to the United Nations. 'It is necessary also to ensure to each man a life conformed to his dignity.'

☆

These notes on Foreign Aid would be incomplete without mention of service overseas by volunteers, of which the Voluntary Service Overseas organization is the best known in Britain. Its more publicized counterpart in America is the United States Peace Corps.[36] (A recent study has shown that of those young Americans contemplating employment in a Federal agency overseas, nearly 21 per cent preferred the Peace Corps compared with some 13 per cent for the State Department.[37]) Other countries share in this task. The German Volunteer Service, founded under the inspiration of the late President Kennedy, is only three years old, but has already sent over 500 of its members overseas. They have the advantage of being free from the stigma of colonialism, but they must shoulder the additional burden of learning English or French, since German is not a world language. The British voluntary organizations are subsidized up to about 75 per cent by the Overseas Development Ministry. The current annual amount is about £620,000, which added to charitable donations supports some 1,500 volunteers. Once in the field volunteers work on their own responsibility, some in conditions both uncomfortable and daunting. They will notify their presence and activities to the nearest Mission or Consulate, which will render them assistance and give such advice as may be desirable. Only the volunteers can decide whether there are not as great problems in their home countries, lacking the glamour of foreign travel. Where they choose to work is their affair, but if they have an avocation, they will help with the minimum of outside support—though one must beware of the occasional tactless enthusiast who does more harm than good. There is much to be said for Volunteers being attached to sound, existing organizations, where they can work under friendly supervision, rather than alone in a strange environment.

Yet, as Briggs has recorded, 'a crusading spirit is no substitute for a foreign policy'.[38] Marshall Aid to Europe undoubtedly worked miracles, because the recipients were highly organized countries and their economies were being restored rather than developed.* It is a grave error to suppose that an unlimited

* It is as well to recall with some humility that what are now the richer European countries only became so because of amazingly generous American help after the war. France received some $7,000 million and Britain $4,000 million; Britain has disbursed in aid less than half this sum in recent years.

outpouring of funds or devoted labour can be equally effective elsewhere. Too much must not be expected and it is more important, as Barnett remarks, that partners should not be treated as pensioners but as real equals.[39] What Bauer (*op. cit.* page 97 above) has referred to as 'pauperization' must be avoided. The resources of donors must also be weighed. It is just as well that every penny of British expenditure should be minutely scrutinized. Further reflection on disbursements and organization is still required. Careful assessment might well show that technical assistance—the field is very wide—could be more effective in the recipient country and less of a burden on the donor than capital aid. It may also come to be realized that dispersion of manpower could be avoided and greater overall efficiency achieved, if there were closer integration of headquarters at home. There can be little doubt that, in Washington and London at least, establishments are luxuriously staffed. In Britain no unification of effort can be expected until the Foreign Office and Commonwealth Relations Office are merged; this will be the moment to include the Overseas Development Ministry in streamlining.

5. SERVICE ATTACHÉS

Having dealt with the main sections of an Embassy (the Chancery and its adjuncts, the Commercial Secretariat, the Information Section and Aid work) that are staffed from the Diplomatic Service, we can now turn to 'attached' and 'seconded' personnel. Only officers from the Armed Services are still 'attached' to British Missions overseas. The term 'Attaché' for a time almost disappeared from the official vocabulary of the British Diplomatic Service, but has now been revived in the form 'Junior Attaché'. The term 'Attaché' is also used for personnel from outside the Service. It is used by many other countries for civilian as well as for Armed Service personnel, sometimes with linguistic variants (e.g., the Spanish *agregado*). The American system of 'secondment' and 'attachment' is considerably more complex than the British.[40]

'Seconded Officers' in British parlance are dealt with in the next section of this chapter.

Nomenclature varies among countries in regard to Service Attachés. The British 'Military Attaché' corresponds to the 'Army Attaché' in the American Diplomatic Service. The United States Marines, that superlative corps, form a fourth arm of the Armed Services and Marine officers often figure as 'Navy' or 'Army Attachés'; but there is as yet no accepted designation, 'Marine Attaché'. France's *Fusiliers Marins* and Britain's Royal Marines come under the respective Admiralties, and some have been appointed as Naval Attachés.

Service Attachés are a comparatively venerable institution. The first to have been so described in Britain was accredited as Military Attaché in Paris in 1858. It was not until July 1862 that the Foreign Office List devoted a short section to Naval and Military Attachés, of whom there were then only three: one of each in Paris and a Military Attaché in Berlin. By 1914 the total number of Service Attachés had risen to twenty-two. Air Attachés are necessarily of more recent vintage, the first one appearing in the Foreign Office List of 1919. In that year, the number of Attachés reached fifty-five. By 1939 the total was fifty-eight, among which were included a few Assistant Attachés. These appointments emphasized the growing importance in a menaced world of maintaining contact with military affairs in the widest sense.

Barnett gives the best outline of American military representation abroad, a clear exposition of the immense American problem.[41] This is a wider subject than Attachés to Embassies since it embraces Military Advisory Assistant Groups, us military personnel in international organizations abroad (e.g., NATO), and military, but non-combatant, support to foreign powers. There are now about 400 American Service Attachés and assistants— slightly less than half of whom are from the us army[42]—and their subordinates are legion. (These figures do not include the vast 'Area Commands' referred to in Appendix A.) In the British Service at the time of writing, there are 199 Service Attachés and assistants (supported by 93 British subordinates); 144 are serving in 51 Embassies abroad and 55 in the Commonwealth. The latter are known as Advisers to their High Commissions, and not as Attachés. The close 'family' relationship with many new nations in the Commonwealth often permits these officers in the British Service to perform the additional, if unofficial, function of giving expert and much-needed advice on military matters, including training and equipment, to the local forces.

Service Attachés in the British system are lent, not seconded, to the Diplomatic Service. They serve not under Foreign Office terms but under conditions laid down by their own departments. The latter will, however, consult the Foreign Office informally about such matters as the cost of living at a post, and pay and allowances will be regulated accordingly. These differing conditions can produce anomalies and occasional complaints, but the system works well on the whole and its retention was recommended by Plowden.[43]

While at their posts Service Attachés are just as much members of the staff of the Mission as their diplomatic and other colleagues. Plowden comments: 'Specialist Officers from home Departments must be fully integrated into the team of the Head of Mission under whom they are to serve. They should not feel either that they are not accepted as members of the team or that they have some kind of independent mission of their own.'[44] Service Attachés are senior officers and have direct access to their chief in writing or in person, though they will be wise (particularly when newly arrived) to ensure that the Head of Chancery is kept fully in the picture. Yet they have not only the right but the duty to report directly to their own departments. Here again, copies of all important letters or memoranda should be shown, if not in draft, at least in final form to the Head of Mission, who is as interested in naval, military and air matters as he is in local politics or economics.

The primary task of the Service Attaché is to maintain links with the armed forces of the country in which he is serving, to exchange information with them and to offer them training facilities in his own country. He can also hope to promote sales of military equipment. This is a reasonable objective in many areas, but in much of the world too many weapons are already in odd hands and the number should not be increased. Regard must also be had to the resources, in finance and intelligence, of some countries, where no economist, let alone humanitarian, can approve the struggle to sell highly sophisticated and expensive arms to drain the budgets of states that should be devoting every resource to peaceful development. A major, but it is to be feared unattainable, blessing in this storm-tossed world would be international agreement about the sale of conventional weapons of all types, in addition to one preventing the proliferation of nuclear armament.

The Service Attaché will advise his Ambassador on the efficiency of foreign forces, and in many countries will try to assess their political ambitions, which all too frequently have led to the violent overthrow of governments. He will play the leading part in arranging naval or other Service visits in his 'parish'. In addition, an Air Attaché (or if there is no airforce representative, the Naval or Military Attaché) can be expected to know something about civil as well as military aviation. (Only the largest British Missions have Civil Air Attachés.)

In British practice Service Attachés take precedence after the No. 2 of a Mission, i.e., the officer who will normally be in charge during the absence of the Ambassador or High Commissioner. Assistant Service Attachés are fitted into the table of precedence lower down the scale according to their rank. British Service Attachés hold Royal Commissions, but are not entitled to the letters 'HBM' or 'HM' before the title of their office. As already mentioned, this privilege is reserved for Heads of Missions and of consular posts.

With the increasing complexity of technical developments in armaments and strategy, Service Attachés have to be expert in their own field but they require, in addition, training in the specialized field of a Mission overseas. The comprehensive training facilities available to personnel in the American armed forces are described in Barnett.[45] The Ministry of Defence in Britain now arranges courses for all Service Attachés, who also receive political briefing at the Foreign Office.

☆

As always, staffs vary enormously. In the British Embassy in Washington there are seven officers representing the three Armed Services as Attachés, and they are supported by over sixty British subordinates. Despite the amalgamation of the British Armed Services under the over-all control of the Ministry of Defence, there are at this Embassy, in addition, more than a hundred Ministry of Defence staff engaged on liaison and research. The Washington Embassy is unique in the British Service in that these attached service personnel outnumber the diplomatic staff.

Many British Missions do not rate a resident Service Attaché, and others are looked after by an officer resident elsewhere but accredited to more than one post. Moreover, if there is, say, only a Military Attaché in the area, he will be expected to do the work of his two missing colleagues. In the past this practice has been carried to grotesque lengths. The record for futility was the appointment of an officer who was accredited to nine different posts and in the process wore nineteen different hats*—some white, some khaki, some blue. In certain of his posts he was the Air Attaché; in others he was the Military or the Naval Attaché; in yet others he was all three. Although he had his own aircraft (a convenience commended by Plowden[46]), the result—which anyone could have foreseen—was that he could not do a proper job anywhere. He covered thousands of miles and could have only a superficial acquaintance with the personalities and tasks with which he was entrusted. In practice he soon had to limit himself to a few key posts and activities, in which he performed admirably. This arose because the Armed Services were unable to extract sufficient funds from the Treasury to cover the world

* A recent letter to the Foreign Office from an Ambassador, in which this phrase was used, proved for a time impossible to trace. It was ultimately found filed by a literal-minded registry clerk under the heading 'Uniforms for Service Attachés'.

properly; they were therefore forced to adopt the ludicrous alternative of spreading their butter so thin on the bread that it was invisible to the naked eye—local or British. As a result of many complaints, wiser counsels have fortunately now prevailed. In general it is safe to say that no Service Attaché should be asked to cover more than three or a maximum of four countries, even if they are reasonably contiguous, speaking the same or not too dissimilar languages, and presenting like problems. Even if countries are neighbours and interaccess is therefore easy, they may be at loggerheads. An officer accredited to and resident in one of them has therefore no chance of establishing friendly contacts in the other. Each party would regard him as a spy, reporting their vital secrets to an enemy. Administrative efficiency must bow before political exigencies and establishments will be more costly.

In 1947 the United States Military Services were amalgamated in the Department of Defense, and later a Defense Intelligence agency was established to superintend activities overseas. It was not until 1964 that the three Armed Service departments in Whitehall were amalgamated into a Ministry of Defence; all British Service Attachés are now controlled by a fully integrated Defence Intelligence Staff. In most British posts where there are several Attachés, there is now a Defence Attaché who is responsible for co-ordinating the work of his colleagues. He and other Attachés are accredited in accordance with the role their Service plays in any particular country. The Foreign Office advises on the number and rank of Service Attachés in each post. Finance, as usual, is the major obstacle in getting all the Attachés needed. The United States can afford to be more generous with manpower.

If in the given area there is, in British parlance, a 'Military Mission' or, in American parlance, a 'Military Assistance Advisory Group', there are additional complexities. Jackson wisely suggests that 'the functions of the MAAG chief and of the service attachés be combined in a single officer, who might be called the defense attaché'.[47]

One admirable Director of Naval Intelligence used to insist that it was over his dead body that he would send abroad officers, however admirable in other ways, whom he regarded as non-exportable. 'We have plenty of skeletons', he said, 'but I prefer to keep them in our own cupboards. I cannot agree to lower the prestige of the Royal Navy by exposing them in shore jobs abroad.'* This admiral was in my experience unique in also enquiring about the suitability of the wives of candidates for the post of Attaché. The other Services did not seem to take the interest in their womenfolk they should. If these precepts were internationally accepted, there would be no further lamentable cases of a Service nominating as Attaché an officer for whom they had no further use, perhaps on a slightly phoney promotion before retiring him. Plowden stresses this: 'Improvements are possible in the system of selecting Service Attachés and Advisers. It is essential to choose the right man. Service Attachés should be ideally men who are going on to bigger things. A tour as a Service Attaché should not be the prelude to retirement, as sometimes still seems to be the case.'[48]

The trouble with this counsel of perfection is the assumption that the post of Attaché is a valuable feather in the cap of an officer of the Armed Services. As these are at present organized in Britain, this is not the case. An ambitious and efficient commander or lieutenant colonel in his early forties is very properly hoping for advancement in his own career. He has half-a-dozen years ahead of him to leap all the hurdles that separate him from the major step upwards, in the career of a promising officer, to rear-admiral, major-general or air vice-marshal. The best men will therefore be highly reluctant to shorten their time for this obstacle race by giving up a couple of precious years to a diversion off the course. They fear, very naturally, that being out of sight—perhaps 12,000 miles from their HQ—they will be out of mind. No enthusiastic private report from an Ambassador will outweigh

---

* There is little new under the sun. Thayer (p. 232) quotes the remark, three hundred years old, of a Duke of Tuscany who, when he complained that the Venetian Ambassador was stupid and was told in reply that there were many fools in Venice, merely said: 'We have fools in Florence too, but we take care not to export them.'

this; he is a member of another Service. These facts are well known and will retain their force until there is some rethinking in the Ministry of Defence. Service Attachés are not, in the old naval phrase, 'pressed men'; they may refuse the appointment without detriment to their careers. Much the same difficulty is recorded by Barnett in the United States: 'Historically, the ambitious officer has not sought assignment as an attaché.' But he goes on to note that the duty has of late been professionalized and made more attractive: 'It is now possible for the most able officers to be made available for the duty and to be content to participate',[49] though an assignment is not compulsory. A similar improvement is surely not impossible in Britain.

The difficulty does not arise so poignantly in the case of junior officers (say, lieutenant-commanders, majors or squadron-leaders) in their thirties. Here the pressure is not so high and good men could be encouraged to take posts as Assistant Attachés. Later they could return in a higher rank to serve again with a Diplomatic Service that would certainly welcome them— thence rising to yet higher appointments, perhaps in the inter- national field.

The confusion of purpose and method in the British system between Ministry of Defence and Foreign Office is the more regrettable because Service Attachés are held in foreign countries to represent not only their particular branch but their country. A fierce and critical light beats on them. Particularly in small or emergent countries, highly skilled and what are called 'representa- tional' officers are even rarer than in large, well established societies—heaven knows they are rare enough in them too. There are not all that many persons capable of carrying out a job efficiently and at the same time impressing on the foreigner that they, and their wives, are charming people, happy to serve in that particular country. Everywhere, and particularly in new countries with their innumerable grave problems, there are more key posts than competent men to fill them. It is readily com- prehensible that you may not be able to spare a good man for work overseas, where he will be much more in the public eye than at home; but never make the mistake of sending a dud to represent you in foreign parts, if only in a minor role. He can wreck what advertising experts call your 'image' more rapidly than you could possibly believe—and it might be many months before news of dire effects trickled back to the home country. It is wise, therefore, to think long and often before making an appointment to a post abroad. If in doubt, send no one.

☆

Nothing I have written above should be taken as implying that it is only in Service Attachés that 'representational' qualities are required; on the contrary, they are needed by all members of any Service working abroad. Members of a Diplomatic Service must be judged to a considerable extent by the ability of themselves and their wives to meet this requirement. There is this major difference between the lives of a home civil servant and a diplomat: once the former leaves his office, he is off duty and can retire to his own little world. The diplomat, the attaché and their wives never can; their very maids are regarding them continuously not only as employers, but as representatives of their country.

It is only too frequent in many parts of the world that a sailor, soldier or airman serving abroad is subjected when off duty to the most cowardly and repugnant assaults,* as are his wife and children. Under more civilized regimes the serviceman is to this extent sheltered, that he can make his home in the ship or cantonment or station, which forms a British enclave in foreign territory. He and his wife need hardly learn a word of the language or have anything but the briefest contacts with the local inhabitants. There are over 50,000 British troops in Germany. It is depressing to read in a recent report in *The Times* on the British Army of the Rhine that 'few even of the officers really speak German and the incentive to learn it is not very great'.

* The Diplomatic Service is not exempt. Since the war, 18 British Embassies and Consulates have been attacked in different parts of the world and some totally wrecked. American establishments have suffered a like fate—libraries, which render precious service, being particular victims.

Nevertheless, and despite the regrettable linguistic barrier, the innate friendliness of the British forces comes to the fore. There is a lot of official and unofficial entertainment of Germans—military and civilian—in officers' and sergeants' messes, and sporting and other events are frequent. It is unfortunate that the popular press does not comment on these good relations and only headlines the rare 'incident'. It is all the more gratifying, therefore, to be able to record how very many members of the Armed Services and their wives rise superior to their difficulties in overseas posts. The strain is perhaps greatest in the case of the clerks of Attachés and their families. Yet many of them, long wedded to the ways of their native land, can and do successfully meet the challenge of a foreign environment and climate, make their own friends and achieve a local popularity that redounds to the credit of their country. More could be done to help them to adjust to the new conditions of their life abroad. Service Attachés and their wives could certainly profit from the Foreign Office's 'going abroad' courses (see chapter VIII, pages 214-17), and above all from courses in 'easy' languages. It does not seem to be generally understood how miserable can be the life of an Attaché (or anyone else for that matter) and his wife, pitchforked into a foreign country with no other basis than a three-weeks' course at an inferior commercial language school. Plowden strongly recommends that 'Service Attachés and their wives should be given tuition in the local language before taking up their appointments'.[50] The Report, however, should have added that similar facilities ought to be provided for service clerks and *their* wives. In contrast, great care has been taken with the 'difficult' or less familiar languages by some of the Armed Services. The new organization of the Ministry of Defence and closer liaison with the Foreign Office should greatly improve preliminary training in all directions, not least in that of language instruction, and increase both the effectiveness and the general well-being of Missions abroad.

The prospect of attachment to an Embassy can be daunting, for it is not only the 'foreignness' that is strange for Attachés and their clerks. It is never easy to accommodate oneself to work with a different Service, with its own rules, traditions and jargon, all meriting the same respect as should be accorded to those of one's own Service. Differences of approach and method can be baffling.

> The civilian is sometimes said to be a horizontal paper-shuffler, while the soldier is a vertical paper-shuffler. The soldier gives orders and takes orders; he asks for advice and receives recommendations from his subordinates, and he gives advice and makes recommendations to his superiors. The civilian, on the other hand, may be less conscious of hierarchy and the lines of authority. In his horizontal consultations, he may, in the eyes of his military colleagues, even verge on being indiscreet.[51]

An Embassy is a machine almost as complicated to a newcomer as a warship to a landlubber, or a military air base to one who prefers to keep both feet firmly on the ground. Adaptability and willingness to learn are therefore as much prerequisite as a determination not to work in a watertight compartment aloof from the rest of the organization. When an Attaché is for any reason absent, some other unskilled member of the Mission staff will cheerfully try to cope. They can expect him to do the same for them, particularly in the smaller Missions, which cannot function unless everyone is prepared to turn his hand to anything. Versatile Service Attachés have been known to play many parts efficiently, from presenting prizes at a girls' school to intricate discussions with trade union leaders.

In one respect British Service Attachés have an immense advantage over their diplomatic colleagues. It is the Treasury practice not to permit any overlap in diplomatic appointments. When an officer leaves a post on transfer, it may be months before his successor arrives. This not only imposes a severe strain on the rest of the staff; it also reduces efficiency. The three Armed Service departments have rightly insisted on a hand-over. This permits the outgoing officer to take his successor on a round of calls on important local contacts and to introduce him and his wife socially. Wise are those who insist on continuity.

☆

It must in conclusion be emphasized that all these Attachés and their clerks belong to other Services. They are lent to the Diplomatic Service, but their main loyalty must be to their own Service and they have their own careers to think of. It would be unreasonable for the British or any other Diplomatic Service to try to impose unworkable conditions on this 'loan personnel' or insist on unrealizable qualifications. There are certain basic requirements—including a knowledge, new or previously acquired, of foreign languages—and agreement on these can easily be reached between the Diplomatic Service and the 'lending' department. Further than that no Foreign Office may go, though it is permissible to express the hope that postings as Service Attachés be made attractive and not detrimental to an officer's career.

The Diplomatic Service is lucky to have officers from other departments to aid in matters beyond the training of diplomats. Complete assimilation is impossible; the objective can only be integration into the team that should be formed at any Mission abroad. This is easier with the small numbers that the British Service—and indeed, most other Services—can afford. More important is a revised outlook at headquarters. The war was only won by the closest inter-Service and allied co-operation. The needs of peace are less obviously pressing, but co-ordination—almost integration—of various Services remains essential if smooth efficiency is to be attained in an Embassy or in larger fields. The difficulties are great, but the overcoming of them will bring immense rewards. One of the best known inter-Service clubs in London is usually referred to colloquially as 'the Senior'. Its official title is not 'The United Services Club' but 'The United Service Club'. Over a century ago that ideal was established. It should now be extended—and not only in Missions abroad—so that factional disputes can be reduced and the common end of united service to the nation be sought by all, no matter what their uniform or designation. International unification of staff was imposed by General Eisenhower within the limits of the possible during the war and has since been continued in SHAPE and elsewhere. Integration of the Armed Services has gone further in the United States than in Britain, and one American Secretary has urged the valuable role that those holding senior political appointments can play in achieving it.[52]

6. SECONDED OFFICERS

In addition to Service Attachés, civilian officers are seconded to the Diplomatic Service. The terms 'seconded' and 'secondment' are not normally used in American parlance; officers lent from other agencies are referred to, rather awkwardly, as being on 'reimbursable detail'. As already noted, the distinction between an 'attached' and 'seconded' officer in British usage is that the former remains under the terms and conditions of his own Service, while the latter during the period of his secondment serves under those of the Diplomatic Service. This is in many ways an advantage; invidious comparisons between rates of pay and 'perquisites' are less likely, since all are on almost the same footing; moreover accounting is simplified—it is wasteful of effort that Attachés should have to run their own imprests.

Seconded Officers are a recent institution in British practice; none existed before the Second World War, but there are now 82 in foreign and 25 in Commonwealth posts, a total of 107 (plus 41 subordinate British staff), as compared with the 199 Service Attachés. As with Service Attachés, Seconded Officers in Commonwealth countries often act as much as advisers to the local government and institutions, as they do to their own High Commissioner. Under the United States system officers from government agencies other than the State Department are much more numerous. Some over-all statistics are set out in Appendix A.

The variety of the callings of British Seconded Officers will surprise many. They include: Agricultural, Atomic Energy,

Civil Air, Colonial, Cultural, Defence Research, Financial, Labour, Pensions, Petroleum, Scientific, Shipping, Supply and Veterinary. The Cultural Attachés are British Council officers who, by exception, are seconded to the staff of an Embassy and not directly to a British Council Centre or Institute, as is the more normal practice. These officers serve under British Council terms and conditions. They are dealt with in chapter VI (3).

What has already been written about Service Attachés in regard to integration into the Mission team and difficulties of adjustment when serving abroad applies equally to Seconded Officers. Though more closely united with the Diplomatic Service in their conditions of service, they too are uprooted from their own country for a brief period of years and placed in a very different environment abroad, where among other things they will have to struggle with the local language (except in the United States and some Commonwealth countries). This alone can be a sore trial for a Seconded Officer (and his wife), who has attained substantial seniority without, perhaps, ever having served or even travelled much overseas. Only volunteers are accepted and they can be hard to come by. It is greatly to the credit of Seconded Officers that they, their clerks and families meet these difficulties so cheerfully and competently. Like the Service Attachés, they can be assured of a warm welcome from their Diplomatic and Service colleagues, to whom their technical knowledge and experience in abstruse fields is invaluable.

American practice is different. The most prevalent method is for the State Department to give training to Foreign Service Officers to take on specialized functions, or to engage experts as Foreign Service Reserve Officers, who might later be integrated as FS Officers; all Labor Attachés are Department of State employees, not seconded from the Department of Labor, and several have risen to become Ambassadors.

Again like Service Attachés, Seconded Officers are only to be found at the larger Missions. In fact there are only 31 posts out of a total of 121 that have resident Seconded Officers. However, they may also cover several neighbouring posts.

Responsibility for the affairs of two or more countries requires flexibility and energy to a high degree. Their home departments are wise not to burden good men to breaking point by acceding to requests that they be accredited to more countries than they can efficiently handle. As for Service Attachés, three or at most four is the limit.

They will have direct access to their Ambassador. They will report to him not only in writing—if they are wise, through the Head of Chancery—but drop in to consult him personally for an exchange of views. An Ambassador who does not encourage this intimacy is, to say the least, unwise. In addition Seconded Officers will correspond direct with their own departments: Ministry of Agriculture, Labour, etc. The Ambassador will only be interested in the broader lines of their work, which he will report to the Foreign Office; the parent department will want far greater detail. They will assist the parent department when foreigners interested in their field visit Britain, perhaps even acting as guides during tours, and they will be called home at intervals for conferences held in consultation with the Foreign and Commonwealth Relations Offices.

☆

In this book it is not possible to go deeply into the work of all these Seconded Officers; its general nature is clear enough from the name of the Ministry from which they originate and from their titles.[53] The importance of their role, for all Diplomatic Services, has been well assessed by Barnett.

It is immediately clear that the role of the expert in overseas representation is becoming more and more important. The Marshall Plan demonstrated that in order to carry out economic-aid programmes involving partnership with recipient countries, it was essential that the United States have highly trained economists on its missions overseas. The foreign information programme has surely demonstrated the importance of the skilled technician and the costs of amateurism in a field calling for specialized skills. In neither case, be it said, can the ultimate policies be left to the expert, but likewise in neither case can the policies be carried out without him.[54]

British experience is similar.

It used to be the British practice for Seconded Officers to be called 'Labour Attaché', 'Civil Air Attaché' and so on. As old habits die hard, these terms are often still applied; officially, however, it has now been decided that they shall be known by their equivalent rank in the Diplomatic Service, plus an explanatory title in brackets; thus 'Counsellor (Labour)', 'First Secretary (Agriculture)', 'Second Secretary (Petroleum)'—this last would be an assistant to a senior officer. Seconded Officers take precedence on the Diplomatic List in accordance with their temporary rank in the Diplomatic Service.

While we need not delve far into the functions of these Seconded Officers, it is appropriate to mention the first of them, the Labour Attachés (it will be seen that I adhere to the now out-of-date nomenclature). The earliest was appointed to Washington in 1942, but organized secondment was set on foot by Ernest Bevin when he became Secretary of State for Foreign Affairs after the war. His heart was with Labour—in the sense of the working man, not solely a political party—and he felt, rightly, that there was a gap to be filled. He did not, like one unloved Labour Party nominee in the Foreign Office, vociferate that no Ambassador abroad had ever spoken to a local Socialist. Ernie knew this was demonstrably untrue, but he quietly decided that more bridge building and greater experience would be beneficial all round. Labour Attachés were the result. They now form a quarter of the Seconded Officers (excluding the British Council 'cultural secretaries') in twenty-one posts covering eighty countries. Trade unions at home are arcane to many of us. Union movements abroad are still more mysterious—indeed experts from home are sometimes confused by the complexities. Any competent Diplomatic Secretary should be able, in the absence of a Civil Air Attaché, to sweat out the difference between the five 'freedoms', but none could have the experience, or the time to acquire it, of labour movements, trades, crafts and legislation required of a Labour Attaché. There is no doubt that Bevin put a finger on the right spot and his idea was then and is now well supported. I may have been lucky, but I have never served with a Labour Attaché who was less than excellent; I could not say the same of my own or any other Service.

This is not to maintain that other Seconded Officers are without value, but in most ways their task is easier in the great international capitals, to which alone they are posted. Such appointments are inevitable; to take an extreme case you would hardly expect to find a 'First Secretary (Atomic Energy)' in a remote African capital. Nor is there anything derogatory in stating that their work is easier. They are apt to find themselves in an English-speaking country, and in any case they have their own common tongue with their opposite numbers. No Scientific Attaché—at any rate so it is believed—ever refers to 'water'; he talks of H_2O and is instantly comprehended by any other scientist in any other language, even without adding a little whisky to the beverage. Petroleum Attachés talk their own 'crude' or 'light' jargon; Financial Attachés of all nationalities are unique in knowing the difference between a tango and a contango. These *linguae francae* are of immense value in establishing rapid technical communication, and it is usually only on this level that work is performed.* All Labour Attachés, on the other hand, like the general run of diplomats, though they have their own technicalities, must learn to cope with the common man at all levels abroad and speak his language.

The ability to make this contact is one of the essences from which a potent diplomacy is distilled and the increasing technical complexity of life today postulates the need for experts in many fields to support a Diplomatic Service. There is thus full justification for Seconded Officers as well as for Attached Officers, and

* There are, of course, some notable exceptions. One British Scientific Attaché is master not only of Russian but of Chinese. No wonder his services are in such constant demand.

the same care is needed in selecting them in accord with the 'representational' functions of husband and wife (and clerk and *his* wife) to which allusion has already been made in the preceding section.

Secondments and attachments are invaluable to the Diplomatic Service abroad and can profitably be extended to wider fields. Plowden mentions particularly the possibility of trained technicians from the Central Office of Information being lent or seconded to Missions to assist Information Officers.[55] Yet secondments *to* diplomatic posts are, or should be, only half the picture. Plowden rightly urges: 'Secondments both to and from the Diplomatic Service are of great potential value, though we do not underestimate the difficulty of arranging them.'[56] Such difficulties exist only to be overcome. It is essential, particularly in the economic sphere, that they should be surmounted.

Valuable though secondments are in both directions, a word of caution must be uttered. It is imperative that no Mission be allowed to overweight itself. The late Christian Herter, formerly US Secretary of State, wrote in his foreword to Briggs: 'There is no doubt in my mind that the American Ambassador of today is seriously over-cluttered with too many people from too many agencies of the Government.' Briggs himself comments bitterly on the *reductio ad absurdum,* a unit of the United States Coastguards attached to the American Embassy in Athens. They had absolutely nothing to do; he tried but failed to abolish them.[57] In the present state of the national finances, Britain is less likely to perpetrate such outrages, but if affluence should ever be attained again, overenthusiasm in this direction must be avoided.

IV

CONSULAR OFFICERS

ONSULS ARE such an integral part of a Diplomatic
Service that they have inevitably already been mentioned
many times in this book. Yet they fully merit a chapter
of their own, for their work is in its way as important as that of
their colleagues in Embassies,[1] and there are in the British Service
four times as many consular as diplomatic posts. It is regrettable that their duties are so little appreciated by the general
public.

Consular work follows an ancient and honourable tradition.
It is probable that the ancient Greeks had the equivalent of
Consuls in Egypt and other neighbouring territories. Certainly
the origins, as we know them, are rooted in the Middle Ages.
The need for a local representative of business interests and an
arbitrator in commercial differences became apparent as the
Mediterranean and the Near East opened up to trade during and
following the Crusades. As his name suggests, the Consul was
originally regarded as a kind of magistrate; one vested with a
measure of authority that enabled him to adjudicate between
the exporter whom he represented and the local trader. He bore,
therefore, the resounding Latin title *Consul Mercantorum* (Consul
of the Merchants) and the function was known among the strong
Jewish mercantile community of Cairo by a direct Hebraic
translation of the Latin as *Peqidim HaSoharim*. For many years,
Consuls were local citizens of high repute. The first recorded
medieval Consul represented Florentine interests in Egypt in the
thirteenth century and was one of the Jewish *Peqidim,* for in

those days nationality was more fluid; it was more important to choose a respected referee of financial probity than to worry about his place of birth.

Early records are hazy, but probably the first British Consul was a local man of distinction in Florence in 1456, while the first Crown appointment as a Consul, with some responsibility to the monarch of the day, was in Pisa in 1485.* The first British Consul of whom official record exists in the Foreign Office was at Aleppo in 1583. There followed Madeira 1658, Salonica 1724 and Oporto 1753. Rio de Janeiro appeared in 1808 and eight years later the first was appointed in the United States at Baltimore, in the same year as one at Le Havre. French Consuls in the Levant had been far more active as a result of the alliance between Francis I and Suleiman the Magnificent. In 1604 the first capitulations were signed between Turkey and France, granting official recognition and immunities to French Consuls. The Anglo-Turkish capitulations did not follow until 1675.

The establishment of career Consular Corps, like that of organized Diplomatic Services, is far more recent. In Britain it dates from 1825, in France from 1833 and in the United States from 1906. The Diplomatic and Consular Services in the United States were amalgamated in 1924; Britain did not follow suit until 1946. Previously, though recruited through much the same examinations, the standards of the two British Services were slightly different. Now there is complete integration and it is on this basis that the work of British Consular Officers should be considered. They are equal members of the Diplomatic Service who happen to be posted to a Consulate rather than to an Embassy or High Commission, and they also serve in the Foreign Office. Later in their careers the more able will rise, like their colleagues in the commercial, diplomatic or information branches, to Head of Mission.

Posts are divided into Consulates-General, Consulates, and

* I am indebted to Sir Francis Evans, a distinguished Consular Officer and Ambassador, for researches into the early history of Consuls, briefly summarized above. The eleventh edition (1910) of the *Encyclopaedia Britannica* is also valuable.

Vice-Consulates, and in addition there are Consulates, Vice-Consulates and Consular Agencies staffed by non-career officers, who need not necessarily be British subjects. Non-career officers hold Letters of Appointment from the Secretary of State for Foreign Affairs, not Royal Commissions. Many have served with immense local distinction throughout the world, little known except to those who travel in distant regions. Apart from outlying posts, every Embassy will have its Consular Section, though its office will not necessarily be housed in the same building as the Chancery. Provided local practice permits, which is not always the case, Consuls serving with an Embassy are given diplomatic rank and referred to as 'Counsellor and Consul-General', 'First Secretary and Consul' etc.

Until very recently there was no British Consular representation in Commonwealth countries, where it was held that British subjects could rely on the normal facilities of the country. This concept, as Plowden pointed out, is no longer realistic and the report recommended that officers be appointed in High Commissions to assume consular duties.[2]

Before a new Consul arrives at his post, his superintending Consul-General or Ambassador will have notified the appointment to the local authorities—normally the Ministry for Foreign Affairs. Strictly speaking, his Commission should be submitted and on this the local government inscribes its exequatur. In common practice, a simple notification of the appointment and a formal reply are all that are required to enable him to carry out his functions. His official exequatur can be granted later.

The main duties of a Consul are summarized by Plowden:

> The Head of a Consular post is responsible for all commercial interests, including export promotion, in his district. He must maintain good relations with the local authorities, keep his Ambassador posted about political and economic developments, support information and cultural activities and provide a focus and rallying point for his local community. Thus,

within his district a good Consul has the same broad representational responsibilities as an Ambassador or High Commissioner in relation to an overseas country as a whole.[3]

The Ambassador is the senior representative of his country in
any particular foreign region, but he will not fail to consult his
consular colleagues in the provinces. As often as he can spare the
time he will visit them personally; at least he will send a senior
member of his staff on tour; or he will ask the Consuls to report
to the capital individually; or hold a private conclave of all
Consuls in his Embassy. The United States Foreign Service is
rightly concerned to promote good liaison between Embassies
and Consulates,[4] and inveighs against any 'poor relation' attitude
between the capital and provincial posts; it is symptomatic that
in American parlance they are known as 'constituent posts'. The
Diplomatic Service of any country will be inefficient if Consuls
are not regarded as members of the 'Mission family'.

Among other duties Consuls record births and deaths of their
nationals. Many British consular posts hold Marriage Warrants
authorizing the officer to perform a civil marriage ceremony
valid in English law; or register a marriage performed in accordance with local law (the intricacies of marriage abroad demand
acute enquiry by the enamoured). United States Consuls are not
authorized to solemnize marriages, but may witness them
officially. Much to their relief, Consuls cannot grant divorces,
though they are not infrequently asked to advise privately in the
most intricate matrimonial affairs. Even more gloomily they can
in certain circumstances conduct burial services and supervise
cemeteries.

Consuls have a great variety of notarial duties. They can be
called on to safeguard estates of their nationals dying abroad and
take evidence on deposition. In ports British Consuls are much
concerned with the complexities of the Merchant Shipping Acts.
These duties call *inter alia* for arbitration in matters of discipline;
investigation of accidents and incidents on board, and of wrecks;
the care of seamen, supervision of their terms and conditions of

service, etc. Agency for the Royal Navy is another interesting port function for a British Consul—agreeable too, because it brings him into close personal contact with a Service as experienced and devoted as his own.

The seals and signatures of Consular Officers are valid in the law of the home country. Fees are charged for such services, but, alas, the career Consul does not benefit personally. Some locally engaged non-career British Consular Officers may, however, be authorized to retain, in lieu of salary, all or a proportion of fees collected; they may also be paid an 'office allowance' to enable them to engage a clerk to cope with the extra work. Until the formation of the United States Consular Service in 1906, no salaries were paid to American Consuls, but they retained all fees. Posts such as Liverpool and London with much traffic were therefore keenly sought after.

All nationals resident abroad for any length of time are advised to register at the nearest Consulate, so that the Consul knows who is in his district. In time of emergency this can be highly important. Consuls issue passports to their nationals and renew them. British Consular Officers may be empowered so to act for other Commonwealth countries and to issue visas for these territories. They stand ready to advise firms in their commercial ventures. They maintain the closest relations with the local authorities and issue visas to foreigners, unless there is an agreement between the two countries that visas are not required.

In the same way that an Ambassador seeks to win the confidence of the central government, so does the Consul with local authorities in his district, which may be much larger than the whole area of some more diminutive country. All capital cities are to some extent artificial. Consuls, stationed in the provinces, are likely to be able to see more of the 'genuine' inhabitants of the country. They live and work where foreigners are rarer than in the capitals and are therefore under closer scrutiny as representatives of their country than they would be in, say, Paris or Washington by the 'international set'. To be thus locally distinguished is a proud responsibility imposing a constant burden. Moreover, the isolated

Consul must be able to make rapid decisions on his own initiative. He cannot, like the secretary in an Embassy, drop into the room of his senior officer next door and seek advice. As the only official of his nationality perhaps for hundreds of miles, the Consul is much in demand. He has a permanent public relations job in addition to his office work. This involves him in much speechifying, often with only the slightest warning, usually in the language of the country and sometimes in circumstances that appear almost grotesque. All this is valuable training for the more staid occasions in which he will take part later as a Head of Mission.

Only if you browse through the massive volume of the consular instructions, can you form some idea of the multifarious duties that fall to Consuls, and even then you will read only half the story. As an example, there are well over a hundred activities in the list of fees that may be charged by British Consuls. The problems that face them are so diverse that no regulations could mention them all. Primarily they are intensely human. The cold or irascible individual cannot play the role of Consul. He is thus deprived of one of the major satisfactions of life—the opportunity to get something done. Only in the Inspectorate, as I mention in chapter VI (1), is there a like opportunity to remedy grievances and smooth the path of others. The basis for the ability to cope with these prickly problems has been summarized by a modest but brilliant exponent as 'willingness to be bothered', and this colloquialism should stand as a motto for any member of any overseas representational service, whether in a consular post or at an Embassy. No Diplomatic Service can afford members who are *not* 'willing to be bothered' by the human problems that afflict all of us sooner or later.

High policy may not come the Consul's way, but he is in daily contact with all manner of men and women of his own and other nationalities. Many travellers, enmeshed—often through no fault of their own—in strange foreign regulations, have had cause to bless the Consuls who came to their rescue, arranged for them to be bailed out or visited them in prison with books, cigarettes and other comforts. Many, too, are the yarns swopped when Consul meets Consul over a drink. To record a small part of them—were it discreet to do so—would require a volume even bulkier than that of the consular instructions, but two or three in lighter vein may be recounted here.*

☆

One day, HM Consul at a French port looked out of his window and was intrigued to observe a man riding an elephant down the street, followed by a woe-begone group of individuals. The elephant was brought to a halt outside the office and the *mahout* entered to explain that they were the remnants of a British circus which had gone bankrupt in France. They sought repatriation to the United Kingdom as Distressed British Subjects. There is a normal procedure for such sad cases; the Consul arranges the passages and extracts a guarantee that they will be repaid as soon as possible. The Consul made ready to cope, but then arose the question of the elephant. The circus manager explained that he had sold all their other animals and indeed all their belongings. No one, however, would buy the elephant, which consumed half a ton of green food a day. He offered to present it to the Consul, who hastily turned down the suggestion. The manager said that in that case the elephant must be repatriated too. The Consul demurred; the elephant was not British. 'Oh yes it is', said the manager. 'It's a distressed naturalized *British* elephant', and he produced a certificate showing its original residence in an English zoo. The Consul was defeated; such a valuable asset could not be left to starve in France, so he agreed to ship it home on the understanding that on arrival it would be sold to defray the cost of the passage of the group. Before a suitable vessel could be found the elephant's food bill mounted in alarming fashion. However, it was ultimately repatriated to the land of its adoption.

Over £60,000 is spent annually on the repatriation of Distressed British Subjects, including the mercifully rare pachyderm. Only about two-thirds of this is subsequently recovered from the

* Thayer (pp. 130–8), with his wide experience as a United States Consul, tells some tales as apparently tall, but just as true, as those that follow here.

beneficiaries. It is startling that over 700 persons are repatriated at public expense from Paris alone during the average year. No taxpayer should complain about the cost involved in rescuing persons left stranded abroad through genuine ill-fortune, but many applicants are feckless tourists and it must regretfully be recorded that there are far too many cases of flagrant dishonesty. The only sanction that can be applied is refusal to issue another passport, until the debt has been repaid.

An Archbishop can be as massive a problem as an elephant. One fine day it entered the head of an Archbishop of Canterbury that he ought to pay a visit to his opposite number, His Beatitude the Patriarch of the Greek Orthodox Church in Istanbul, so off he flew on this goodwill mission. He was met by many bearded clerics, the British Consul hovering tactfully in the background. After a few days of no doubt fruitful intercourse, the Archbishop went to the airport to continue his journey. Now, the Turks are Muslims and not really partial to any Christians; in particular they dislike Greeks and the Greek Church. The Turkish officials at the airport were therefore ostentatiously unimpressed by the Arch-bishop and the black-robed farewell party, the Consul again hovering tactfully in the background. It was as well he was there, for a senior official spotted him and, waving the Archbishop's passport, said: 'Where's the woman?' The Consul was scandalized. 'There is', he said, 'no woman.' 'Oh yes there is', said the Turk, and triumphantly showed the Archbishop's passport, which was valid also for his wife and bore her photograph. The Consul explained that the lady had not accompanied her husband. The Turk persisted that she must have done and that she must leave too. 'No woman, no go', he declared, glaring banefully at His Grace who, in ignorance of the crisis, was conversing animatedly with his hosts in whatever tongue they shared. The situation was saved by the Consul's Turkish chauffeur, who had overheard the conversation. As the official stamped off, he plucked the Consul's sleeve and asked for the passport. Within minutes he was back with two exit cards, one for the Archbishop and one for the 'woman'. The Archbishop was instructed to present both these when called to the aircraft and did so innocently enough, as he could not read Turkish. The Consul's only printable comments afterwards were that he wished the Archbishop would have a real splash and buy a second passport for his wife; and that he was glad to have a chauffeur whose aunt's cousin's niece was married to a Turkish immigration officer.

The most startling Consular problem I ever shared in myself was when a largely constructed, tweed-clad lady called without notice at the Embassy in Tehran. She announced that she represented the Royal Society for the Prevention of Cruelty to Animals and that she proposed to do something about the appalling cruelty to animals in the Middle East. I asked the lady how she proposed to effect a cure. 'I shall reason with them', she said, adding darkly, 'if that fails, I have my own method.' This was intriguing, but I did not take her very seriously. All she required of the Embassy was help to engage an interpreter and a car to take her to Isfahan, her base of operations.

A week later, the Consul-General in Isfahan telegraphed that he was returning the lady to Tehran, escorted by his Vice-Consul. He advised that she be at once deported from the country. All agog, we awaited the Vice-Consul and his report, which was sensational in the extreme. The lady had indeed encountered much cruelty practised on animals. If she saw a donkey so overladen that its legs gave way beneath it or a mule covered with gaping sores, she 'reasoned' with the owner, who paid no attention other than to address to the interpreter remarks so offensive that he thought it wise not to interpret them literally. Persuasion having failed, the lady had recourse to her 'own method'. This was as simple as it was effective. She produced a revolver from the capacious pocket of her skirt and with unerring marksmanship shot the suffering animal dead. She then moved on in search of another victim. After she had dealt with a dozen cases in different parts of the city in two days, terrified owners were observed reducing the loads on their animals and even attending to their sores, casting anxious glances around lest the assassin descend on them.

It was, however, too good to last. Complaints were made to the police and the lady brought down a final storm on her head when she stopped a portly *mullah* tittuping along on his donkey. He impelled this not with a whip, but by sticking into its withers a sharpened skewer. After the usual fruitless argument the animal was despatched, but the lady was arrested. The Consul-General had procured her release on the ground of insanity, after having compensated the outraged *mullah*. His report concluded that he had persuaded the lady to leave the country. On arrival in Tehran, she insisted, before departing for England, on seeing the Ambassador, who reluctantly agreed. In fact, Rex Hoare thoroughly enjoyed that interview. He used to recount afterwards his admiration for the lady's command of genteel invective. 'Lily-livered' was about the least biting epithet she applied to him and to all British officials in Persia. She left for England the next day and we wrote mildly in protest to the RSPCA. They replied wearily that, while they knew the lady very well, she had no connection with their organization. In their letter was noticeable a slight hint of regret that she would soon be back in the United Kingdom.

One mystery was left unsolved: the tactics used by the Consul General to persuade so masterful a woman to leave the country. When asked by the Ambassador, Ernest Bristow replied silkily that he too had his 'own method'. Months later he told me that he had taken her to inspect the men's prison in Isfahan and that his wife, suitably primed, had said that she would not again face the horrors of the women's prison (which did not, in fact, exist).

These frivolous stories illustrate the qualities of alertness, of experience and of humanity so often displayed over the centuries by Consular Officers—and so often unthanked. Such work breeds in the men and women who undertake it a stamina and value that should be more widely recognized. In earlier days, before career Services were set up, they were engaged *ad hoc*. Among the British one of the staunchest, who led a life of almost unbelievable adventure, was Walter Plowden,[5] Consul to the Emperor Theodore of Ethiopia in the fifties of the last century.*

* It is pleasant to record that HM the Queen paid a visit to his grave at Gondar during her recent state visit to Ethiopia.

THE CRAFT OF DIPLOMACY

The renowned name of the missionary explorer Livingstone will be found in the Foreign Office list for 1864 as Consul for Central Africa; the prickly Burton held consular posts in four continents, dying as Consul-General at Trieste; and Beau Brummell, when Prinny had tired of him, did a stint at Caen in Normandy—not, one imagines, with notable assiduity.

☆

Until 1920 there was not only a British Consular Service (as distinct from the Diplomatic) but several such Services. The Levant Service covered North Africa, the Eastern Mediterranean (Greece, Turkey, Syria and the Lebanon), the Arabic speaking countries, Persia (though the Persian Gulf and East Persian Consular posts were the perquisite of the old Indian Political Service) and finally Ethiopia. The Chinese, Japanese and Siamese Services covered those linguistic areas; the General Service the rest of the world. If only because of the language problem, there was little interchange between the Services. When a man had learnt Chinese or Arabic, he tended to remain in the Far East or Levant.

The advantages of such a system are manifest: the Service acquires a group of men who are deeply expert in a particular region and who speak the language or languages—many of them extremely difficult—with impressive fluency. The disadvantages are two-fold: there is a tendency for all experts in a limited area to become blind to wider fields, they come to 'know more and more about less and less'. Secondly, it can be stultifying for a good man to be forced to serve during his whole career in a certain part of the world and in a branch of the Service so small that promotion is much slower than elsewhere.

Those in favour of the 'compartment' system point out that many officers rose to positions of the greatest importance in consequence of their expert knowledge. Attached to British Embassies, they formed what was called the 'Oriental Chancery', which worked in parallel with the Chancery proper. The Head of the Oriental Chancery, who was probably a Counsellor in rank, could wield enormous influence, because the Ambassador would rightly depend on him as an interpreter and contact man. In the Constantinople Embassy this officer bore the title of 'Chief Dragoman',* responsible only to the *Büyük Elçi*, the Ambassador. Men like Eliot in Turkey, Teichman in China and Sansom in Japan, to name only three, attained immense local prestige—but only the first ever became an Ambassador himself. These individuals may have preferred to enjoy only their pre-eminent local expertness; assuredly they rendered great service in that capacity; but given wider fields, they could have shone as brightly anywhere —indeed Sansom did so in his later educational and historical work. In the General Service it was happily more frequent for Consular Officers of outstanding ability to switch to the Diplomatic Service and attain the highest posts.

By 1935 the separate British Consular Services had been integrated as far as new entrants were concerned, but it was not until after the Second World War on the amalgamation of all the Consular Services with the Diplomatic, that this rigid specialization came to an end. Something has been lost, but there is now a career open to the talents, and linguistic and other training for 'difficult' areas can be provided.

I have mentioned a few of the great names in the old British Consular Services, but there were many others who attained fame, sometimes in very different ways. Men serving in remote posts, often hardly in communication with the capital, had to be remarkably resilient and self-reliant. They acted as they thought best, without authority if necessary, and developed into pretty tough and sometimes odd characters, who earned deep respect in their districts. Sometimes, however, curious situations developed as a result of individuality.

One famous character was Mr Consul Chick of Shiraz, widely known as 'His Majesty's Chick'. He had retired years before I served in Persia, where his fame was still widespread, but he left us an awkward legacy. He had become very friendly with a Shirazi of

---

* This word is a corruption of the Arabic *terjumeh*, meaning interpretation. The French call him a *Drogman*.

immense wealth, whose only son had died leaving two children, to whom the old gentleman determined to leave his vast fortune. He distrusted his relatives and discussed safeguards with HM Chick. The latter blithely proposed that they be made wards of the British government and drew up an imposing document to this effect, bedight with consular seals and stamps. This was entirely bogus in law, but no one in Shiraz was able to query the legality, so, when the old boy died, the Legation in Tehran found themselves charged with the administration of a massive estate for the benefit of two infants. Always known on the file as 'the Chick Twins'—though twins, in fact, they were not—they used in later years to demand larger allowances at the instance of a horde of greedy relatives. These incursions became a considerable nuisance and it was a great relief when they successively reached their majority and the Minister could disembarrass himself of their affairs.

Curiously enough the only other Consul known to bear the sobriquet 'HM' before his name was also avian. He was widely known as 'His Majesty's Finch'. A person apparently of the mildest disposition, he outfaced a raging mob that attempted in 1941 to storm his Consulate in Iraq. By sheer personality and brilliant oratory, he persuaded the mob to retire. Moreover, he collected all the British and American nationals in the area and despatched them, in a large convoy of over a hundred men, women and children under charge of an American oil man, to Syria where they eventually arrived unmolested and, indeed, well-fed on camels' milk carefully boiled by the American.*

I have mentioned isolation, but this is not easy to grasp, accustomed as we are to convenient methods of transport, to the

---

* After the war, the American was awarded a decoration for his conduct of the successful evacuation. I happened to be in charge of the Embassy in Baghdad at the time and it fell to me to present him with the medal. He was very obstreperous when baldly asked to 'call at the Embassy'. (Somehow or other, the reason for the call was not explained to him.) He had a train to catch and he was damned if he would miss it for a stuffed-shirt Limey diplomat. In the end, however, he was persuaded to present himself at the British Embassy. When he realised what was afoot, he was deeply moved by the unexpected recognition. 'Think nothing of it', he said over the champagne. 'But it's good of your King to remember. I guess someone must have told him, but still he remembered and after all these years.'

proximity of shops and cinemas and above all to the company of our fellows, speaking the same language and thinking much the same thoughts. It is true that we sometimes announce that we want 'to get away from it all'; some of us even actually go on a walking tour or camp in a remote place. Artificial solitude can thus be found, but on the mainland of the United Kingdom only Cape Wrath is more than forty miles from a railway and this because the open sea lies on three sides of the promontory. If you search Europe outside the Iron Curtain and below the Arctic Circle, you will find no place more than forty miles from a train, except perhaps some remote spot in Spain. In countries outside Europe isolation is easier to achieve. There used to be a British Consulate-General at Kashgar in Sinkiang. Admittedly there was a railway 120 miles away, but this was in Russian territory. The Consul-General and his family reached his post after a journey of many weeks over the passes of the towering Karakorum range, the fabled Roof of the World.

The most isolated Consulate I have myself visited lies over 300 miles as the crow flies from the nearest railway or made road and yet further from an airport or harbour. It is in a village called Mega—I leave you to try and find it in your atlas. For half a century a succession of British Consuls functioned there. The tides of war have swept over the area, but little has changed since Sir Arnold Hodson, the first Consul, laid out his nine-hole golf course.[6] He could not construct smooth greens, so the 'holes' were animal skulls—when your ball hit one, you were 'down'. The house is now comfortable, with all modern conveniences that are very welcome to visitors, but one gave thought on departure to the Consul who had provided such generous hospitality. The traveller was heading for the fleshpots of civilization; the Consul would be thrust back again into his African solitude with no standby other than his own rich resources. Fortunate is the Service that can attract such men.

In earlier days Consuls from Britain and some other countries had to face yet another problem in their daily duties. Westerners in their conceit and perhaps in their wisdom, inclined to view with suspicion the process of justice in less developed areas. In China, and in the old Ottoman Empire and some of its successor states, foreigners could elect to bring their suits or be tried before 'mixed' courts, where a majority of the judges were not nationals of the country and where the procedure was more western than oriental. Consular Officers of foreign powers sat in these courts, though the higher posts were held by qualified lawyers appointed as judges. These extraterritorial judicial rights existed until after the First World War in some areas, and indeed persist today in the sheikhdoms of the Persian Gulf. They were carried to extremes in Persia where Nasir ud Din Shah presented the whole village of Gulhek, six miles north of Tehran, to Queen Victoria—inhabitants and all. Until the capitulations were abolished in the 1920s, this area was a British enclave on Persian soil. The lovely summer Legation was constructed—it is still in use by what is now an Embassy—and the Persian writ did not run in the surrounding village. The unfortunate Consul had therefore to add the duties of magistrate to his labours. Emotional matrimonial disputes were brought tumultuously before him, complicated claims over the precious water rights, and occasional cases of violent assault.

All these paled, however, before the file I once discovered in the Chancery in Tehran, when weeding out archives. A forgotten chest contained the 'black sheep' files and one thick bundle of documents provided enthralling reading. It was the tale of the Legation murder. In those days, it seemed, the bachelor Military Attaché had a roving eye that fastened on the attractive wife of the Vice-Consul. Much was the talk in such a small community and the Vice-Consul not unnaturally took the affair amiss. One night at a stag party he announced that he was going off to shoot the Military Attaché. No one took him seriously, though all sympathized. He did in fact proceed to do so, frankly admitting his guilt to the Minister and apologizing for the embarrassment. The Attaché was heartily unpopular and the verdict of all was 'good riddance'. Justice, however, had to be done and the Minister reported the matter to the Foreign Office. There followed in the file a diverting exchange of telegrams. The Consul flatly refusing to sit in trial over his junior, who, he stated in a minute to the Minister, ought to be decorated rather than tried. As the charge was capital the Foreign Office said that the Minister himself (in his other capacity as Consul-General) must take the case. The Minister had no objection until it dawned on him that, as the culprit had declared his guilt, there was under English law, as it then stood, no alternative to the death penalty. The Minister protested to the Foreign Secretary that he had no intention of condemning to death a colleague for whom he had a high regard. This brought a fulminating reply from the Foreign Secretary instructing him to do his duty. The Marquess Curzon of Kedleston was not a man to be trifled with, but Sir Percy Cox was emphatically not a man to be bullied. He duly presided at the trial, declared the Vice-Consul guilty and condemned him to the out-of-date penalty of 'two years imprisonment in a fortress'. Curzon raged, but he was helpless; under the capitulations no appeal to a higher court was possible and the judgement could not be reviewed.

This, however, was far from the end of the file. The nearest British fortress was Gibraltar, some 3,000 miles away, and there was no air travel in those days. Clearly a convicted murderer could not travel unescorted, but Sir Percy stoutly maintained that no British member of the staff could be spared to conduct him to jail. The Vice-Consul was therefore entrusted to the care of two Sikh troopers of the Legation Guard. In fact the roles were necessarily reversed. The poor *sowars*, heartily sympathizing with the plight of the Vice-Consul and speaking no word except their own language and Persian, had to be escorted by him. From every stopping place he sent a telegram reporting progress and sometimes his difficulties owing to the dietary exigencies of his escort. Weeks elapsed before the party reached Gibraltar, but the Vice-Consul's trials did not end then; he still had to arrange for the repatriation of the escort to India. The last telegram on the file announced happily that he had put them on a troopship bound for Bombay and asked that the authorities there meet the pair.

Extraterritorial murders are, one hopes, uncommon nowadays, but there is still plenty of spice in the life of a Consular Officer. There is also ample scope for initiative, intelligence and humanity. If, for instance, he is stationed at Innsbruck, which tourists invade in thousands, he will be appealed to by those who break their legs ski-ing on remote glaciers and by those who run out of money. In the Barcelona district the glaciers are less visited, but the picture will be varied by persuading the police to release young women so ill-advised as to wear bikinis on public beaches. Plowden comments tersely on the trials inflicted by tourists on Consuls: 'We are strongly of the opinion that consular officers must not be expected or encouraged to provide round-the-clock travel agency service.'[7] The report also suggested that, since this pressure was largely seasonal, arrangements should be made in busy posts to recruit temporary assistance locally or from Britain during the busy periods.

Perhaps most important of all, it is to the Consul that his nationals turn in case of natural disaster or internal strife in a foreign country. The Consular Section of an Embassy and the individual Consulates themselves will have in their safes plans carefully prepared and kept up to date at regular intervals for the protection of their nationals in case of emergency. These schemes will frequently have to envisage evacuating them, perhaps in conjunction with nationals of other nations. In some consular districts the colony may number several thousand, so the problems can be grave. Planning is inevitably complex and liable to violent disruption in the event, owing to unexpected moves by the opposition. The balance between not causing alarm by taking measures publicly (such as assembling the colony in 'safe' areas), or leaving matters until it is desperately late is extremely difficult. Usually several stages of alert must be envisaged. In the first only the staff are in the know and making surreptitious preparations; in the second a few others, who can be counted on to keep their mouths shut, will be roped in. A further complication can well be the inquisitive noses of newspaper correspondents, only too apt to cable their editors either that the Consul is asleep and taking none of the proper steps, or that he is an alarmist, sowing unnecessary panic in all directions. Outlying Consuls can have the worst time. Communications may well be difficult and perhaps have to be conducted by apparently innocuous coded messages conveyed by telephone or telegram. Frequently communications are completely cut and a level head has to be combined with initiative and ingenuity, often buttressed by great courage.

☆

The picture I have painted of Consular work would be misleading without mentioning that in the British and American Services, and rarely in others, there are women Consular Officers, who have won deep respect overseas for their conduct of duties requiring both meticulous accuracy and humanity. I have been privileged to serve with one, who was elected President of the local Consular Corps, of which all the other members were men. Such recognition that she was *prima inter pares* in a very 'masculine' country was a proper tribute to her efficiency and devotion.

Consular wives, too, may often play a more prominent role on the local stage than their colleagues in Embassies. The wife of a British Consular Officer has allowed me to quote what she once wrote from the woman's standpoint:

In some ways the consular wife will play a role similar to that of a parson's wife. She will listen to tales of woe, visit the sick, sustain the bereaved at the graveside. She will sit on, and chair, committees, and must be prepared for public speaking. Side by side with this, she must be at ease with the wives of foreign colleagues. In out of the way places, her house will be a hotel and she will entertain visiting firemen in all walks of life with an enormous range of interests and topics of conversation.

Yours are the obligations of a big frog in a small pond. You are the custodian of British prestige. You will sit, as of right, in the front pew in church, and must learn not to catch your husband's eye when he is reading the lesson.

My next point represents a woman's view, and may be slightly controversial. The man in the street is less concerned with the successful conclusion of a Treaty of Friendship and Navigation than with the fact that when his passport and money were stolen the Consul was more or less effective. 'What did the Consul do? Nout!' Or else, 'Eee, the Vice-Consul and 'is wife weren't 'alf kind to us'. You stand or fall by the help you can give to people in distress at any time of day or night. One of the things they want most is to hear their own language spoken.

So, if the consular post comes your way, go for it with open arms. It is hard work, varied, interesting, sometimes frustrating, sometimes rewarding. You get out what you put in. You will come out a tired person, but a fully rounded personality.

Few in any walk of life achieve such an ideal; the best, who may rise to fame in wider spheres, have these guiding principles deeply implanted in them.

V

SECURITY

F ROM EARLY days use has been made of espionage as
distinct from military scouting, which must date back to the
most primitive ages. The first Ambassadors were regarded
as licensed spies and were indeed to some extent forced into the
role by the efforts made by their often reluctant hosts to prevent
them from establishing any contact with the natives of the
country. Communist countries still maintain such prohibitions,
abandoned centuries ago in more courteous lands.

Hundreds of books have been written about efforts to extract
information, with a vast variety of methods, from sundry governments at different periods. They will continue, no doubt, to be
avidly read, even if they are by self-confessed liars. The better
thrillers, though not purporting to be anything other than fiction,
are often more solidly based on experience than some of the 'I
was there' fantasies purveyed to gullible readers by irresponsible
publishers. There is a succinct account of the real problems faced
by the British Diplomatic Service since 1939 in Watt[1] and the
Radcliffe Committee Report on *Security Procedure in the Public
Service*.[2]

Up to 1914 the British and Americans were remarkably naïve
about the dangers of diplomatic espionage. In a highly revealing
passage in a secret memorandum of 1899, the German Chancellor,
von Bülow, wrote of the British: 'They find it difficult to credit
really bad intentions in others.' Almost complete complacency
prevailed in British diplomatic circles up to the outbreak of the
Second World War. The practice of appointing foreign nationals

to posts that gave them access to confidential documents was widespread, partly because funds were not available to employ British, but primarily because of lack of suspicion. The Second World War loosed graver menaces than the First, but the lessons were even then slow to penetrate. It is true that a Security Department was established in the Foreign Office and that for the first time British Security Guards were employed in Missions abroad. However, with the advent of peace the warnings sometimes tended to be forgotten. Rude shocks were in store and the Burgess–MacLean conspiracy, revealed in 1951, at last made the Service sit up and think. It was realized that constant vigilance was required, but it was not until some time later that other departments of state with officers attached to Embassies abroad adopted adequate security measures. By then further damage had been done.

A major difficulty here lies in the entire attitude to life of Western countries. On the human side complete security will always be unobtainable, for not even the most ruthless dictator can control all the minds and actions of all his slaves all the time; but in totalitarian states repressive measures against the population as a whole are possible that would not be tolerated in democratic countries. Expense, carefully scrutinized with us, is immaterial to them. In the employment of manpower (e.g. secret police, who certainly number at least a quarter of a million men and women in the Soviet Union alone), in the construction of machinery (e.g. transmitters to jam foreign broadcasts), and in money supplied for perversion, the Communist 'repression budget' is, by civilized standards, not only unlimited but fantastic.

Every time there is a case of defection from the West to the East, there is an outcry; questions are asked why it was possible and demands are made for preventive measures. Such complaints are entirely justified, but before criticizing we must think coolly—which is not easy in the heat of emotion and abhorrence. One can have a regimented state with every policeman regarded as an enemy, and plainclothes snoopers behind every bush. Mihajlov, recently gaoled in Jugoslavia, where sympathy for the forbidden may not be expressed, reported (this was one of his first offences) what happened in Moscow to the Russian Dudintsev, who was under a cloud. Unknown people in trams would squeeze his hand stealthily without looking at him. 'For that sort of thing', Dudintsev said, 'it is worth while enduring anything.'[3] A Communist power should nevertheless be able to boast of a security system as efficient as man can make it. If, on the other hand, we prefer freedom of thought and word, we must face the fact that such safeguards against espionage as we can devise will fall short of the totalitarian ideal. The choice is ours and we in the West have made it. We have preferred that the main stream of our lives should flow unmuddied, and we cannot reasonably complain if we slip occasionally in matters less essential to our general way of life. We must not hope to have it both ways.

This is not in any way to excuse security lapses, some of the utmost gravity. It reminds us that we have to seek balance between freedom and repression. Each will have his own view, and in the West will be entitled to express it. The only people with whom I have little patience are the non-thinkers who rate the problem easy and rouse themselves from mental lethargy to brief heat when afflicted by 'surprises' that could have been foreseen and perhaps forestalled under a tougher regime.

Let us examine this horrendous subject more closely within the limits that discretion imposes. We can make a distinction between the 'palpable' and the 'human'. Although this is blurred because the human invades the palpable, the outlines of the distinction are clear.

By 'palpable' security measures I mean such everyday things as doors with locks; the sort of precautions that every sensible householder employs. The doors must be stout and the locks not easily pickable. Though the expense is great, combination locks are less vulnerable than key locks. If you are designing an Embassy or Consulate office, you should have a secure zone or 'keep' to guard your deeper secrets, which no unqualified person is permitted to enter, and ensure that it is always locked by the last to leave. The codes and cyphers, which must be devised to be 'unbreakable' by foreign experts, must be safeguarded with special care. All confidential papers must be held in the 'keep' and only removed during the day by the officer entitled to work on them. If he leaves his room temporarily while they are on his desk, he must lock the door and it is his duty to ensure that they are returned to the 'keep' at the close of work. A member of the staff should at least once a day inspect all rooms, including the Ambassador's, to ensure that no confidential papers are left out. Later a night watchman should patrol the premises. Again the householder comes to mind: 'Darling, have you locked the front door and fastened the windows?' shouts the wife from upstairs to the husband still reading before the fire. The answer is often 'No, but I will'—and may be even then he forgets. This is where the 'human' side impinges so devastatingly on the 'palpable' and why casualness in the Service is rightly counted a serious offence.

These are sins of omission. The opposition can be relied on for crimes of commission undreamt of thirty or even ten years ago. They will pounce on any papers that you are unwise enough to leave unsafeguarded or on notes that you have thrown into the wastepaper basket, photograph them and return them in a matter of hours. All 'confidential waste' (including typewriter carbons) should therefore be collected and destroyed under careful supervision.

They will plant microphones in your office and house; as your local servants will probably be in the conspiracy, this is very difficult to prevent. A considerable discretion in conversation is thus imposed. Moreover, unless you are a highly trained expert with complex technical equipment, you have no hope whatever of discovering built-in plants and you run a risk with transitory devices. For instance, your suspicions may be aroused by the gift of, say, a pink china elephant. You have it examined and it is innocent. A month later, when your fears have been lulled, another elephant is substituted, with a mike in its stomach. Similarly with your car; you scrutinize every cubic inch of it, but your actions have been anticipated. It will not be for some time that a 'bug' is planted in it. This can be battery operated and switched on when you turn the ignition key—a little trick work with wiring that only an expert constantly on the alert will spot. In Bolshevia petrol stations are scarce; you form the habit of refilling at a convenient one where the service, for good reason, is excellent. You may report to friends at home that they not only clean the windscreen but look underneath the car to see that all is well. You recall that the Bolshevian mechanic even refuses the tip you offer—but you do not notice the minute recording device he extracted and stuffed into his dungarees while grovelling in the mud. You are more likely to relate that he said there seemed to be a slight oil leak from the differential and could he have the car for an hour one day when it was entirely convenient to you to replace a godwit, sprue or other technical bit of your vehicle. The convenience is all his, to insert a freshly charged recorder.

The opposition will record your telephone conversations and, contrary to popular belief, there is no audible click to warn you that their machine is being turned on. Once at least the victims of telephone tapping really enjoyed themselves when the staff of the British Embassy in Tokyo was interned in the Compound after Pearl Harbor. After some months of confinement we tried to leave all in good order for our successors when we had won the war. It was easy to inspect the internal telephone system linking all the houses and offices and leave it in good repair, because we had an enthusiastic technician on the staff whose time lay heavy on his hands. He soon discovered two taps, one on the telephone in the Ambassador's study and one on mine. We spent all one night linking these two together and connecting a third line so that we could listen in to the resulting exchanges, which in those primitive days soon became audible. Ignorance of Japanese deprived me of that amusement, but a few nights later, ensconced under a rhododendron, I enjoyed watching a mystified trio of Japanese come over the wall to trace their wires—unavailingly, because we had dismantled everything twenty-four hours before. Little did they know that our real anxiety was for the safety of the small radio concealed in a nearby attic.

This is all on the palpable side; far more subtle and dangerous are the attacks on the human front. Any failing is observed and exploited, sex, drugs and drink being favourite targets that can lead to blackmail. Financial embarrassment is another weakness, eagerly seized on. This may perhaps arise from pathetic family circumstances, perhaps from high living or gambling, or perhaps more prosaically because someone, unfamiliar with conditions abroad, becomes confused with strange currencies and a different standard of living and runs into debt. Those suspected of curious tendencies will be offered various forms of debauch in a room where photographs can be secretly taken. When confronted with these one Oriental diplomat in Bolshevia easily defeated the ploy. It was suggested to him that unless he 'co-operated' prints would be given to his Ambassador. 'Don't give them', said the Secretary, 'sell them; they are just the sort of photographs he likes.'

A particularly low trick is the appeal to human sympathy. You are approached by an agent who confides that he has an aged aunt in France, destitute but affectionate. Could you smuggle a letter through the Iron Curtain to her? Or he has an even more aged aunt in Zbrsk, destitute, affectionate and dying for lack of aspirin. Could you smuggle in some of this miraculous Western drug of which he has read in clandestine news sheets? If the sucker is unwise he falls for such lures. Just as he reaches out to accept the clandestine letter or hand over the forbidden medicine, Secret Police will pop out of every cupboard, photographs will be taken and he will be brusquely requested to 'co-operate'. The diplomat may accept damnation; if he refuses he will be declared *persona non grata* and have to leave. If the victim is a tourist or visiting student and still has the courage to refuse to submit to blackmail, he will be tried (after months of delay to soften him) and the Public Analyst of Zbrsk will state irrefutably that aspirin (as manufactured in the West) is exclusively composed of arsenic and strychnine.

Do not think that these are frivolous examples of duplicity; they have all happened—the unbelievable included. In the latter category enters the woman who, just as you are getting into a taxi to go to a museum, begs you for a lift, as you are by sheer chance going past the house where her aunt is dying. If you are a sucker you accede to this pathetic suggestion. Within a mile the woman will utter piercing screams, rend her loosely sewn raiment in the manner of a strip-tease dancer and accuse you of attempted rape. Nor are women members of Diplomatic Service or female tourists immune from insidious attentions. Contact with attractive young men, including domestic servants, will be arranged in the hope that they will fall.

Anyone who thinks he is being got at should remember two precepts—and these are applicable whether one is a member of the Service or not. First, don't try to be clever. Communist intelligence officers are very highly trained and you are not; don't think that you can outfox them on your own. Secondly, if your suspicions are in the slightest aroused, report at once to your superior officer, or (if you are a private individual) to your Embassy abroad or some competent authority at home.

Most insidious of all, and the most difficult to detect, is the successful ideological assault that induces a hitherto loyal officer to commit treason, not for gain but because he has been brought to believe it is 'right'.* It may take literally years to spot the defection and months to trace the source. In one bad case during the war it was known in London within forty-eight hours of a leakage that it had occurred—for the British employed agents against the Nazis more efficient, I venture to say, than theirs against us. Counter-measures were developed that soon put an end to the leak, but it was not until after the end of hostilities that we learnt definitely who was the source.

On the palpable side extreme vigilance must be exercised; on the human side observation and training are required. This means not only the vetting of the background of new entrants, but a continuous eye kept on officers by their seniors throughout their careers and the results carefully recorded in jealously guarded files. This sounds distasteful, but in fact the eye should be friendly and

---

* Rebecca West's *Meaning of Treason* (revised edition, Pan Books, London 1956) is required reading for the student of these abhorrent matters. Pages 274–314 are a particularly pertinent warning to a Diplomatic Service—indeed to us all.

part of the general education of any member of the Service, without which he cannot hope to eliminate faults and improve himself. Throughout this book I have insisted that Heads of Mission and Heads of Chancery fail if they do not help their juniors. No matter their renown in the art of diplomacy, they must give equal weight to this aspect of the craft. The essence of good security is not to try to catch people out—even the most honest may slip sometimes—but to *prevent* error. There should be no witch-hunting. Confidence in a happy team, each helping the other not to forget his duty, is paramount.

Up-to-date training courses in security are essential not only for new entrants, but to warn older hands of the latest devices and stratagems adopted by adversaries without scruple or pity. Wives too should be made familiar with the dangers they can incur. After a lecture on security problems that gave chapter and verse for much varied devilment in different parts of the world, I have known officers with many years of service to leave muttering that they had never believed such things were possible. As long as there remains any tendency to 'find it difficult to credit really bad intentions in others', such education is imperative.

Bumbledom in Britain would insist that observance of the Official Secrets Act should become as much a habit as the bodily functions. All members of the Service must subscribe to the Act, but it is turgidly drafted and could obviously be used in ill-mannered hands to 'crime' you for doing anything normal—such as mentioning to your godmother that the Foreign Minister of Barataria was tiresome—because you acquired that information 'as a result of your official position'. It could legally be argued that this subject of conversation was indictable, although 392,178 of the 392,179 inhabitants of Barataria were acutely aware of the tiresomeness of their Foreign Minister (the exception being the Minister himself). It is the principles *behind* the Act that are far more important. They should be observed closely and implicitly. Watt writes:

The substitution of security procedure for trust, formal communication for informal social relationship, can lead to a paralysis of judgement, freedom of comment and recommendation which would greatly impair both the internal workings of the Service itself and the role of the Service in the defence of the national interest. The experience of the German Diplomatic Service under Nazism and the more recent Calvary of the American Service under Scott MacCleod and McCarthyism are terrible warnings of the pitfalls which the Service may have to face in the next few decades.[4]

Such cogent warnings are necessary. I would only disagree with the idea that it is impossible to establish 'trust and informal relationship' in the larger post-war Service. The close intimacy of a very small Service may have passed, but even when a diplomatic family grows and far more of its members are initially inexperienced in work overseas, superiors can nurture trust and cordial informal relationships throughout the larger organization.

It is not disrespectful to say that official supervisory bodies, like the imposing three-man Standing Security Commission set up by the British government in 1964, should be less important than the everyday awareness of pressing danger by all members of the Service. Only their united vigilance and intimate contact can guarantee the security of the national secrets with which all are entrusted. The disease of disaffection must be diagnosed at source and remedies instantly applied lest corruption gain its sinister hold. Guidance on technicalities, ever refreshed, must be available and every other precaution that tragic experience has shown necessary must be taken. Basically, however, the problem is 99 per cent human and therefore not insoluble by humanity in any Service in any country.

VI

THE INDISPENSABLE
AUXILIARIES

ESSENTIAL TO the success of overseas representation are four auxiliary systems: the inspectorate, the diplomatic messengers, cultural representation, and the housing and equipping of Missions. They are grouped under this chapter heading because they do not entirely fit the general pattern of the book. The Corps of Inspectors for the British Diplomatic Service is based in London, but its personnel are regular members of the Service who spend so much of their times travelling abroad that they must be included in any consideration of overseas representation. The Queen's Messengers are not members of the Service but, though based in London, their sole duty is to serve Missions and Consulates abroad. The British Council is a separate Service, working partly at home and partly overseas. The Ministry of Works is generally regarded in Britain as a purely 'domestic' department of government, yet its staff overseas play an important role in the successful running of Missions.

Mention could be made in this chapter of the Diplomatic Wireless Service, but its personnel, while attached to Missions, are members of the Diplomatic Service whose work is so closely connected with that of the Chancery of a Mission that it was more convenient to deal with them in chapter III (see page 68). These nimble-fingered technicians, trained to miracles of deftness and sensitivity in the arcane craft of communication through space, deserve a study all of their own, but this could hardly be written except by one fully initiated into their guild.

The four auxiliaries we are now going to examine are not unique to the British Service, albeit the matter of this chapter is drawn from British practice. All competent Diplomatic Services employ highly trained officials to fulfil the duties of these four agencies. I regret that lack of space prevents detailed comparison with the methods of other Services.

I. THE INSPECTORATE

This home-based branch of the British Diplomatic Service has an influence on the work of Embassies, High Commissions and Consulates that is as profound as it is often unrecognized. British Consulates, as opposed to Missions, were subject to inspection as far back as the last century, but there was only one Inspector. However willing, he could not possibly cover efficiently 600 or 700 posts all over the world. One legendary character preferred to live in Paris and restricted his inspections to the more civilized European posts, which he took care to visit at the best seasons of the year in his Rolls Royce. Far more strenuous is the modern method. The Corps of Inspectors was first established in the Foreign Service in 1946. In the integrated Diplomatic Service it now consists of one Senior Inspector, grade 3 (i.e. of ambassadorial rank), and nine colleagues. There is an additional Inspector, who deals solely with commercial and economic matters, particularly the promotion of exports. The junior Inspectors are ranked grade 4 (i.e. Consuls-General or Counsellors). The United States Foreign Service Inspection Corps numbers sixteen officers.[1]

High policy is not the concern of the Inspectors, but they have a large responsibility for the efficient functioning of Missions. They travel the world, being absent from London on their journeys for seven months of the year on the average. It is their duty to make recommendations to the Chief of Administration, as the administrative head of the Diplomatic Service is now known. (Until 1965 his title in the Foreign Office had been 'Chief Clerk' and this will be slow to die in colloquial use.) In the early days of the Inspectorate after the last war, the most important task was probably the calculation of adequate allowances to be given to officers of different grades in each post (basic salaries in each grade are the same). These financial calculations have now been simplified and the Inspectors rarely have to deal with cases of officers trying to make do on totally inadequate emoluments. For some time, however, they will still be fully occupied in bringing into force all over the world the new system of allowances established in accordance with the recommendations of the Plowden report. (See Appendix B.)

The most important part of the work now is that connected with the staffing and organization of a post and the efficient distribution of sparse manpower. It is remarkable how often a fresh eye directed at a problem can find a solution that has eluded those working on the spot. On occasion the Inspector may recommend that a Consulate be closed if the small amount of work does not justify the expense, or he may suggest that a new post be opened. The Inspectors also examine Security; the scale of rent allowances, if accommodation is not provided; the grading and pay of locally-engaged staff; the condition of office premises and furniture, etc. In addition, they occupy themselves with matters of personnel, welfare and health. An Inspector's visit gives an opportunity to all members of the staff and their wives to discuss any personal private problems with a home-based officer. Even in a 'happy ship' people are glad to be able to pour out their woes —frequently trifling, sometimes grave—into a sympathetic ear known to be in direct contact with headquarters. Inspectors collaborate intimately with the heads of posts and other senior officers. With the integration of all the overseas representational services of the Crown, more Inspectors will have to be trained for a job that demands a human approach as well as a thorough knowledge of the new regulations.

The work is gruelling. The frequent change of climate; the tiresomeness of constant travelling (indeed, its precariousness in some areas); the separation for long periods from one's family—

all this imposes a strain that is not lightly faced. In addition there are the often intricate discussions that take place at home when the weary Inspector returns to his desk, not only to report to the Chief of Administration and the Head of the Personnel Department, but perhaps also to confer with other Ministries, whose officials serve abroad, about matters of particular interest to them.

Outsiders who incline to the view that Inspectors are an unpopular bunch are overhasty in judgement. In the early days there was no occasion when inspection was not asked for by the post itself—inadequate staff or allowances being the most frequent cause of complaint. The Inspector was thus always welcome and, while one cannot claim that he was able to satisfy everybody or that there were no rows, it would be fair to say that it was rare for him not to leave a post happier and more efficient than he found it. Now visits by Inspectors are more regular, but equally welcome and more productive than during the initial post-war gropings. As one Inspector commented on leaving the Inspectorate:

The rewards of this work are great and do much to mitigate the strain. None see more of the Foreign Service at home and abroad than Inspectors and none can be prouder of it with more justification. It is a pleasure to deal with such a machine. Personally I regret the increase in its size and the loss to some extent of the family atmosphere. I hope, however, that given a few years of peace we can build that up again, not on a spoon-fed basis, but encouraging full bent for individuality in all ranks.

It is of the nature of foreign affairs that it is rarely possible to feel that anything has been accomplished. The work is a continuum; obstacles may be surmounted, but others are immediately disclosed beyond. An Inspector can, however, achieve something durable, particularly on the human side. He can right grievances, reorganize so as to increase efficiency and well-being, and often pride himself privately that he has left the staff at a post more cheerful and in better shape to face an arduous future. It is impossible to exaggerate the satisfaction derived from such a job well done.

The disadvantages are severe, nevertheless, and I quote from the same memorandum as above:

> It is in many ways one of the charms of Inspection that the problems are always new, but the mental effort required to face these ever changing landscapes, personalities and problems is severe. After sleeping every night in a different place one comes to dislike the mental prostitution and longs, as Mrs Patrick Campbell is alleged to have remarked, for the comfort of the marriage bed after the hurly-burly of the chaise longue. This kaleidoscopic life is frustrating, because one can never really develop an interest in the intricacies of, say, Mexican policy, though it is going on all around and is the major topic of conversation at any table. The Inspector knows only too well that in a fortnight he will be grappling with another continent and another set of problems. This is most unsatisfying because administration, though vitally important, is not an end in itself and it is difficult to be enthusiastic about it for long.

While there is no doubt that work in an Inspectorate is highly educative, it is wrong to employ good men indefinitely on such a job. Too much absorption in administrative detail is stultifying. If you hope to use a razor blade to shave with, it is a mistake to sharpen too many pencils with it.

Other countries have Corps of Inspectors with whom it is useful to maintain contact and exchange views. The British Inspectors for long had a unique advantage (now adopted by others)—they travel with their Personal Assistants. These are hand-picked; they need to be if they are to face cheerfully the appallingly long hours inflicted on them. The overtime clocked up by my Personal Assistant was fantastic. On our last tour she averaged over fifty-eight hours a week, including long stints on Saturdays and Sundays—nor was this exceptional. We travelled over 90,000 miles together at an average rate of 180 miles a day, including non-travelling days.* A lady in the United States was

---

* This was c. 1950. The pressure of high-speed travelling is now heavier on all ranks. Her Majesty's Secretary of State for Foreign Affairs covered over 60,000

once ill-advised enough to ask me what my wife felt about my travelling round the world with an attractive girl in what she clearly regarded as undesirable propinquity. It was difficult not to reply that my wife's mind was not as dirty as hers. When I retailed the remark to Valerie, my Personal Assistant, she looked wearily up from her portable typewriter in a compartment in the 'California Zephyr' and remarked crisply: 'Does the woman think we have time for that sort of thing?' I can never pay sufficient tribute to her and her colleagues for their staunchness and good humour.

Inspectors, perhaps even more than their colleagues leading a more 'normal' diplomatic life, are great yarn swoppers, but for reasons of delicacy these should rarely penetrate much beyond the inspectorial gossip circle:

> A tell-tale in their company
> They never could endure;
> And whoso kept not secretly
> Their mirth, was punished sure.

Perhaps, however, I can properly release to a wider public one inspectorial 'true adventure' story. On this particular tour the Inspector had visited Nepal, which has no rail connection with India. On completing his task, he had therefore taken plane to a railhead, where he found that he and his Personal Assistant were to share a commodious four-berth sleeper for the overnight journey to Delhi. Very early next morning he rose and went to the communicating bathroom to perform the usual ablutions. While he was thus occupied, the train stopped at a station and he heard a considerable commotion next door in the sleeping compartment. The train had restarted by the time he could properly present himself and then, to quote his bleak words: 'I found the compartment occupied by my PA in bed, sixteen other persons and a parrot in a cage.' In England if someone knocks at the shuttered door of a sleeper, you may well open it without undue

---

miles in 1965 burdened with infinitely greater responsibilities. Few adding machines provide enough noughts to clock the mileage of any American Secretary of State.

anxiety. This is not necessarily so safe in other parts, as any experienced Inspectorate PA knows full well.

☆

No Service can fail to benefit from proper, intimate and efficient supervision of its methods and conditions—provided always that those responsible for the task have in them the milk of human kindness, behind them the requisite training and that they themselves are ordinary members of the Service, who will later revert to a 'normal' Service life. The latter point is vital. No organization will do otherwise than regard with suspicion and dislike 'efficiency experts' foisted on it from outside. The name of Bedaux and 'time and motion' studies once stank in the nostrils of all who were subjected to the process, and outside experts can expect little success in the small units of which a Diplomatic Service is made up overseas. In larger organizations, such as the Foreign Office itself, Organization and Method experts have a part to play, for guarding the nation's purse is a difficult and thankless job. There is little awareness in some government departments of the need for close scrutiny of capital and recurrent expenditure, perhaps on a vast scale. The attitude seems to be, 'let's try it on and leave it to the Treasury to object'. This is crass; a heavy-spending department should take pride in not putting up such proposals.

British Railways have been in a parlous state and Dr Beeching was called in to produce remedies. I have never met him, but I know where he went for advice and he did not hire a firm of managerial consultants to snoop. It may not be generally realized that the worst problem of the Railways was not that, for instance, there were twenty-seven sources of supply for tarpaulins (now reduced to three), but the low morale among railwaymen. The way to raise this is not to employ outsiders to pry into their work, but to train selected men in the problems and let them go out among their colleagues. If railwayman talks to railwayman, he can—this is an actual case—reduce the number of men in a plate-laying gang from fourteen to seven without outcry. An outsider trying to enforce the same regulation would provoke a strike. As usual it is flesh and blood, the human being, that counts much more than machinery. The British Armed Services have adopted the same wise course. They do not employ outside experts; instead they send officers to be trained in what is best called 'work-study'. Such men know the particular needs and traditions of their own Service, they are 'insiders' not 'outsiders', can speak the right jargon to their colleagues and gain their confidence. All they need is specialized training.

In general, those selected for organizational or administrational duties should be chosen, not because they are misfits, but because they are outstanding men who are expected to go very high in the Service. In fact, it is the 'men who cannot possibly be spared' who should be chosen. Ideally they should be not much over the age of thirty-five—in the British Diplomatic Service, a small, compact organization, they tend for good reason to be rather older—and experience has shown that they need not be scientists even in the most technical Service. Cross-fertilization with the humanities seems highly beneficial in any team. None should have to do more than a stint of two, or at most three, years before reverting to normal duties—in which, as experience has also shown, they will go far, after a training that is primarily designed to teach a man to think methodically and logically.

I have maintained that the Foreign Office's Corps of Inspectors has done sterling work. After much trial and error in the early days, the Inspectorate learnt as it went along. The Diplomatic Service could now well take a leaf out of the book of the Armed Services and establish with outside help a 'school' at which members of the Service could be trained for specialized duty. Any Diplomatic Service has much to learn about administration and it should keep abreast of modern methods and devices in a rapidly changing world. Above all, an eye should be cast on the central organization of the Service—Foreign Office, State Department and their equivalents in the various countries—leaving Missions and Consulates until later. The procedure should operate from the top downwards and not make the mistake that is made all too often of beginning at the bottom with the nuts and bolts rather than with the over-all functioning of the machine. A profitable moment for this will come in Britain when the Commonwealth Relations Office and the Foreign Office are at last amalgamated. I revert in more detail to the question of training in chapter VII, where it is argued that it is both desirable and possible to have an 'administration section' in the Diplomatic Service Staff College that is there proposed.

The Diplomatic Services now springing up in newly independent countries all over the world would be wise to set up such 'schools' from the outset, or to send their men to be trained at those already in existence elsewhere. The governmental organizations in London are accustomed and glad to give assistance and advice to the administrative services of new states in the Commonwealth. If the Foreign Office had such a 'school', it would benefit the Diplomatic Services, not only of Britain, but also of many other countries.

2. DIPLOMATIC MESSENGERS

All Diplomatic Services must maintain couriers to carry from the capitals to their Missions and Consulates and *vice versa* the official correspondence that passes, often in great volume, between a government and its representatives abroad. Though these services are based on the home country, they are such an important feature of diplomacy that they must be treated here.

'Bag days' are important in the Embassy calendar; the days when the official mail arrives with the latest instructions from the home capital, or the more flurried days when the outgoing mail has to be ready on time. In large Embassies—such as those in Washington and Paris, where the bag is a daily affair—there is no excitement, but if your post receives and despatches only one bag a fortnight, pressure is high and staffs may have to work late to have all ready for the Messenger, who is probably leaving next morning at some hideously early hour. Ambassadors as well as lesser mortals should learn to accommodate themselves to this timetable. One of my first chiefs had only one vice—he loved to go on titivating his drafts and writing more and more letters until the last minute. It was seldom that we could close a bag before midnight. The record was 5 a.m., an hour before the Messenger was due to leave. On that occasion, the Chancery came near to mutiny. Protests were tactfully made; the Ambassador was contrite and reformed—for about a month.

☆

Though basically similar, details of the courier system vary in different government services. The British diplomatic messenger service is probably the most ancient in origin and may be taken as the type-example.

The story of what is now the Corps of Queen's Messengers begins in late medieval times.[2] At least as early as the middle of the fifteenth century, the Exchequer had messengers. The first mention of a King's Messenger is in 1485; he enjoyed a salary of 4½d a day—then worth very much more in purchasing power than today. By the restoration of Charles II in 1660, pay had risen to £45 a year. The King's Messengers for long acted not only as couriers but also as a kind of special police; it was part of their duties to arrest wrongdoers in Britain, particularly those accused of serious crimes against the state, such as High Treason, and the Messengers might be required to keep them in custody in their own houses. It is on record that, during the Napoleonic Wars, a French general and his servant were thus held for ninety-one days. The Messenger was granted an allowance of £1 a day for the subsistence of the general and 10s 6d for the servant.

One of the consequences of the accession of the Hanoverian dynasty to the throne of England in 1714 was a heavy increase in official mail traffic with Europe, but it was not until 1772 that Messengers were divided into 'Home' and 'Foreign' sections. This may be considered as the date of the official foundation of the Corps of King's Messengers. For many of those tempestuous years, when all Europe was riven by war, they ran grave risks. During the French Revolution and while Napoleon was in full march, no less than ten perished—by disease, by accident (a wheel would come off a coach at speed, so that it was hurled into the ditch), by attack from highwaymen in England (how disappointed the robbers must have been to find, instead of jewels, a mass of correspondence unsaleable in local pawnshops), and by enemy action (one King's Messenger disappeared on a journey in Germany and his end remains a mystery, while others were killed in defence of their mail). It seems odd now that in those days there was no regulation that Messengers must be British. One reason was that then (as unfortunately often now) the British had little training in foreign languages. A reliable polyglot was therefore often preferred in an age when men on their travels had to be able to cope with every emergency of the long road. Many of these foreigners rendered invaluable service.

Expenses were high. There is a record of one journey in 1780 from London to Petersburg, which cost £459 3s 4d. This would be the equivalent of at least £5,000 today. The present first-class air fare to Moscow is £83, so it is agreeable to reflect that some things are cheaper now than in the time of our ancestors. Governments, however, do not change much; George III's Messenger had to argue lengthily over his accounts before he could get his money back. Messengers were required to maintain their own carriages (which they usually kept at Calais) and were encouraged to find reliable travelling companions to add to the safety of the journey. These escorts could often be induced to contribute to the cost. In 1850, however, it was laid down that a King's Messenger might not take with him his wife 'or any other female'. The Messengers also had to show before they were engaged that they were accomplished horsemen, since on the wilder routes, such as those through the Balkans, no wheeled traffic was possible. In 1824, the Corps was remodelled and the eighteen Messengers were placed under the Foreign Office, to serve exclusively overseas.

Some prodigious journeys are on record. One from London to Tehran overland took from December 10, 1833 to March 8, 1834—some 3,000 road miles at the highest speed, but with many vexatious delays. If enforced halts are not counted the Messenger was averaging forty miles a day in midwinter over rough and dangerous country. Probably the outstanding performance is one mentioned by Temperley.[3] This was the journey of Captain Townley in October 1849 from Belgrade to Constantinople— 592 miles in five days eleven hours, averaging 106 miles a day. The best of the Turkish Tartar messengers, also a *corps d'élite*, probably covered as much as 120 miles in a single day, but there is no record of such a lengthy journey as Townley's at such speed by a single Tartar. Horses were changed as frequently as possible and the Messenger had an escort of one or two men, a led horse for his personal baggage and a spare animal in case one of the others went lame. The *Yam* (message service) of the Mongol rulers is described by Marco Polo, but his statement that a courier could travel 200–250 miles in a day must be discounted, as must be Ossendowski's graphic story of the Mongol who, he says, rode 1,800 miles to Peking from Uliassutai in nine days.[4] In fact the distance is more like 1,400 miles, but even an average of 150 miles a day by one man is very difficult to credit. The famous 'Pony Express' of the American West, before the telegraph reached the Pacific, also produced some fantastic speeds, though liable to interruption by hostile Indians and other hazards of the road. It covered nearly 2,000 miles from the Missouri to San Francisco in eight days. Staging posts were twenty-five miles apart and each rider did three before handing over the mail bag to the next.

My own family have always had an interest in these matters because, in the last century and more rarely in this, it was necessary to employ what were known, perhaps a bit disparagingly—but the Corps of Messengers is a body jealous of it's prerogatives—as 'Casual Messengers'. My great-grandfather was a British merchant resident in Russia and he was often called on in the forties and fifties of the last century to perform this duty by the Ambassador in Petersburg. If a British vessel were available, he could travel by sea, but then he was subjected to the vagaries of wind and if the Baltic were icebound, no ships called. The alternative was overland. It was 700 miles to the railhead at

Warsaw and, as the Messenger had first call on the horses at the frequent posting stations for his carriage or sleigh, he could cover the distance in nine days on an organized and policed route, very different from the conditions faced by the dauntless Townley. Nature and climate were the worst enemies. In the spring thaw and in the mud of autumn before the heavy frosts, thrice as long might be required.

'Casual Couriers' have their full share of misadventure. Between the wars, before there was an air service to Persia, the bags went from Baghdad to Tehran by road. There was no permanent King's Messenger, so they were placed in the charge of one of the officers serving in the RAF station at Hinaidi. In summer, when Iraq was a furnace, the duty was popular and many volunteered; in winter it was another story. One January a junior officer set forth on his 500 mile journey in the car hired for the purpose, accompanied by an Indian trooper of the Legation guard. He crossed happily two of the great passes, reaching successively the British Consulates at Kermanshah and Hamadan. As he set off northward to face the Aveh pass, beyond which lay Kazvin and Tehran, it began to snow. When he was forty-eight hours overdue at the Legation and confirmation had been obtained that he had left Hamadan, search parties were sent out from each end. He and his derelict car were found four days later. The bags were intact and the courier, though very cold and hungry, was cheerful. He had been lucky to find a shepherd's hut close to where the car had finally stuck in the drifts, and there he had sat out the blizzard with his own meagre supplies of food supplemented by what the shepherd could spare. Such were the conditions that he had to struggle for three more (happily better-fed) days to reach Tehran, where every care was then lavished on him. Even after less perilous journeys, Messengers fully deserve some hospitality from the Ambassadors and the staffs they serve so devotedly. There is at times and in various places a tendency to take their prompt deliveries too much for granted.

Much false glamour has been attached to Diplomatic Messengers by romantic novelists. It is assumed that they are often approached in sleeping-cars and hotel bedrooms by scantily dressed Ruritanian countesses, so avid to purloin their despatches that they will pay any price. I am sorry to report that members of the Corps are unanimous in regretting that no such romantic adventures come their way. This does not mean, however, that there is no danger to the official mail bags; in many countries the slightest inattention would result in the vanishing of one or all of them. Attempts more sordid than amorous are made. A remarkably fat bribe was once proffered in the hope that a back would be turned long enough to permit the substitution of a fake bag. I have always regretted that this gambit was not more subtly checkmated. The bribe should have been accepted to increase Britain's reserves of foreign currency and a bag passed over with contents that would have kept the Kremlin mighty puzzled for some months. Constant vigilance must, indeed, be exercised, but in general the work is as dull and exhausting as it is responsible.

Nowadays one of the worst burdens is the irregular behaviour of aircraft. Delays in the weirdest places require experience and patience to deal with. Missed connections are not only wearisome, but arouse anxiety for the safety of the bags. The unpunctuality of aircraft is also hard on the staff of Missions, for Messengers must be met at airports and conveyed to the Embassy, which may be many miles away. Junior officers on the duty roster spend dreary hours in inhospitable surroundings waiting to meet or see off a Messenger on an aircraft as reluctant to start as a recalcitrant horse.

☆

I have dwelt on the British Corps because of its ancient history and proud record; other Diplomatic Services will recall the work of their own Couriers with equal pride. Nomenclature varies. In Britain we speak of a 'Diplomatic Bag'; this in the United States becomes a 'Pouch' and in France a '*Valise Diplomatique*', transported by a *Courrier*. The *Valise* is in no way to be confused with a '*Serviette diplomatique*', which is not a napkin but one of those slim briefcases busy continentals carry under the arm. All members of foreign Diplomatic Services and their Couriers are supplied with special diplomatic passports differing in colour or other ways from the normal ones of the country. It is not generally realized that members of the British Diplomatic Service hold only ordinary passports, which sometimes involves them in difficulties with suspicious foreign immigration officers.* Only for Queen's Messengers is an exception made; they are furnished with red passports instead of the normal dark blue, and these describe their status.

In Britain the Corps is recruited largely from retired officers of the Armed Services or the Colonial Service. Its personnel are not members of the Diplomatic Service. Despite the long hours and fatigues of travelling and the enforced separations for much of the year from wives and families, there is a long waiting list and intense competition for these posts. The pay is not high and subsistence allowances, particularly in countries suffering from inflation, are far from generous, but most Messengers draw pensions in addition. In 1966 members of the Corps were at last recognized as established civil servants and on retirement they draw a pension.

During the last war there were twenty-seven Messengers. The number had risen to over forty by 1951 and now stands at fifty-four. The rise is due partly to the larger number of countries that must be covered and partly to a similar increase in the weight and number of bags. In addition to the Messengers proper, Escorts have to be provided on some routes. These are usually recruited from former police officers and accompany Queen's Messengers on long train journeys, where a man cannot be immured for days without ever leaving his compartment.

* It is also not understood that members of the British Diplomatic Service (and Queen's Messengers too) are not entitled to freedom from customs duty on their personal effects when entering the United Kingdom. Unthinking friends often ask one to convey cameras or bottles of perfume to their relatives at home and demonstrate frank disbelief when informed that the bearer will gladly perform the service provided he reclaims the duty paid.

In other countries Messengers are often serving officers, who volunteer for a period of duty under the Ministry for Foreign Affairs. In the United States, there is a special group of Messengers attached to the State Department. They have to be young college graduates and bachelors. They have been known to regard with some distrust the 'decrepit old gentlemen' charged with the Queen's mail bags. The task of the youngsters is easier in one way, since the United States maintains a comprehensive system of military courier aircraft that convey official mail to key points. It is therefore only the local or *comparatively* short-haul journeys that fall to their lot, tedious and tricky though these can be.

It is the proud boast of the Corps of Messengers that, even in the dangerous days of the last two wars, they have never lost a confidential bag, though government messengers of other departments have done so. There was, for instance, a case in the First War when one such courier travelled by sea across the Mediterranean. His ship was held up by a German submarine, so he threw the bags overboard. Alas, they floated and were picked up by the enemy. Thereafter bags were perforated and weighted. In 1951 a small British coaster travelling between Hong Kong and Tientsin was similarly held up by Chinese pirates. The King's Messenger was about to throw his bags over the side when the pirates swarmed on board. He had just time to retreat to his cabin and cover the steel box in which he stowed the bags with a curtain torn from the doorway. When the pirates reached him they merely removed his watch and signet ring. His claim for the value of these was refused by the Treasury. As has already been remarked, governments do not change much. Even life insurance (apart from injury) must be found by the individual. Insurance is necessary; since the war three Queen's Messengers have been killed in aircraft accidents. The mortality incidence is fortunately not high. The average Messenger will cover 180,000 miles a year, so the annual total for the whole Corps is little short of 10 million man-miles, nowadays mostly by air.

Even more prized by the Corps than the red passport is the insignia awarded to each of the regular members. Early in the last century, the Messengers had a uniform, which was unpopular because it made them conspicuous on their travels at times when, for reasons of safety, they preferred to look as nondescript as possible. A yet more ancient practice was to furnish Messengers with a badge that would ensure their recognition and give them priority in such matters as post horses, when the need arose to change animals. The history of the badge goes back at least to the reign of William III. The earliest still extant consisted of the Royal Arms with the supporting lion and unicorn surmounted by a crown. From this escutcheon was suspended a silver greyhound at full stride. The silver greyhound figures in all the later badges, though the badge itself has now been simplified to the Monarch's initials surrounded by the Garter motto *Honi soit qui mal y pense*. A collection has been made of them; it will be found by visitors to the Foreign Office in a glass case at the junction point of the main staircase. Queen's Messengers do not now carry their badges on their journeys, but they are worn on ceremonial occasions.

Should you ever be travelling in the same train or aircraft as a Queen's Messenger, you will recognize him because the seat next to him in the aircraft or train will be piled with lumpy, not over-clean, white canvas sacks labelled 'OHMS' and addressed to Embassies and High Commissions at his various ports of call. There will be others of a less confidential nature in the hold or van; these too are under his general charge, though not a responsibility of vital importance. Do not be misled by his age and apparently sedentary occupation into supposing that he is in his dotage. In fact he has to be very fit and he has eyes all round his head. He is so alert that he does not find it necessary, when he dozes in an aircraft, to copy the Russian Couriers reported by Eric Linklater,[5] who chained their despatches to their ankles. If you are a Ruritanian countess or even an untitled willowy blonde with a roving eye, you may attempt to seduce the Queen's Messenger. You have no hope of success, but you will probably find him an entertaining and experienced companion, so inured to the weariness of travel that he will lighten the journey for you.

To conclude on a more intimate note, the bags themselves are so highly convenient that they are apt to be borrowed by members of Embassy staffs to carry home from the office parcels that have arrived or even for more exotic purposes. I hope that the Communications Department of the Foreign Office still preserves a photograph I once sent them of a mountaineering camp in the Andes at 14,500 feet featuring a bag prominently stamped 'FO' and labelled more discreetly 'ropes and crampons'. I hasten to add that the invaluable bag was returned, after laundering, to the Administration Officer of the Embassy. It has no doubt travelled many more thousands of miles since then, but it has rarely contained a more important load.

3. CULTURAL REPRESENTATION

In the concluding paragraph of section 3 in chapter III, it was noted that in British practice a distinction is made between 'information work' (largely political and necessarily changing according to the circumstances of the day) and 'cultural work' (which suffers less from diurnal variation). In many countries these two aspects of diplomatic life are considered so closely linked as to be indistinguishable. This is particularly so, to take an extreme case, under any Communist regime, where culture and science are subordinated to political ends with a disregard for truth and for those who support it that leaves the Westerner aghast.

The British combine information and cultural work in small Missions, where everyone must be able to turn his hand to anything; but in larger posts the practice is for government information work to be dealt with by members of the Embassy staff and for cultural work to be passed to the local representatives of the British Council, which has branches in over eighty countries. It may happen that there is no Information Officer in the Mission in a particular country, but there may be a British Council representative and office. Nevertheless, the latter will not be charged with any information work, though in some countries (about twenty in all) the British Council Officer is a member of the staff of the Mission and is described as a 'Cultural Attaché'. Under the British system there is inevitably some overlap between the work of the Information and Cultural (British Council) Officers abroad; the closest liaison between the two is thus necessary to avoid waste of effort, though their offices may be widely separated. Other Western countries claim that the 'combined' system is more economical and efficient. The United States has its own distinctive practice; information and cultural work overseas are combined under the US Information Agency, an organism separate from the State Department and Foreign Service. In the Washington headquarters cultural work is divided between the State Department and the USIA, the former being responsible for educational exchange programmes and cultural presentations abroad. For a description of American governmental cultural relations with foreign countries, see Barnett.[6]

Before, however, we discuss the mechanism, we should ponder whether cultural propaganda is necessary. Every culture or civilisation tends to a conceit, justified or not. The United Kingdom demonstrated during the nineteenth century a *hubris* so supreme that no need was felt to advertise the worth of British achievement or culture. Only later was it realized that some publicity was desirable if foreigners were to be convinced of Britain's high standing. Meanwhile other nations had long grasped the need to spread their influence abroad, linguistically and culturally as well as politically. As Harold Nicolson pointed out in his history of the British Council, French and German schools had been established in foreign countries long before the turn of the century.[7] Other nations followed and the American Colleges in Istanbul (founded in 1863) and Beirut should be specially mentioned. The French effort is particularly praiseworthy. Under the auspices of the *Alliance Française* or the French government, first-class educational institutes are provided, sometimes in the most unlikely places. Whether in London or Addis Ababa, parents need look no further than the *Lycée* for standards higher than most if not all local schools. Not until 1934 was the 'British Council for Relations with Foreign Countries' established.

Its first budget amounted to £881; the following year it rose to the princely sum of £13,947. By the end of its first decade the £3 million mark had been passed. The estimates for 1966–67 mount to nearly £11 million, plus £790,000 received as earnings and donations.

Before the British Council was five years old, war had broken out and Britain was not only facing military dangers, but a vast and efficient Axis propaganda machine. Throughout this period the British Council fought to maintain its independence from the enormous Ministry of Information. Cultural matters, it was then and is still maintained, should be treated separately by experts, who must be subject to no political pressures. In this lies the difference from the practice of most other countries. While this practice can be queried, most competent British observers feel that, for Britain at any rate, the divorce between culture and politics should be maintained absolute. Culture in this view demands and can receive long-term planning, unshaken by the often hand-to-mouth treatment of politics; it should not be subjected to the cold efficiency striven for, but not necessarily achieved, in political circles.

Nevertheless, it is an illusion to maintain, as do some unrealistic purists, that the British Council, functioning separately from an Embassy, is free from official taint and regarded by the locals as utterly independent. Though the British Council is not in fact a government department, not even the most gullible thinks of a British Institute in a foreign capital as supported solely by charitable contributions in Britain. *The Times*, perhaps because until recently it printed the Royal arms on its front page, is held by a majority abroad to be a government newspaper, and so are the *Daily Mirror* or *Daily Express* if they happen to venture the slightest criticism of the local regime. I was once privileged in the Foreign Office to be the recipient of a violent complaint from the Ambassador of a Latin American country against something that had been written in a British philatelic magazine. He professed his entire inability to understand why the item had been allowed to pass the censorship.

It should not be assumed that Council work smacks of a desperate attempt to impose on reluctant foreigners a 'culture' alien to them and heartily loathed. The merciless days of the *propaganda fide* are past. The historical example is rather that of the early Christian missionaries in China, who could not impose their will and yet found, even in that enclosed society, great receptiveness among a population enjoying a civilization ante-dating and in many ways superior to that of contemporary Europe. Make no mistake; the demand for 'culture' (taken in its wider sense to include education and the sciences as well as the arts) is immense in foreign parts. There is a natural thirst in less developed regions to share the knowledge that has led others to an easier way of life; and the initial pathway to this goal must be linguistic. It is easy to teach an intelligent Lukonjo boy carpentry or a bright Dyak girl the elements of midwifery, using their own tongues as the medium of instruction, but neither will really advance into the world as we know it and as they fervently wish to know it, until they can read a world language and assimilate what we are pleased to call 'civilization'.

We cannot seriously suppose that a universal world language is imminent, despite the hopes of the Esperantists, but we can be confident that English in all its many forms is well on its way to becoming the auxiliary tongue of the world, learnt in addition to the native language of a region in order to permit wider contacts.[8] The enthusiasm to grasp the lower rungs of the ladder is astounding to those with no personal experience of it. In Africa and Asia the pressure can almost be felt. I rejoice that in one British Embassy we were able to meet a crowding need by establishing English classes for all adult local employees. I have never seen such a concentration of effort—or gratitude, though each student according to his salary paid his mite towards the cost. We were delighted to receive a report ten years later showing how effective this long-term scheme had been in producing men fully instruct-ed and literate in their own language and in English, and now capable of filling positions of responsibility. Even in more developed areas a similar enthusiasm is manifest. In 1965 an

English course run by a commercial agency in a Latin American capital advertised 100 vacancies. By nine next morning there was a milling crowd at the door. Police were called to organize a queue, soon 3,000 long. The first to enrol were the twelve policemen in charge. It is permissible to doubt whether such numbers would have sought to join a course in French or German—or Russian or Chinese.

In the early days of the British Council one of the first chairmen, Lord Lloyd,* insisted that the teaching of English was its primary task. There was a period after the war, infuriating to the staff and to outsiders alike, when London decreed that lessons should not be given to beginners, only to advanced pupils. Fortunately commonsense and the increasing clamour of the unlettered reversed this ludicrous policy. Now English is not only taught on the Council's own premises, but also by Council staff in local educational institutions from secondary school up to university level. The concentration is on training teachers, as the demand for English cannot be met by direct instruction. This accounts for three-quarters of the Council's work overseas. Direct teaching is, however, still carried out in many Institutes and Centres and in Anglophile societies assisted by the Council, where modern methods, including 'Language Laboratories', are used. In this respect many foreign students of English—even in countries we tend to regard as primitive—are better off than the majority of students in Britain learning a foreign tongue, no matter how high the fees paid by their parents. The Council is also co-operating to an increasing extent in the production of 'English by TV' programmes. In addition it recruits teachers of English and other subjects on behalf of many overseas universities, colleges and schools.

In most of the world's main capitals nowadays there will be a British Institute or Centre as headquarters, and it will be crammed from early morn until late at night. Among other facilities it will

* It is interesting to speculate what would have happened if Lord Beaverbrook had been appointed the first chairman, as he himself suggested. Certainly the British Council would not have been under such continuous attack by some organs of the press.

provide a library of high class, including not only works of reference, but fiction, periodicals and gramophone records. There will probably be only two or three British staff, but they will be supported by others locally engaged for their knowledge of English and also for the considerable administrative work. The Council is now maintaining 141 libraries of its own and directly supports another 55 in 83 countries. In 1964, 250,000 books were supplied to these, and they lent 4½ million books to some 330,000 readers.[9]

Members of the Council staff may be much involved in technical assistance to foreign countries and here there is a risk of overlap with the Embassy. I have dealt with this matter in chapter III (4).

In one respect the Council staff overseas are less trammelled than their Diplomatic Service colleagues. Once on the job abroad, they can get down to it without being so closely tied to the home headquarters. The Chancery, which spends so much time coping with telegrams and drafting reports, envies the British Institute where a man, within broad directives, can devote himself to his work in his own way. He, too, will meet much frustration and the results may not be as creative as he would wish, but he paddles his own canoe. Only in Consulates or the smallest diplomatic Missions is this freedom possible.

The representatives overseas of the British Council are not concerned only with English language and other teaching. To them falls the organization of travelling exhibitions of British art and books, of tours by theatre or ballet companies and of lectures by specialists in many fields from the United Kingdom. These activities probably absorb less than 5 per cent of the budget, but they are none the less valued—and onerous. Each problem differs from its predecessor, and much ingenuity and patience is required to solve the difficulties. The whole weight of the Embassy may have to be employed—as when, for instance, the local Customs authorities suddenly refuse to admit the scenery of Hamlet and the costumes of the cast, until the Ambassador has personally signed a guarantee that all will be re-exported after the performance. Every British Head of Mission is faced sooner or later with the problem presented by the arrival of a ballet or a Shakespearian company touring the country to which he is accredited. Whether you like it or not, these people—charming, appreciative and gifted though they are—cannot be handled in the same way as a trade delegation. The wise Ambassador is happy to be guided by a patient and unfailingly courteous member of the British Council staff, trained to deal not only with the artistic temperament but with the (mercifully rare but highly explosive) artistic temper, which can be as devastating as a terrorist's bomb hurled at the Embassy. Having said this, one must pay tribute to those who undertake such burdensome tours. Often they may be doing only 'two-night stands', preceded and followed by long and tiring flights. At the end of a couple of months of such travelling, the theatrical company or individual lecturer is justified in feeling exhausted.

☆

The British Council is often thought of as an organization working exclusively abroad; in fact it is as busy at home. Though this book is designed to deal with overseas representation, brief mention may be made of this work.

Beginners in English overseas soon make progress and yearn for the opportunities of higher education in the United Kingdom. The Council grants scholarships and takes under its wing not only students it has trained, but thousands more who come under their own steam or at the expense of other organizations. They are met on arrival, hostels are provided or accommodation is found for them. It is noteworthy that, though there are individual misfits, whole groups of students do not riot against their hosts and clamour for repatriation as they do in Russia and China. That students received in the United Kingdom have risen from 10,000 in 1950 to 64,000 in 1964 gives some idea of the extent of the demand. Meanwhile some 78,000 foreign scholars and students were being accepted in the United States, and the intake is increasing by 7 per cent a year.[10] The general organization of selection is important, but so is the 'follow up', when those who have received grants return to their country. Much thought is given to these problems by American Heads of Mission.[11]

These students require specialized teaching. They are adults, not children, and elementary or secondary school methods are not applicable. Many may require training in what may be called 'vocational English'—the technical language talked by nurses, policemen, engineers, agriculturalists or what have you. This education will include many terms unfamiliar to the non-expert in America or Britain. Highly specialized courses are required, and here the British Council has done much valuable pioneer work. Its journal *English Language Teaching* is authoritative and influential. In selecting students for grants, regard must be had both to the facilities available in Britain and to the needs of recipients. It is probable that developing countries are best served if scholarships are reserved for post-graduate work. There is more risk of wastage with juniors.

In addition to students proper, the Council cares for a stream of visitors of higher age, who are often eminent representatives of their nations. The subjects in which they are interested are amazingly diverse, even esoteric; their courteous demands for help, to see this, to meet so and so, are difficult to manage. I remember two men, in different continents, whom I pressed to let me have privately their preferences for a short visit to England. One ran something like this (not necessarily in order of precedence): 'A day in the X Laboratory at Y; the Festival Ballet; and meetings with Sir A.B., Professor C.D., and Dr E.F.' The other list, also by a scientist, was similar, but instead of the ballet he had 'a visit to Madame Tussaud's'. Both returned delighted with their stay in England and expressed gratitude for the efficiency with which their fruitful if hurried tours had been arranged by the British Council.

☆

The path of the Council and its staff has been far from as smooth as one could wish. During the tremendous stresses of war there were many who mocked at those who strove in an alien and often hostile world to hold high the torch of British culture. Even when hostilities had ceased there were violent disputes about the utility and methods of the Council. At intervals government commissions reported on its work—favourably—but the die-hards would not be convinced and the Treasury was reluctant to sanction expenditure. This uncertainty and the constant sniping by ill-wishers was hard for the staff to bear. There was no real permanent cadre; financial cuts led to the dismissal of men with long service; British Council posts abroad were closed, others reopened, and then switched again owing to the vacillating policy dictated from above. At times the very survival of the organization appeared in peril. The critics ignored the immense dissatisfaction caused in foreign countries by the sudden withdrawal of British Council staff, whose work was widely appreciated overseas. The USIA has had, and is still facing, similar difficulties, as mentioned in chapter III (3).

The first eight or ten years after the war were hard and it says much for the staff that their morale, though seriously shaken, never cracked and that able recruits still came forward. All who have had much to do with the Council abroad will agree that, then and now, the staff have, with only the rarest exceptions, shown themselves capable and devoted. Now, in easier waters, a high tradition has been built up and none will doubt that it will be maintained in all quarters of the world—not least by the wives, who play as important a role as their colleagues in the Diplomatic Service.

It is essential that British Council establishments should be apart from Missions. If they are to attract young and perhaps timid students, there must be easy entry and no security guards. All, including the occasional local crackpot, are welcome to drift in, read books, attend classes or merely gossip. The same separation between Embassy and Library of Information is widely adopted by the USIA, and also by the French, Italian and German counterparts.

The British Council staff are not members of the Diplomatic

Service, but the 'divorce' I have referred to between culture on the one hand and political and economic work on the other has been by consent. There is the closest possible collaboration between the British Council Representative and the Embassy's Information Officer, though they work in separate buildings. The 'divorce' did, however, mean that the British Council was not included in the terms of reference of the Plowden Committee. To many observers this omission was unfortunate. Though not of the same Service, the British Council abroad co-operates with diplomacy in a common effort, and even the Home Division of the British Council must maintain contact with HM representatives in the countries whence the students working in Britain are drawn. Fortunately, however, individual members of the Committee took the trouble to talk with British Council staff at posts abroad, which gave them much useful information and as a result certain reforms are being extended to British Council staff overseas.

After the First World War, the staffs of the Foreign Office and Diplomatic Service, which had existed separately, were amalgamated. Thenceforth all members had to assume the obligation to serve either abroad or at home, as required. The same regulation exists in the British Council, but complete interchangeability is not feasible, because the overseas personnel for the most part are educationalists while the home staff is mainly administrative. Nevertheless, more frequent transfer could not fail to be beneficial and the indirect influence of the Plowden report is beginning to be felt in this direction. It is difficult to expect the essential cordiality and understanding if men responsible for the administration, including finances, of the British Council Representatives in, say, West Africa have never had to travel much further than Guildford. All British Council staff abroad are faced with immense administrative problems. It would be beneficial if they had more tours of duty at home. The purely administrative staff of the Council in London would be more difficult to place in British Council establishments abroad, but some could be seconded temporarily to British Embassies as Administration Officers. The best of them would not only profit by the experience, but enjoy their richer comprehension of the problems to be faced in foreign parts. American practice is superior in this respect. Information and cultural work are the responsibility of the USIA and the staff are more frequently interchanged between home and overseas.

In addition to further integration between the home and overseas staffs, the British Council faces another type of personnel problem. The Diplomatic Service has decided that on balance a variety of experience is preferable for its officers rather than too much specialization. It is arguable that this mobility should not be sought by the British Council and that the staff should not be moved too freely from area to area. It can indeed be maintained that it takes a British Council officer longer to find out how to teach English in Malaya or Madagascar and to penetrate the academic circles in those countries than it does a diplomat, working a great deal of the time with his own people, to perform efficiently in an Embassy. On this assumption the British Council man should be transferred less frequently from post to post abroad, and this is another argument in favour of not amalgamating the Diplomatic and British Council Services.

In the article from which I have quoted in chapter III (3), Professor Beloff has drawn attention to yet a third personnel problem—one which is little understood in Britain because of lack of familiarity with the systems of other countries.

The fact that the teaching profession in Britain is not part of the service of the central government has other consequences as well. It is not easy to obtain from hardpressed local authorities a massive secondment of teachers such as the French have made in order to secure the perpetuation of the French language in their former imperial possessions; nor can those who go overseas receive such ready assurances that their career-prospects will remain unchanged. Similarly the British Council cannot call (as can the *Relations Culturelles* of the Quai d'Orsay) upon British university teachers to spend part of their career directing Institutes abroad.[12]

179

It would be profitable to Britain, in educational and also other fields, if security of employment at home could be combined with the enlarged horizon offered by temporary service overseas.

What is still needed is a lot of thoughtful planning, which should include—not only in Britain—a fair deal for those who undertake the work. The total British 'London appointed' staff (which corresponds with the 'UK based' of the Diplomatic Service) of the British Council abroad is now some 400, who work with four times that number of locally engaged staff. Some 1,600 serve the British Council at home. The Council does not function in the United States; representation here would involve too large and expensive a commitment and there is no need of English teaching. Like Information Officers in Embassies, British Council representatives —and their wives—have to be on duty all round the clock. This is a commonplace abroad, but it is also true at home; if you are concerned with the well-being of foreign students in Britain you must be accessible and sympathetic at all hours. In terms of cash or personnel the British effort to meet a great and growing need is small.

An experienced judgement may be quoted in conclusion: 'The teaching of the English language and the attraction of students to England, now the main activities of the British Council, can do as much for British influence abroad as almost any activities of HM Government.'[13] The same applies *mutatis mutandis* to the work of the USIA and similar organisms established by other Western powers, which help to disseminate the languages, culture and technical knowledge of Western civilization.

4. Housing and Equipping of Missions

Yet another small group of officers, not members of the Diplomatic Service, work in or for Missions overseas and must therefore be included in this chapter. The Ministry of Public Building and Works maintains a number of area offices with regional responsibilities, as well as many resident Clerks of Works, at overseas posts. Although some of the more senior of these officers figure in the Diplomatic Lists at their posts, their role is little known to the public, but a moment's reflection will show how important it is.

Many Embassy and High Commission Residences and offices are owned by the British government. In some cases, particularly at the older established missions in Asia and Africa, 'compounds' are maintained; these are large areas in which are placed not only the office and Ambassador's Residence but houses for the staff. In Addis Ababa the compound extends to eighty acres and includes a village for servants. In Tehran there are two compounds, one in the city and one a few miles away in the foothills. Originally, the latter was purely for summer use; now it is occupied all the year round with permanent residential accommodation. The Communist Chinese obliged the Service to vacate the famous compound in Peking, but the one in Tokyo still stands.

Many Residences and office buildings have been expressly built for the purpose from plans prepared by Ministry of Works architects. This is a grave responsibility, for such work is on display to a public perhaps more critical than at home. The Embassy buildings in Tokyo had to be constructed to withstand earthquakes. A mesh of flexible steel rods was therefore interlaced in walls and roofs. The resultant style is known as 'Shock-proof Queen Anne'. The proliferation of steel had tiresome results when the staff were interned during the war. The Japanese removed all external aerials and a team trying to run a clandestine wireless set needed three laborious months to rig a concealed aerial. However, the buildings withstood the devastating American incendiary raids on Tokyo. Apart from those built expressly, many Residences and some office buildings have been purchased by HMG. Even when they are rented, the Ministry are responsible for them and will have had a large say in their selection and lay-out. Housing for the staffs of the Missions is also on occasion designed and built by the Ministry of Works and is quite frequently purchased by it for HMG.

In addition, the Ministry supplies furniture and domestic

equipment to all Embassy and High Commission Residences, and furniture to all offices and to government-owned staff accommodation and those hirings taken on long unfurnished leases. This is a formidable task, sometimes bedevilled by the very different tastes of officers and their wives as compared with those of their predecessors. Unfortunately there is in Britain no *Garde-Meuble National* as in France—a depository where is kept furniture, often including pieces of great merit and value, that can be issued to official residences overseas. It has often been suggested unavailingly that items, including pictures, held but not on public exhibition in Britain's museums and galleries should similarly be made available.

These buildings and their contents merit expert maintenance, and any purchases of property require expert appraisal. This dictates the need for professionally trained officers of the Ministry of Works overseas. At posts where HMG has a considerable estate they supervise the maintenance of it; or, stationed at strategic points, they at need assist Administration Officers in more than one capital or territory. These Ministry of Works officers serve under the terms and conditions of their own department. Their work is supplemented by visits from headquarters—particularly to posts which cannot be serviced by the officers stationed overseas—and by the special short term appointment of Clerks of Works for new building projects. The latter are normally designed by the Ministry's staff in London, in consultation with the Diplomatic Service Administration and with frequent visits to and consultations with the post in question. Employment of, or at least consultation with local architects of high standing in an advisory capacity, is also valuable; they obviously have deeper experience of regional conditions—prevailing winds, temperature, rainfall and other vital factors—than any expatriate.

VII

PERSONNEL, RECRUITMENT
AND DEPLOYMENT

W E HAVE now studied, if only in outline, the trunk and interlacing branches of the diplomatic tree; but without roots and active cultivation it cannot grow. It is now necessary to revert to the beginnings.

How are the methods of entry into the various grades of a Diplomatic Service to be chosen? What additional training should be furnished at various stages to members of the Service? How can the general welfare of officers, their wives and families best be safeguarded? These important matters will be dealt with under three main headings: 1. Selection; 2. Training; 3. Welfare. The first section will be further divided to cover the different methods used with candidates for the various grades of the British Diplomatic Service. These grades are explained in Appendix A.

Although the following survey is based mainly on British practice, it indicates the general nature of a problem faced by the Diplomatic Services of all states. References to the methods used in the United States and some other countries are included.

1. RECRUITMENT AND SELECTION

Only outlines of the examination and Selection Board methods can be given here. Entry can be at different ages, with different qualifications for the various grades. The Civil Service Commission,

THE CRAFT OF DIPLOMACY

Savile Row, London W1, can supply details, and full information about work and conditions in the British Service in all grades, at home and overseas, is available from the Personnel Department of the Foreign Office. Methods of entry into the United States Foreign Service are described in papers in the series "Foreign Affairs Personnel Studies" (FAPS) published under the auspices of the Carnegie Endowment for International Peace.[1]

Selection in Britain is carried out, not by the Civil Services of the Crown themselves, but by the Civil Service Commission established for that purpose in 1855. This method ensures a non-political and independent judgement by persons with long training and skill in this art. In the past the Civil Service Commission was not responsible on any scale for recruitment, that is, endeavouring to induce people to apply for entry into the Services.[2] Recently two members of the Commission have been specifically charged with recruitment from universities and publicity is being improved, but much recruitment is rightly left to each individual Service. Recruitment for any Diplomatic Service is best done by personal contact between the Service and the universities. This is one of the innumerable duties of an efficient Personnel Department, but it is a grave problem affording no easy solution. In Britain it has been found that sheer ignorance of the possibilities of government service—and, in our particular context, of the Diplomatic Service working largely overseas—is prevalent among students in universities and colleges, and that at a time of full employment many and diverse are the positions offered to promising graduates. The Diplomatic Service examination has a daunting repute—largely undeserved, for over 30 per cent pass. In the United States 25 per cent pass the written examination and only 17 per cent of these are accepted by the Foreign Service. In Britain it is still widely assumed, perhaps largely because of ignorant or malevolent press comments, that the Service requires private means and anyhow is only poodlefaking. It is certain that many excellent candidates are deterred from applying by this antipropaganda and that even more do not have brought to their notice the great opportunities offered to the intelligent, enterprising and trustworthy.

Similar problems face the US Foreign Service, but on a vaster scale because of the extent of the United States. In one respect there may be a difference. Mobility of labour is a pronounced feature in North America. Britons seem to prefer to select their career at an early stage and stick to it despite adversity. Americans, early or late in life, are more footloose; they welcome change, provided it offers opportunity. Such activity and intelligent restlessness could be encouraged in other continents. Yet that does not solve the problem for the American Service.[3] There remains an untapped pool of talent there, as in the United Kingdom. If American experience is a guide, it would be preferable to direct 'recruiting agents' from the Foreign Office or State Department not towards the students themselves, but to those who teach and influence them in college. The small geographical extent of Britain should make this easier. It is encouraging that Mr Michael Stewart, when Secretary of State for Foreign Affairs, devoted personal attention to the problem and found time to talk with heads of universities and colleges. Another difficulty in both Britain and America is the reluctance of potential candidates to face the considerable interval that may occur between applying to take the examination and actually entering the Service. In the United States this averages ten months, and many candidates drop out between the written and oral examinations.

In Britain the manpower problem is likely to be a major bugbear for at least a decade. Even if a hundred brilliant recruits were accepted tomorrow, they would require years of training, and would later form a lamentable promotion-block, as they clustered at the top end of the Service. There is already such a mushroom in France under the present system of absorbing 'ex-colonial' officers into the Diplomatic Service at all levels. In Britain the Plowden Report recommended a 10 per cent increase in manpower; the Treasury at once whittled this down to $7\frac{1}{2}$ per cent. Meanwhile demands on the Service will increase in ways unpredictable and uncontrollable by Whitehall. There will be a crisis here, the emergence of a new state there, and always the clamour of many Ambassadors that they simply cannot carry on without an increase in staff. These demands are difficult to meet, though the last is handled by listing all posts in order of priority of importance to the United Kingdom under different headings, and then firmly maintaining decisions reached after full consultation. Ambassadors are also asked to report on which of their activities are essential and which less so. The ideal would be at least sufficient 'slack' to form a reserve—a sort of fire-brigade to cope with perilous outbreaks—but even this is likely to prove very difficult. It is therefore all the more important that the Service should build up to its meagre permitted level.

One measure that could be highly profitable both in the Service and outside is being explored. Many young men, assured of entry into business concerns, would be glad to join the Diplomatic Service in a temporary capacity to widen their experience, particularly overseas. An accession of temporary officers would reduce the tautness in the Service and they would be better fitted for their own later responsibilities.

The problem of recruitment having been thus briefly discussed, we can now proceed to the equally important matter of selection.

(i) *The Administrative or Senior Branch (Grade 8 and upwards)*

Here it is unnecessary to go further back in history than the First World War. The methods of selection of candidates for entry into the Service from the earliest days until 1939 are well set out in Nicolson's *Diplomacy*.[4] Outlines of procedure for entry into the American Service are available for comparative purposes.[5]

With the Armistice in 1918, the now combined Diplomatic Service and Foreign Office staffs found themselves desperately short of men. Practically no permanent recruits had been accepted during the war and the needs of an expanding Service had been met by drawing on temporary officers, often no longer young. The thinned ranks were now made up from demobilized officers, who were allowed to deduct their years of war service from their actual age. This rule still exists. Any Navy, Army or Air Force candidate up to the age of thirty-five can deduct his previous years of service from his age; in certain special 'lateral' methods of entry, between the ages of twenty-seven and thirty-five; even older candidates are accepted with a similar reduction, starting at First Secretary level. You can serve for twenty-five years in, say, the Royal Air Force. You are then forty-five, but your 'examination age' does not exceed twenty-seven, although you happen to be an air vice-marshal. It might seem crazy then to enter the Diplomatic Service near the bottom, but it is not unknown—which at least shows that the Service holds some interest even later in life—and you draw your air vice-marshal's pension in addition to your meagre subaltern's pay in the Diplomatic Service. This accretion of mature minds can be most beneficial.

In 1919 the examination had to be very easy, since in most cases the candidates had gone straight to the war from school and had had no chance of a university education. There was also an interview before a board. The intake from this method between 1919 and 1921 was so substantial that for the next few years no recruitment was necessary. Even when the doors opened again, there might well be only two or three vacancies each year. It was not until about 1928 that a larger flow of entrants was required. These were selected through a written examination, with a preliminary and a final interview before boards. This system endured until 1939. The examinations were conducted by the Civil Service Commissioners. The Preliminary Board was supposed to decide whether a man (no woman was then eligible) was acceptable in general terms as a candidate for the Service. If he failed here, there was no appeal; if he passed, he could attempt the written examination three times in successive years between the ages of twenty-three and twenty-five. The standard of the Preliminary Board was lenient and a blind eye was sometimes turned to the rules of entry—which required, among other things, that both parents of a candidate be of British birth. At least one entrant was infinitely relieved to find that a mother of American origin did not disqualify him.

The Preliminary Board was in no way to be compared with the

unnerving interview I encountered when, as a boy of sixteen, I applied to enter New College, Oxford. The Warden presided. He was the famous Spooner, originator of spoonerisms. Like many albinos he had for long been very short-sighted. In old age his brilliant blue eyes gave an appearance of vision that was woefully deceptive. He peered at my laborious filled-in form and then beamed at me in the most endearing fashion. 'Ah, Mr Dirk', he began. 'Not Dirk, Busk', whispered the don next to him. 'Ah, Mr Busk', continued the Spoo without any obvious gearchange, 'I am so glad to see you are going to take Modern Greats. Now I always say that Modern Greats is one of the best Schools that this University. . . .' 'History', murmured the don. 'As I was saying', continued the Spoo unabashed, 'History is one of the best schools. . . .' He then asked me one or two personal questions and endeavoured to inscribe the answers. It was to say the least disconcerting that he jabbed his pen not into the inkpot but on the table. The nib was spread like a bird's claw. The alarm of the candidates must have been comprehended, for the kindly don next to the Warden held up his pen and winked to indicate that he was writing the answers on his own copy of the form. None of this was deliberate testing of the candidate, for, as we all subsequently discovered, the Spoo was the kindliest Warden that his college had had for many a day.

I can recall no one, not even the lucky ones who passed, expressing anything but disapproval of the interwar Foreign Office examination. It was vast in scope and lent itself to cramming. There were half-a-dozen compulsory subjects—including reasonably enough, European history, French and German, and a third language at a lower standard. On top of that another three or four subjects had to be taken, up to a certain total of marks. The pass mark over-all was 50 per cent and in French 60 per cent, which sounds easy, but the marking was so severe that no candidate, no matter how brilliant, ever received 80 per cent for any paper. The highest percentage for any candidate for the whole written exam was under 70 per cent—and some of the candidates were outstanding. Moreover, a mere pass was not sufficient, for you might pass fifth in a year when there were only four vacancies. The strain was increased by the long time required to complete the papers—over six weeks in all, but not of course every day for every candidate. Only once were those long sessions enlivened. We sat in a large hall in Burlington Gardens at flimsy little desks spaced carefully apart to prevent cheating. Linoleum was laid to protect the parquet flooring. On one occasion my neighbour was an old friend. In the throes of reflection he tilted his chair back on its hind legs and gazed pensively at the ceiling—but not for long. The rear legs of his chair suddenly sank six inches into the floor under his not inconsiderable weight. He did a painful back somersault, his feet upset the table, and papers, pen and ink cascaded in all directions. Invigilators rushed up convinced that some nefarious plan to outwit them was in play. Investigation disclosed that under the linoleum the gratings of the central heating were placed at intervals. The sharp chair legs had penetrated the linoleum and sunk deep into the slots. Despite this painful experience, the candidate duly passed and ended his career as an Ambassador.

This system of examination, though academically highly testing, was not nearly so effective as one might suppose. Candidates could, and did, pass who subsequently proved entirely unsuitable and had to be ejected. In one year, 30 per cent of those accepted did not, despite intellectual brilliance, survive more than two or three years. This was an unusually high level of failure, but the method of selection was so obviously chancy that wise heads began to ponder.

In the Second World War, all recruitment was again suspended for permanent membership of the Service. Eventually the Eden–Bevin reforms were implemented which, among other things, amalgamated the Diplomatic, Consular and Commercial (i.e. Department of Overseas Trade) Services that had regrettably been separate hitherto. The combined Service was thenceforth to be called 'The Foreign Service'. The new regulations also standardized the examination system. Previously candidates for the Consular Service had taken much the same examination as those for the Diplomatic Service, but the pass marks had been a trifle lower and a man who failed for the Diplomatic could be accepted for the Consular, or he might for personal reasons opt only for the Consular Service.

During the war much experience was gained by the Armed Services in methods of selection of officers from among the vast numbers of men who volunteered or were conscripted. The result was the establishment of the War Office Selection Boards (WOSB for short). The object was to devise a system of tests that would disclose the quality of leadership and—ghastly catchword —'man-management'. Candidates were not examined exclusively on their academic ability, but grouped together, often under conditions of stress, for as long a period of time as possible. Their performance was closely observed and they were interviewed. The results on the whole were excellent—far better than previous methods of selection of British officers in the 1914–1918 war. This did not pass unnoticed by those who had already been worried about recruitment for the Diplomatic Service. Clearly the individual tests and the approach must differ somewhat between, say, candidates for infantry officers and diplomats, but in general the same principles could be adopted. Recent experience has shown that the method can be applied to many different Services—the police for instance.

In 1946 the new combined Service found itself in much the same lamentable position as its divided predecessor in 1919. Its ranks were depleted, while its responsibilities had increased. There was an urgent need for new recruits, hundreds of them. Fortunately many who had served in the armed forces during the war wished to apply. (In the United States during the war, any new personnel brought in came under the designation of Foreign Service Auxiliaries. This category was discontinued soon after hostilities ended.[6]) The so-called 'Reconstruction Examinations' were therefore established, based to a large extent on the WOSB system and with allowance made for the fact that candidates had been far too busy fighting for their country to have enjoyed the higher education they might otherwise have aspired to. This system, continually modified and improved, is the basis for the present series of tests for entry into the British Diplomatic Service of today.

A prerequisite of this type of test (known as Method II) is a First or Second Class Honours degree from a university.* The educational standards for entrants into the United States Foreign Service are not set so high. Only 65 per cent have a college degree; on the other hand more have done post-graduate work up to and including the Ph.D. than is the case with British candidates.[7] Alongside Method II, there is Method I, a shorter form of the inter-war examination described above. This examination, which is also taken by candidates for the Home Civil Service, has no obligatory academic qualifications. Until 1957 the Foreign Service (now the Diplomatic Service) refused to accept candidates by Method I. But in that year the government ruled that 25 per cent of vacancies could be filled by Method I, because it was feared that some good candidates might otherwise be lost.

In Appendix C will be found a note giving an outline of the tests to which candidates for the Administrative Grade are submitted under Method II by the Civil Service Selection Board (hereafter referred to as the CSSB). They are so designed that agreement can be reached after full discussion on a rating for each candidate, compared not only with others in the same batch, but with many entrants in earlier years. The age-limits are from 20 to 27 years (in the American Service, they are from 21 to 31). The upper limit may appear high; it is enforced by the immaturity of many candidates, to which attention is called elsewhere (see page 210 below). It is profitable to allow late developers their chance. The CSSB procedure concludes with a decisive interview before the ominously named Final Selection Board (FSB). In the last few years, of those who attempted the CSSB tests 71·7 per cent passed onwards to the FSB, and 30·9 per cent of the total entry to the CSSB were accepted for the Service.

The same method is applied to candidates for the Administrative

* From a British university, that is; the equivalent from an overseas university is valid.

Grade of the Home Civil Service. Indeed, there is nothing to prevent a candidate from applying for both Diplomatic Service and Home Civil Service and he may well be marked differently in respect to each application by the CSSB and the FSB. This is right. Wide though the sweep be of the present Diplomatic Service, the Home Civil Service provides a greater variety of subjects. For the Diplomatic Service 'good-mixing' is required in addition to intellectual ability. The 'backroom man' is frequently unexportable, and indeed might not wish to be exported. Admirable in general though a candidate may be, he can be a liability in one Service and an asset in the other.

The question of tests, to which Plowden devotes a whole section,[8] requires two points of view—the examinees' and the examiners'. There is a natural tendency to stress the former, because far more of the human race have been guinea pigs than have acted as examiners. The less studied aspect, the problems facing examiners and the methods to be used in the testing of candidates for any Diplomatic Service, is more important.

It is interesting to compare statistically the follow-up results of Method I and Method II, based on recruits who entered British government service between 1948 and 1961. In the Home Civil Service they were reported on by their seniors after some experience of their work as follows:

	Very good indeed %	*Distinctly above average* %	*Well up to standard* %	*Below standard* %
Method I	4·1	27·9	54·7	13·3
Method II	13·6	39·3	41·0	6·1

In regard to 'future promise', recruits were graded on whether they might ultimately be expected to reach a rank *higher* than Assistant Secretary (equivalent to Counsellor in the Diplomatic

Service). The results gave: Method I candidates 31·0 per cent; Method II candidates 48·9 per cent.

As already mentioned, recruitment to the Foreign (now Diplomatic) Service was, until 1957, exclusively by Method II. The results between 1948 and 1956 showed the following percentages:

Very good indeed %	Distinctly above average %	Well up to standard %	Not quite so good as most of his rank %	Among the less able %
9·9	31·2	41·6	13·4	3·9

For 'future promise' it was reported that 62·4 per cent should rise *higher* than Counsellor in rank: i.e., become Heads of Mission.

To summarize: for the Home Civil Service, Method I produced 4·1 per cent of outstanding men and 13·3 per cent below standard; Method II produced 13·6 per cent and 6·1 per cent respectively. In the Diplomatic Service, Method II produced 9·9 per cent outstanding and 3·9 per cent in the bottom category. The 'future promise' statistics are also illuminating.

It would be extremely valuable to examiners all over the world to have tables such as these from several countries so that different selection methods could be compared. Such information is unfortunately lacking for other countries.

I have been privileged from time to time in the last fifteen years to sit on these Boards or to act as an observer, and have also had the opportunity to note results in the Service. It is dangerous to be dogmatic, because the craft of diplomacy requires no easily standardized and 'examinable' qualifications, such as one may associate with a university degree in, say, music, physics or the classics. But I have personally no doubt that Method II is better for assessing candidates for this flexible career, which cannot be called—as it sometimes is in the United States—a 'profession' on an exact analogy with, say, medicine or law, because diplomacy does not require the long years of specialized and prescribed study at an early age demanded of a doctor or lawyer.

It is impressive at the CSSB and FSB to observe the high quality of the selectors and the immense pains taken to arrive at honest results, bearing in mind not only present performance but future potential. In Britain all the tests are held in London (fares and subsistence of candidates being paid for), so uniformity is easier to achieve. In the far vaster United States the oral examinations are held in some 290 centres, and it is suggested that there is a considerable variation in the standards of the different boards.[9] Examinees naturally feel that they are under great strain. I can only assure them that their sufferings are nothing to those of good examiners, who work under higher pressure with greater anxiety; for it is a severe responsibility to make for another human being a decision that may change his whole life, and perhaps the lives of many others. Candidates may feel that it is hard on them to have to spend a couple of days going through their paces at the Civil Service Commission, but on recent visits I noticed that with the resilience of youth they all seemed as fresh as paint at the end and expressed the view privately that the experience had been 'stimulating', 'exciting' or at least 'interesting'. At the end of the week, during which fifteen candidates will have been put through the mill in groups of five, the three assessors in contrast will be limp.

The FSB is presided over by the First Commissioner of the Civil Service Commission or a deputy. There are six other members, of which one will usually be from the Personnel Department of the Service and another a retired Ambassador. Other places are filled from universities, the House of Commons, trade unions, business, industry and so forth. There is thus a double check in the search for pre-eminence—a quality that recalls a remark by the American poet Edwin Arlington Robinson about his own art, that it 'has two outstanding characteristics. One is that it is, after all, undefinable. The other is that it is eventually unmistakable.' It is the 'eventual' that should worry selectors. It would be interesting, if it were possible, to keep track of the failed candidates and see how they fared elsewhere in later life.

Plowden maintains that it would be a serious mistake to lower standards of entry.[10] The Service needs an annual intake in the Administrative Grade of twenty-five to thirty by examination,* but it is unrealistic to imagine that all of these will reach the highest rank. At present the tests seem too much designed to ascertain whether every corporal applying has a marshal's baton in his pack. A very high standard of recruit is certainly produced. As already noted, 62·4 per cent are assessed after their three-year probationary period as likely to rise to one of the top three grades, and experience with later assessments has shown that, though some resign or fall by the wayside, reports on good officers tend to become increasingly favourable; after five to ten years the figure might well be 70 per cent. However, an army needs few marshals but many colonels and captains; without the efficient service at their own level of these, the marshals would be helpless. It is true that any Diplomatic Service has a high proportion of Heads of Missions or Under Secretaries to subordinate ranks, but in the British Service only 14 are Grade 1, 30 Grade 2 and 119 Grade 3—a total of 163, or 5·5 per cent of the 'officer' grades of the Service (i.e., grades 1–8). There is a cavernous discrepancy between 5·5 per cent and 62·4 per cent, even admitting that most officers who reach Grade 3 or above are likely to spend ten years (over a quarter of their service) in these grades.

The question of standard is one that preoccupies all concerned. The present pass mark at the FSB is 240 out of 300. At the moment a sufficiency of recruits is forthcoming—and a plethora would produce grave promotion problems in later years. Should the flow show signs of diminishing, I would venture to suggest that the Board could be more adventurous and reduce the pass mark to 230. This would produce perhaps a dozen new entrants a year. Of these some would fail early, but some who did not reach ambassadorial grades (1–3) would still render useful service for many years within their capacity. Such a lowering of standard

---

* There are other methods of entry into the Administrative Grade, some 'lateral' (as they are known in the American Service), and some by 'bridging' from the Executive Grade. These provide another fifteen to twenty officers annually. In the United States Foreign Service no less than 75 per cent of entrants are 'lateral', some at very high rank (see FAPS 6, ch. V). The total US annual intake is about 200.

could be counterbalanced by greater severity during the new entrants' probation. Their showing would have to be reviewed ruthlessly at the end of the three year period and obvious weaklings could be weeded out even earlier, so that their time and that of the Service was not wasted. A trial of this lower standard of entry could be made for five years and then the over-all results— 'progress reports' of new entrants—reviewed. The Service might well profit from such an experiment.

This brief exposition of the present series of tests for Grade 8 entrants into the Diplomatic Service leads to consideration of the qualities sought by the selectors. For centuries attempts have been made to define these.[11] Any assessment will inevitably tend to be subjective. Everyone will have his own views, but at least the more important qualities may be suggested as a basis for discussion.

I am not being flippant when I suggest that the single most valuable asset for a diplomatic career is the possession of a cast-iron digestion, which is likely to carry with it the ability to sleep like a log anywhere in the world. The intellect, the imagination, the tact, the . . . well, all the rest of them, are not in constant, hourly employment; there are whole days off. The digestive tract is on continuous duty and sleep an essential requirement of the human frame. I do not think I rate my two blessings too high. In well-ordered Britain with a food Inspector lurking near every counter, in much of Europe and the United States, it is easy to overlook the fact that in some countries your cook will strain the soup through one of his old socks and that every time you go out for a meal it is wise to take precautions before and after. Nor indeed is this merely a European conceit or lack of resistance. It can be as difficult for an African or Asian to adapt himself to our firmly entrenched system of meals, or even to the glories of the French cuisine, as for us to enjoy without ill effects *Nasi Göreng* or *Couscous, Sukiyaki* or the ominously named *Olla Podrida*. The happy owner of a copper-plated gut can absorb these without ill effects and is not alarmed by experiment. While others are existing on food tinned or flown frozen from remote places and consumed in a self-imposed diplomatic ghetto cut off from contact with the local inhabitants, he will be eating like a horse, enjoying all nature's vitamins without taking handfuls of pills, sleeping dreamlessly and rising with a song in the morning. Unfortunately no medical examination has yet been devised, or at least practised, that can test this quality. I have toyed with the idea that, twenty-four hours before the Final Selection Board, the candidate should be given a Borgia draught guaranteed to impart to him the trotting malady known vulgarly to the British in Eastern parts as 'gippy tummy' and more elegantly to our American friends, suffering stomachically from more frequent contact with Mexico, as 'Montezuma's revenge'. Candidates who even so much as appeared before the Board next day would be given bonus marks; those who seemed unmoved would be passed immediately, even if they did not know what Queen Anne said to Washington when she found that her favourite cherry tree at Balmoral had ceased to yield.

Physical stamina is of paramount importance in the Service. Later in life the strain of jet air travel (to which Professor Parkinson has called attention not entirely whimsically and on which the American Secretary of State is reported to be brooding) can be severe. The menace of late or irregular hours is less recorded, but none the less vivid to those who, year in year out, have had to participate in these obligatory manifestations.

I would link a well-developed, if at times necessarily concealed, sense of humour with the physical blessings, because it is difficult to maintain if one is feeling wretched inside, and because those of the medical profession who have studied such matters maintain that the mere act of laughing produces unconscious physical reactions that prevent ulcers. The sense of humour will be required in order to laugh at oneself far more than with others. Laughing *at* others is to be deprecated; even in private it is habit-forming. A sense of humour should also prevent worry in all directions. One of the worst menaces on any Embassy staff at any level is the knitted-brow fusser.

These are preliminary considerations of 'diplomatic assets'. Let us return to the examiners.

Integrity: how are they to assess this vital quality on which, as is well known, one can be disastrously deceived? A candidate's past record and letters from referees may give some indications.

Imagination, which I would rate very high in the sense of the ability to comprehend the motivation of others, will perhaps have been disclosed in the course of the selection tests. The same means may also reveal the presence or absence of the qualities of patience, particularly required in negotiations, and of tact and humanity. Persistent fortitude in time of personal strain and official stress is a precious quality, less easy to spot in the short period of candidate-testing.

The level of intellectual quality should certainly have emerged from a candidate's earlier career and his showing in the tests. What the Selection Board will be seeking is not merely high mental attainment, but evidence that the candidate has the capacity to think for himself and receptiveness—the quality that Sainte-Beuve referred to as '*des ouvertures tout autour de la tête*': the ability to observe and absorb.

Versatility can also be divined in youth; and if present, it will advance with age. Sometimes this is required in the oddest ways. One young Ambassador at a new African post recently prided himself that, after long personal labour, he had managed to reorganize the plumbing of his house so that at last it worked. He then visited the nearest British Embassy, some hundreds of miles away, only to find the incumbent busily rewiring with his own hands an electric motor sent out from England by the Ministry of Works for the wrong voltage. Versatility should *not*, however, imply slackness of mind.

Ignorance and lack of experience are pardonable among new entrants, but not inaccuracy. A well-known traveller and historian recently wrote: 'In diplomatic communications imprecision is seldom a fatal defect. Ambiguities can be clarified in later exchanges.' He continues that, on the other hand, imprecision in military matters is highly dangerous. His first statement is astonishing. Imprecision in the running of even a village shop is at least tiresome and probably dangerous to the shopkeeper—which matters both to him and to the community. It is more widely menacing in diplomacy. Even if, which is not always the case, there is time to correct the ambiguities, imprecision of thought is unpardonable and the importance of accurate drafting is paramount. Watt comments: 'Actions in the field of foreign affairs can rarely be recalled or repudiated.'[12]

These are some of the 'qualities' that require discernment by the eye of the examiner. Everyone will wish to make up his own list. I hope that all would add that outside interests were helpful. The officer who is too buttoned up in his work can be a menace. The examiners will be hoping to note some exterior activity, mental or physical—not necessarily superlative but at least enthusiastic; something that will offset any danger of lethargy. Allied with other interests at times when pressure is less, comes the potential influence of marriage and family*—but now we are in a future hardly to be described by even the most discerning assessor or CCSB with the latest electronic crystal ball. He will concentrate on the facts—disclosed by the record of the candidate at school, university and in the tests. He will try to draw him out in kindly fashion. He will seek for indications of good leadership. He may take *suaviter sed fortiter* as a good motto for the potential diplomat—once translated by an American friend as 'smooth but tough'.

I was careful to write my own impressions of 'diplomatic qualities' before rereading Nicolson on the subject.[13] He mentions the following: truthfulness, precision, calm, patience, good temper, modesty, adaptability, imagination and loyalty. I do not think we differ overmuch and I am sure that we both sympathize with the examiners who are expected to divine these qualities in youthful candidates. At the end of his chapter on this subject in *Diplomacy*, Sir Harold says that he has taken for granted:

---

* During the last three years, 8 per cent of new entrants into the British Service were married. In the United States Foreign Service, 23 per cent are married when they enter the service.

199

intelligence, knowledge, discernment, prudence, hospitality, charm, industry, courage and tact. At this point, one could hardly blame an examiner for resigning and devoting himself to the far easier problems of nuclear physics or bathyscaphal exploration.

Sir William Hayter regards the selection of candidates against a wider background. He bases his observations on British practice, but his views are generally applicable.

The question of entry into the Foreign Service has been much bedevilled by ignorance and confused thinking. . . . Between the wars entrants were mainly the products of a few public schools, while since the Second World War, in spite of a change in the system, they have almost all come from Oxford or Cambridge. The blame for this . . . lies not on the Foreign Office or on the Civil Service Commission but on the British educational system. Those schools then, these universities now, have produced the best candidates. It is a question of what you want. Are you thinking of social justice, or of building up the best possible Foreign Service? These aims conflict. The Civil Service Commission, and the Foreign Office too, to my personal knowledge, lean over backwards to encourage suitable candidates from other sources, and welcome them with open arms when they appear. But they do not appear very often.

The phrases 'best possible Foreign Service' and 'suitable candidate' of course beg the question. What do you require? Integrity, first of all. This may be found anywhere. Then brains. Of course these are not a monopoly of any school or university, but it must be admitted that the British educational system does tend to channel the best brains towards Oxford and Cambridge. Then, self-confidence and social ease. These qualities are not always admired, particularly the latter, and they are not necessary for all professions. They are for diplomacy. It is not, alas, the case that this is a democratic world, governed by ordinary people. Countries, whatever their regime, are governed by politicians; it is with them that diplomats have to deal and they must not be intimidated by them. For this purpose the secondary, perhaps even second-rate, qualities of self-confidence and social ease are essential. If you insist in the interests of social justice on admitting into the Foreign Service people who lack them you will have a worse Foreign Service. You have to choose. So far the Civil Service Commission, as is their duty, have chosen to go for the best available Foreign Service. . . . The Foreign Service that has resulted from these principles of selection has not always been popular with the British press and public. This is not altogether surprising. There is, I am sorry to say, a rather unpleasing envious element in the public reactions of the modern Englishman [*], which might be expected to take exception to the very qualities, integrity, brains, self-confidence and social ease, which ought to be conspicuous in a well-selected diplomat. The British Foreign Office and Foreign Service, on the whole, seem to command more respect abroad than at home, and this is perhaps what matters most.[14]

I have only one gloss to add to this comment. It is a general experience that, like integrity and brains, self-confidence and social ease are the product of no particular background. Often only a little training gives the necessary polish.

Criteria used in examining candidates for the United States Foreign Service have been closely studied by what is known as the 'Job Analysis and Interest Measurement' system, under which the subjects fill up forms posing certain questions.[15] Comparisons have been made, for example, between Foreign Service officers and members of other professions, and between 'superior' and 'weak' Foreign Service officers. Of the latter test it is noted:

The officer with the superior rating is optimistic and self-confident, is interested in data and people, sees himself as imaginative and ingenious, takes personal leadership, likes a great deal of activity and excitement, and wants to be recognized as a success. He prefers an autonomous, rather than

* It is noteworthy that similar prejudices flourish in some other highly democratic countries, e.g. the United States and, for different reasons, Switzerland.

hierarchical, relationship to the formal organization and tends to be methodical in his information processing behavior. Approval from others and social service are less important to him than resourceful accomplishments and formal status.[16]

As compared with other occupation groups

the FS officers report that they like the kind of work that includes the interpretation of data and the influencing of other people. Their style for analysing information tends to be impressionistic and intuitive rather than formal, methodical and statistical. Their preferred style for working with a formal organization is to do the work themselves rather than to work through a hierarchy. They greatly value personal intellectual achievement and place a moderate value on formal status, social service, and the approval of others.[17]

Tests of this kind have not been carried out on British Diplomatic Service officers. The second analysis reflects the officer's impression of what he is like. What others thought of the individual might be different.

The qualities mentioned, and others you will think of yourself, are also required in fields other than diplomacy. A good man is a good man in any walk of life, and I am far from suggesting that all members of Her Majesty's Diplomatic Service manifest these virtues every day and all day. The oddest comment on the qualities required in diplomacy remains that of the *Daily Telegraph*. When reviewing the report of the Plowden Commission, this journal summed up the need for contortionists: 'Men who can box and bicycle and put an ear very close to the ground may be as necessary as the brilliant scholars.'

So much for qualities; to be objective we ought also to discuss disqualities, difficult though they are for the examiner to spot. Among these, prejudice should be ranked very high. We all have our personal tastes; but diplomats, dealing for much of their official lives with foreigners, must learn early that they cannot afford prejudices, unless of the most innocent personal kind—a disinclination towards shellfish; a reluctance to go bathing in cold water; a preference (not too strongly manifested) for brunettes, and so on. Tolerance of the attitudes of others is even more essential abroad than at home.

About the worst 'disquality', which may only develop later, is a tendency towards pomposity, often allied with didacticism. It is all very well to be proud of a Service—any good officer believes his own regiment to be the best in the world—but this becomes intolerable if carried to a personal level. In another connection Koestler once wrote: 'Myths grow like crystals, according to their own recurrent pattern; but there must be a suitable core to start their growth.' Diplomats of all nationalities are often accused of being conceited and haughty—and the core, alas, is there. But Koestler is wrong when he continues: 'Mediocrities or cranks have no myth generating power.' It is precisely the mediocrities who seem most likely to perpetuate the myth by exasperating displays of pomposity. As the Service is much in the public eye, such behaviour is widely noted and commented on. It is one of the first duties of an Ambassador to check such a tendency if he observes it in any member of his staff.

☆

Before concluding this section I must, with considerable trepidation, mention the question of the admission of women to the Administrative Grades of the Diplomatic Service. This has long been a matter of contention, probably first treated by the Dutchman Wicquefort in the seventeenth century under the titles: *Si l'Ambassadeur se peut servir de l'entremise des femmes pour le progrez de ses affaires* and *Si les femmes peuvent estre Ambassatrices*. In brief, his answer to the first proposition was 'yes' and to the second 'no'.

Today the Foreign Office and its Missions and Consulates abroad are admirably served by many women in the secretarial, clerical and executive grades, but it has always been a matter for argument whether women should be admitted to the administrative grades, as they have long been in the Home Civil Service. Up to the Second World War the Foreign Office resolutely set its face against the recruitment of women, but in 1946 they were allowed to enter the 'Reconstruction Examinations' and may still do so by the present method of selection,* and they at last receive the same pay and allowances as their male colleagues. From then until 1964, thirty-three were successful of whom nineteen are still in the Service. The percentage of women entrants has always been low in the British Service. (It is much higher in the American.) During the same period 1946–64, 634 men were accepted of whom 536 remain. The highest rank so far attained by a woman is that of Counsellor/Consul-General, but one of outstanding ability was tragically prevented by crippling illness from taking up the ambassadorial post to which she had been appointed. No woman career officer of the United States Foreign Service has yet achieved such a nomination, though some women have proved highly remarkable—to say the least—as Ambassadors after political appointment. One woman career officer has held four Head of Mission posts in the Canadian Diplomatic Service.

As far as the over-all picture is concerned, women form 30 per cent of all grades (including the Secretarial) in the British Diplomatic Service. This compares with 28 per cent in the American Service and 36 per cent in the French (though not one of these is in rank comparable with the British 'officer grades' (1–8), of which some $1\frac{1}{2}$ per cent are women in the British Service). The German figures are 25 per cent over-all and 7.5 per cent of the 'officer grades'. The highest rank so far reached by a woman officer in the German Service is Senior Counsellor, of whom there are two.

Whatever views one may hold about the suitability of women for diplomacy, the difficulty remains that they are attractive to the opposite sex and are therefore likely to embrace matrimony. The Diplomatic Service Regulations set out certain regulations governing marriage of officers.[18] Marriage by women officers need not necessarily be a bar in the Home Civil Service. If a

* Candidates in the written examination do not put their names on papers, only numbers, so that their identity is concealed. I was impressed recently by one examiner, who wrote that one 'had a rather feminine mind'; the candidate was in fact a woman.

stockbroker in London marries a woman officer in the Ministry of Defence, there is no *prima facie* reason why she should have to resign; husband and wife could each carry on their separate jobs, at least until maternity loomed large. Abroad this might theoretically be possible for a time, but later it is another matter. If a woman Third Secretary marries a local doctor (British or otherwise), what is to happen when a year or so later she is transferred to a distant part of the world? Can the doctor expect to practise there in an entirely different language? The British regulation is that women members of the Diplomatic Service must resign on marriage. For the woman in government service the choice must often be heart-rending. The first to reach the rank of Permanent Under Secretary in a government department in Britain recently said: 'I should have preferred to have been a man; then I could have had a career and marriage too.'

In the early 1930s the State Department decided to admit women as career officers to the Foreign Service. The first to pass naturally received much publicity and yet more when, after a period of training in Washington, she was posted as Vice-Consul to Beirut. Within six months she married the British Vice-Consul and was lost to the American Service. The British Service, in which her husband later rose to high rank, was delighted to acquire such a well-qualified wife. Washington has not yet got its own back on Whitehall.

Nubility is not only acceptable but desirable in ordinary life; it is a persistent difficulty in all Diplomatic Services. In a recent conversation about candidates for junior executive grades, a senior official in the Civil Service Commission remarked: 'The girls in that batch were all better than the men and we've taken them, but', he added morosely, 'it's no good. They were far too attractive. They'll all be married within the twelvemonth.' One sees his point. Of those accepted for the Service during the last decade, 15 per cent of the men dropped out for one reason or another and 42 per cent of the women. The wide disparity between these percentages is due largely to resignation by women on marriage.

Between the wars there was a feminist movement in Britain strong enough to put the Secretary of State for Foreign Affairs under uncomfortable pressure. As a result he wrote annually to Heads of Missions asking their views on the admission of women to the Service. One of my Ambassadors wrote in reply:

> In diplomacy we bow to the inevitable, we accept injustices which revolt us if we allow ourselves to think about them, we are courteous to men who utterly disgust us, we accept compromises despite all logic, we burden our minds against our consciences and we are right to do so. At the same time, if we aspire effectively to serve the state, there must subsist under a heavy armour of cynical pose, a hatred of injustice, a contempt for the despicable, a loathing for bad compromise. I believe this sort of mentality to be utterly alien to the vast majority of women; they are not likely to make good diplomats.

Whether you agree with the last sentence or not, the whole passage shrewdly summarizes some of the personnel problems in diplomacy.

As far as capacity goes, I have served with many highly capable women officers, whose departure on marriage was widely regretted; but in general the right type of mind is rare in women and they are difficult to place in many posts abroad, no matter how able, owing to local prejudices and circumstances. As Plowden points out this should not be taken to mean that women are 'tender plants': 'We came upon not a few instances in which, to put it no higher, they had withstood disagreeable climatic, political or living conditions with fully as much resource and fortitude as their male colleagues.'[19] This verdict is not unexpected; during the war women imprisoned in appalling conditions showed at least as much courage and stamina as men. It is no more than justice that women should be allowed the right of entry into the Service, no matter the administrative difficulties.

(ii) *The Executive (Grade 9) and Clerical (Grade 10) Branches*
Much of what has been written above about the Administrative

Grades—particularly the qualities required—applies with equal force to members of the junior branches of the Service. The academic requirement and ages of entry are, however, very different for Grades 9 and 10. Only an outline is given below. Full details can be obtained from the Civil Service Commission. In this and succeeding sections of this chapter, I refer exclusively to British practice.

The normal competitive entry for Grade 9, open to both men and women, is for those aged between $17\frac{1}{2}$ and $19\frac{1}{2}$. The majority of vacancies are in the Home Civil Service. The educational requirements are similar to those demanded in Britain for entry into a university, but they include qualification in one foreign language for candidates opting for the Diplomatic Service. There is no written examination. Candidates appear before a selection board; those who have expressed a preference for the Diplomatic Service and who have attained a high mark in the first interview appear before a second board which tries to explore the candidates' interest in the Service, their personality and adaptability to conditions overseas. As an observer, I have been flummoxed by candidates who, when asked why they wanted to join the Service, merely thought that it would be 'nice' (which I hope it is), and had not bothered to ascertain what it did. Here again poor publicity is to blame in part, but not entirely, for a cheerful ignorance prevailed during the Reconstruction Examinations for officer grades in 1946 and later. One new entrant was summoned by the head of Personnel Department and informed that his first overseas posting was to be at Baghdad. He answered blithely that he had always wanted to serve in Persia. Having mastered these geographical obscurities, he has now attained ambassadorial rank.

In addition to this competition, candidates in the twenty to twenty-eight age group are accepted for Grade 9 if they have obtained a university degree or diploma. (Second Class Honours are not, however, required for this grade as they are for the Administrative Grade 8). There is no written examination; selection is by preliminary and final interviews before a board.

Finally, candidates are recruited from the armed forces and the Overseas Civil Service (Colonial Service). Here there is no age limit and no educational qualification. The written examination comprises papers in English, arithmetic, general knowledge and intelligence tests. Those who qualify go before a selection board.

About fifty are recruited annually into this grade of the Diplomatic Service. Men and women may enter all these competitions, but married women are not accepted in the Diplomatic Service, though they can be for the Home Civil Service.

Selection of candidates for the Clerical branch (Grade 10) is roughly similar to the foregoing, but the qualifications are naturally lower. Those who enter in the 16–20 age group either take an examination in English, general knowledge and figures,* or, if they have the General Certificate of Education in specified subjects, are exempt from the Civil Service examination. In either case, they are selected by a board. The 20–39 age group can be similarly exempt from examination, but candidates opting for the Diplomatic Service must pass before a Foreign Office board as well as before a Civil Service board. Candidates are also accepted who are serving in the Armed Services or the Colonial Service, or who are over 40. About 200 are recruited into Grade 10 of the Diplomatic Service every year. As with Grade 9, men and women are eligible but, again, married women are not eligible for the Diplomatic Service.

(iii) *The Secretarial Grade, Branch S*

Selection into Branch S (formerly known as Branch C) is not through the Civil Service Commission but by the Foreign Office. It is by personal interview only, at which time the girls must pass tests in shorthand and typing (or the latter only if they are applying as copy typists). Every applicant is warned of the liability to serve anywhere in the world, though full notice is taken of preferences for any particular area. Candidates can be between 17 and 38 years of age (in the case of copy typists, the upper age limit can be 45),

---

* A word ('numeracy' has been suggested) is needed to convey a counterpart to 'literacy'. Both qualities are required in all walks of life.

but none are posted abroad before the age of 21. One of the reasons for this is that in the case of minors the permission of parents must, under British law, be obtained before a surgical operation may be performed. An acute case of appendicitis could therefore be extremely dangerous.

After a brief period of temporary service, a shorthand typist may sit for an establishment examination conducted by the Civil Service Commission. For this she must be recommended by a superior officer. The examination includes further shorthand and typing tests, and papers in English, arithmetic and general knowledge. Knowledge of a foreign language is not a prerequisite but, as it is so essential in the Service, facilities for instruction are arranged. More efforts could be made in this direction, but the Secretarial grade is so stretched that it is not easy to arrange for spare time. Members of Branch S are encouraged, if suitable, to transfer into the Clerical (10) or Executive (9) grades of the Service, in which they can rise to high rank.

About 130 are recruited annually into Branch S.

(iv) *The Security Guard, Branch SG*

Branch SG (formerly known as Branch D) is unique in the Service in that its members serve only overseas. Candidates are usually between 30 and 50 years of age with long service in one of the armed forces or the police. There is no examination; selection is by a Diplomatic Service board.

All appointments are temporary in the first instance, but can be made permanent (and pensionable) after three years' satisfactory duty. There are possibilities of 'bridging' into the Clerical Grade (10), which opens up further fields of promotion.

Applicants are very numerous for posts in Branch SG. The standards are high and only about sixteen are recruited annually.

2. TRAINING

Our new recruits have now entered the Foreign Office, filled— let us hope—with curiosity and anticipation. If that notoriously incommodious architectural survival does not alarm them, they can stand anything the future offers. It is a comparatively recent novelty that, instead of being thrown straight into the machine, they are now faced with a brief period of high-pressure training, designed to introduce them to the tasks awaiting them in their different grades. This is the more necessary because they tend to enter the Service nowadays with less experienced backgrounds than their less numerous predecessors before the war. Plowden comments that, with the disappearance of National Service—the Draft or Conscription as it is called in other countries—'greater numbers of relatively immature candidates are appearing'.[20] A witness before the Estimates Committee stated that junior officers in the Civil Service knew very little about life, except what they got from the files. They worked side by side during the day but lost contact out of office hours and were 'cut off from what makes life "tick" '.[21] The cure is easier in the Diplomatic Service because, once abroad, life and work are blended into a continuing whole.

Again I write primarily of British practice, but the problem of training is a universal one, preoccupying those who direct Diplomatic Services all over the world because, for all new entrants, the course they must navigate is more exacting than in the past. In this race many start further back than was the case heretofore, and all have further to go past reefs more daunting. The interests of the Service—not to speak of common humanity— demand that novices be given a fair wind at the outset.

Plowden devotes a whole section to training.[22] Written in 1963, the report begins by making the point, so painfully obvious to all members of the Service during the preceding five or ten years, that if manpower resources are overstretched in relation to commitments, training goes to the wall. The Foreign Office spent less than £25,000 a year on training programmes and the Commonwealth Relations Office another £4,000. (This compared with the annual budget of £1,600,000 allotted to the United States Foreign Service Institute.) The importance of 'career management' is stressed. 'Introductory' and 'Language' and 'Functional' training are then discussed; followed by 'Refresher' training in mid-career.

The section concludes that the *extra* cost of carrying out training programmes on these lines would be in the order of £50,000 annually, and in the proposals it is implicit that the total staff should be increased to free officers for this.

Watt writing before the integration of the overseas Services, implies the importance of selection and training:

> The process of posting from the Foreign Office to Embassies abroad, and back, the mechanism which makes of the Embassies abroad the channel of communication with foreign governments, as well as the providers of information on the country to which they are accredited, even with the twentieth century vogue for ministerial diplomacy, combine to make the personnel of the Foreign Service a crucial and permanent element in the formulation of British foreign policy; while their position in London very often makes for the closest personal contacts and friendships between them and their political masters.[23]

It is against this background that we should consider the training methods now taking shape in the combined Diplomatic Service that came into being on January 1, 1965 as a result of the Plowden Report.

Space does not permit a comparison with the methods of the United States Foreign Service, which have been worked out with thoroughness, are in a permanent state of transition and perhaps more complicated than the British. Those closely concerned can however undoubtedly learn much from studying the State Department systems.[24] In France and Germany the emphasis in training inclines to be academic. Something like post-graduate courses are given to new entrants before they take up their posts. In France the hundred or so (out of 700–800) who pass the examination for entry into the senior grades of the Civil Service spend the next twenty-eight months at the *Ecole Nationale d'Administration*—the first year working on practical problems in a provincial *préfecture* and the rest at the School itself. The French Diplomatic Service recruits annually about ten entrants from this source and a few more who, after obtaining a university degree, have gained

211

diplomas in at least two difficult languages. In Britain a brief introductory course, 'training on the job' and specialized courses at intervals throughout an officer's career are preferred. This view is shared in informed quarters in America. Jackson's comment is: 'On-the-job training and experience are likely to be more "educational" for Foreign Service Officers than a year at an educational institution.'[25] TWFM devotes space to such training overseas in the context of American Embassy organization.[26]

The New Entrants Course for the recruits to the Administrative Grade 8 lasts for seven working days and is usually held in September, when they assemble. It is presided over by an experienced ex-member of the Service and sessions are conducted by serving officers or by visiting speakers, such as a Minister of the Crown, a Member of Parliament or a High Commissioner from some other Commonwealth country. As befits a beginners' course, the range of subjects is wide. The present organization of the Service; office work at home and abroad, divided into political, economic and consular; Commonwealth and Colonial countries, and aid to developing states; security; information, cultural work and the press—these are some of the matters dealt with, inevitably superficially but each expounded by an expert in his own field, with plenty of time for discussion. Brief visits to other organizations are also in the programme, including the BBC, the Central Office of Information and the British Council. Other Embassies, particularly the American, also open their doors. The last session is entirely devoted to a discussion of the course. The comments are informative, if sometimes politely restrained. Each future course benefits from the impressions formed by earlier participants, argued and discussed freely. Progress in training methods is thus improved year by year.

The reaction of the recruits revealed in private talk and in the many searching questions they put to speakers is instructive. In general, the course appears lengthy for those anxious to get down to the job and often matters are discussed that inevitably seem remote or not readily comprehensible to new entrants lacking experience of work in Whitehall or in the field. The duller parts of organization could be dealt with concisely in a few pages issued the evening before, to be assimilated in advance of each lecture and retained for future reference. It is above all noteworthy that what youth enjoys and profits from is a description by youth on what youth actually does on the job.

The need for training has not been ignored in the Home Civil Service, which established in 1962 a Centre for Administrative Studies. A member of the Diplomatic Service has now been seconded to the directing staff of the Centre. All new entrants, except those on 'hard language' training, attend a three-week introductory course at the Centre to familiarize them with the governmental machine. Every year about sixteen Diplomatic Service officers in the fourth or fifth year of service attend a twenty-week course, in which the emphasis is on teaching the students to think analytically and to raise their eyes from the narrow limitations of their immediate job to the enormous sweep of horizon that surrounds them. Courses are also arranged in the Foreign Office about six times a year for the larger intake into the Executive and Clerical branches (Grades 9 and 10) of the Diplomatic Service to fit them for duties they will be called on to perform. Branch S and Branch SG officers also attend courses.

Despite such an introduction, the new entrant will soon realize that, as in almost all forms of human activity, it is only actual experience that helps him to play his part and develop his own quality. No matter how good the initial training, much will still depend on the Head of Department in Whitehall or Head of Chancery in an Embassy, who will have to try to spare time to guide the new entrant. This is not easy. Pressure today is high, particularly in the Foreign Office. Seniors are often so immersed in their jobs that they cannot run their departments as they would wish. In earlier days it was possible for the head of a department to tell a 'new boy' to draft a telegram and, if the results were not satisfactory, explain why and tell him to do it again. Nowadays there can often be a temptation for the senior to redictate the draft himself and rush it to its destination; this tendency must be resisted. All Western Services complain of pressure, which makes instruction of subordinates by their seniors so difficult. The best seniors of any nationality somehow find the time.

Before an officer of any grade is posted abroad for the first time, he attends a 'Going Abroad' course, which occupies nine full afternoons. Wives are also invited. This deals with such questions as: how posts abroad are organized; health; team-work, representational duties and etiquette; domestic problems; and commercial, consular and information work. The concluding session is designed to elicit response to the question 'Have we overlooked anything?'—for in informal courses such as this the instructors can learn much from the intelligence of those taking part and omissions can be rectified next time.

It has so far proved difficult to arrange for Service Attachés or Seconded Officers and their wives to benefit from these courses, because they are not yet held frequently enough to coincide with their postings to Missions abroad. Further inter-Service integration is required in such matters.

☆

Language instruction must be particularly mentioned.[27] Between the wars the standard required for the Administrative grade candidates in the so-called 'easy' languages—French, German, Spanish and Italian—was very high. Today candidates for the Service cannot for the most part be expected to speak, read and write fluently a couple of the more familiar languages, because they have not had time to spend abroad the many months necessary. In the past instruction in the less usual and sometimes more difficult tongues was dealt with on the spot. No previous training was given in London and tuition abroad was somewhat haphazard, except for those learning to read and write, as well as speak, Chinese, Japanese and Arabic. It is still as important today for a member of the Service to command a medium of communication with other races. An officer (and his wife) in the Administrative Grade is profoundly unhappy if he cannot cope fluently at an early stage in his career with at least two languages other than his own. If he is to play a full part he will later learn more, in some of which—the less used and less universally useful —he will pick up only an adequate smattering. A sound grounding is never completely forgotten. Years later he may be posted back in higher rank to the region where he once gave up so much of his precious spare time to acquire competence in the vernacular. He will find that fluency will return and that his hosts are gratified by his stumbling recollections of their tongue. He will very soon be as much at home with them as he was twenty years earlier.

In the Executive Grade and in Branch S and Branch SG (again I refer to Appendix A), the so-called 'gift of tongues' may appear less essential, because these officers are not hob-nobbing with foreign personages of high rank. Here lies an illusion. A common language is vital in dealing with persons of any class and the ability to convey your ideas is just as important in an Administration Officer, Head Chancery Guard or typist—how, for instance, is she to buy her personal requirements if she can only make faces? Languages are one of the indispensable tools of diplomacy. St Paul recognized this: 'If I know not the meaning of the voice, I shall be unto him that speaketh a barbarian, and he that speaketh shall be a barbarian unto me.' There are maddening difficulties in Britain. The Treasury will permit payment only for 'authorized' courses. One officer was not unreasonably infuriated when told that he must learn Russian in London, though he lived near and had arranged to attend a course in Oxford, where there happens to be a university of some repute.

For some years the weight will be heavier, because the integration of the Commonwealth and Foreign Services into a Diplomatic Service has produced many officers who had previously tended to conduct their intercourse overseas in English. They will now wish to fit themselves for wider tasks by acquiring a modicum of 'world language' fluency. It is encouraging to see the vigour with which this problem is being faced. Enquiries were initiated in all government departments in London as to their need for linguists and the steps taken to produce them.

This had the immediately useful result of disclosing that one Ministry was running two courses in Russian, the organizers of neither being aware of the existence of the other. It is to be hoped that rationalization will range throughout Whitehall. Meanwhile the Foreign Office has started its own 'Language Laboratory'. This efficient organization is already beginning to instruct members of the Service, their wives and other officials (particularly those attached or seconded to the Diplomatic Service) in the essential basis of French, German and Spanish.

Even so, we are far behind the Americans in this form of training; the methods of the State Department—and of Moscow— could profitably be studied in Whitehall. Facilities for language training must not only be available, but time allotted for it. It is preposterous to expect a man and wife with little or no experience of foreign tongues to absorb an adequate knowledge of, say, Italian in five hours. Modern 'crash courses' reduce the time enormously, but even if taken just before departure for the 'new' country, they are only a tenuous base, not a real linguistic strong-point—rather like being parachuted into enemy territory with only light weapons and hoping for the arrival of artillery when you have had time to clear an airstrip. Even for an 'easy' language with expert tuition and modern methods, three or four weeks of concentrated work six hours a day is not too much for a basic knowledge.

Less familiar tongues, ranging from Arabic to Chinese, Amharic to Finnish, have long been a familiar problem. There is no common centre for instruction—indeed this would probably be wasteful if not impossible to organize—but the teaching of even the most obscure language is arranged, partly in Britain and partly in the region concerned, with increasing efficiency as experience is gained. The Middle East Centre for Arabic Studies, run by the Foreign Office in the Lebanon, is famous and much used by representatives of commercial firms (which repay in fees three-quarters of the total cost). Though systematic training by modern methods is only now beginning in the British Diplomatic Service for all ranks, the position in the Officer Grades (1–8) is encouraging. Full statistics are not yet available, but a recent check showed that all spoke at least one foreign language 'professionally' and many several. The percentages were: one language 25 per cent, two languages 37 per cent, three languages 22 per cent, four or more languages 16 per cent. In 'hard' languages—best defined in this context as those lying outside the Romance, Teutonic or Scandinavian groups—36 per cent of all officers had passed higher standard, 21 per cent intermediate standard, and 5 per cent lower standard examinations. The last percentage is known to be misleading, since many had reached the standard, but had not taken the examination.

In comparison with the British Service, where every officer speaks at least one foreign language, in the American Service 70 per cent are proficient for 'professional use' in one language, and only 14 per cent have attained proficiency in 'hard' languages, which did not include a single African tongue.[28] No statistics are published for the number of officers speaking more than one language, though there are many such. Since the war the French have made great linguistic efforts. No statistics are available at the Quai d'Orsay, but there has always been a high standard of proficiency in 'hard' languages—among which the French and Americans include, as the British do not, Scandinavian tongues. It may be doubted whether the French proficiency in familiar languages, up to 'professional standard', is as high as the British where two or more languages are concerned. In these tongues the smaller countries are remarkably efficient, partly because their own are so little known elsewhere. It would for instance be difficult to find a Dutch or Norwegian diplomat who could not speak fluent English, French and German and frequently other familiar tongues. They may, however, have less training in 'hard' languages.

We must now deal with the question of specialization on which Plowden has this to say in general:

One of the principal tests of an effective Diplomatic Service is its ability to find the right man with the right qualities, experience and knowledge and send him to the right place at the right time. This is a particularly difficult test for any overseas representational service to pass. Probably no question affecting representational work is argued over more hotly than what is the best means of solving the problem of specialization.[29]

Before the war, when the British Diplomatic Service was separated from the Consular Services, the latter each in its own territory— China, Japan, Siam or the Levant—provided a cadre of local experts with notable linguistic proficiency.* These high experienced men were invaluable, but they were almost all compelled to spend their entire careers in one area and the opportunity of promotion to the highest ranks was very limited. This disability was removed with the amalgamation of the Services after the war, but there was then a grave risk that local expertness would vanish. This was a sad prospect, because, though the British are widely considered (particularly by themselves) to be bad linguists, they are as a race far better than most.[30]

Some degree of specialization is therefore essential. This involves considered prognostication. How many 'Chinese' and 'Magyars' does the Service require today? How many 'Turks' and 'Swahilis' will it need in five years (bearing in mind that an excellent 'Turk' may meanwhile develop even more important qualifications in other directions and not therefore be available for Ankara)? Shall we have an Embassy in Tibet in ten years' time? If so, should someone be assigned to learn that language now? or when? and can a suitable man be spared for months to study this abstruse tongue? and, if so, where? There are in the Foreign Office adept crystal gazers who ponder on such matters and draw up hopeful charts. They attempt to

> Describe the horoscope, haruspicate or scry,
> Observe disease in signatures, evoke
> Biography from the wrinkles of the palm

* As noted in chapter VI, there was also the 'General' Consular Service covering the rest of the world.

And tragedy from fingers; release omens
By sortilege, or tea leaves, riddle the inevitable
With playing cards, fiddle with pentagrams . . .

So, anyhow, it is widely believed; but they do not, as T. S. Eliot
continues, include barbiturates in their pharmacopoeia. With the
'future needs' charts as a framework and making full use of the
'Post Preference' cards* filled up by all members of the Service,
planning can proceed and officers can be allotted to countries or
areas considered 'difficult', linguistically or otherwise.

However, this does *not* mean that a man is condemned to serve
all his career in China or even in the larger Arabic-speaking area.
What he will be told is that his next assignment will be to Jargonia:
so notorious a trouble spot that, even if it does share a language
with its neighbours, it is never on speaking terms with them.
He may be taught basic Jargonese in Britain or he may be posted
there without an introductory course. He will then labour more
at the language than in the office. A friendly Jargonian family
may be found to take him in, so that he can absorb as much of
the atmosphere as is good for him. These tribulations are not
without reward. He will, it is true, be faced with the additional
trial of an examination, probably in the 'lower standard' at his
first shot. He will then gain an addition to his pay—a 'language
allowance'[31] varying in amount according to the difficulty of the
language.† This he will continue to enjoy as long as he maintains
proficiency. He should then have the beginnings of the 'Jargon
expert' in him, linguistically and otherwise, and may attempt the
'higher standard' for which the pecuniary rewards are greater.
After his tour of duty of two or three years he will be transferred
to other posts and perhaps very different activities. Later, however,

* The Department of State for long had 'Officer Preference Reports' to serve
the same purpose. They became known as 'April Fool's Reports', partly because
they were unwisely called for on April 1 each year, but also in sarcastic allusion to
the extent to which officer's requests for future assignments actually bore fruit. A
more elaborate system is now to be adopted.

† Wives are not yet, as they should be, recompensed if they attain a standard of
fluency. This is very wrong when one reflects on the immense efforts many of them
make and how proficient they become in the weirdest tongues. It is high time that
this devotion, so valuable to the State, was recognised.

he can hope to serve for another tour in Jargonia, to which he will return with much local knowledge. Once again he will be posted away from that country, but, provided he has shown his quality in higher ranks, he may come back once more, perhaps this time as ambassador.

To some extent 'linguistic' specialization is linked with 'regional' specialization—Spanish and most of Latin America, for instance, or Arabic in spacious areas of Africa and Asia. Regional specialization may, however, overlap languages— Persian and Turkish, even Kurdish, will also be required for an overall view of the Near East. That at any rate, is the theory behind the crystal gazing. As no method of prognostication can be adequate, it stands open to criticism, but after some experience it is difficult to suggest fundamental improvement within the narrow limitations imposed by shortage of men and money.

In addition to initial courses, others are provided in the Foreign Office that may be taken fairly early in an officer's career, or later when he is to be appointed to a particular post. These cover 'functional' specialization. The most important are for Consular, Commercial, Information and Administration Officers. Officers may often be called on to take these courses while on leave between posts. The time spent on the course does not count as leave and those who live outside London are granted a subsistence allowance payable while they work in the capital. Commercial affairs are so important nowadays that special courses are arranged for 'locally engaged' officers, whether of British nationality or not, who deal with this work in Embassies abroad. Their journeys to the United Kingdom and subsistence there are paid. These courses, of which there are eight a year, last for seven weeks.

A greater effort is now made to familiarize 'Attached' and 'Seconded' Officers from other Services with the conditions they meet when serving overseas. The Ministry of Defence runs its own fourteen-day courses for all Service Attachés (Naval, Military and Air). This is a marked improvement over the previous system whereby Admiralty, War Office and Air Ministry each indoctrinated its own nominees in splendid and frequently very uneven isolation. In addition they are briefed in the Foreign Office on diplomatic life and work. The language training of Service Attachés is a matter for the Ministry of Defence; it may be hoped that the FO initiative towards rationalization will raise standards in 'easy' languages and give greater opportunities to acquire some of the less familiar tongues in which Service Attachés, like diplomats, are perforce acutely interested. The Ministry of Labour briefs its own staff admirably, in close liaison with the Foreign Office for local details, but Labour Attachés would benefit by more unified direction of language teaching. Other Seconded Officers are much rarer. Their own departments brief them and they apply to the Foreign Office for local information. The time will no doubt come when all these 'Attached' and 'Seconded' Officers and their wives, will be included in the regular Diplomatic Service 'Going Abroad' courses.

Most of the training described so far is for new entrants, but education can never cease. For more senior officers (Grade 5 and above), courses are arranged in spring and summer on special subjects or areas. In addition, officers are seconded, for periods varying between six months and a year, to educational institutions, including the Imperial Defence College, the Joint Services Staff College and the Canadian Defence College at Kingston, Ontario. These courses are particularly valuable because they promote inter-Service liaison. Nor are these the only external contacts. Some British commercial concerns accept Diplomatic Service officers at their courses, and universities in Britain offer them seminars. The German and Austrian governments grant scholarships to the diplomats of some foreign powers. All these contacts can be expected to increase as the integrated Service gets into full stride and it is to be hoped that officers can be spared for secondment to American establishments—particularly the Foreign Service Institute. The determination of the Service not to lead a closed life but to profit from wider experience is shown by exchanges with industry whereby the Foreign Office accepts (usually for one year) employees of firms who work in political or economic departments. Similarly, officers from the Foreign Office are attached to firms (not necessarily the same as those with employees on short-term attachment to the Foreign Office). This recent scheme promises to be most valuable. Hitherto, it has been found easier to fit the businessman into the Foreign Office than *vice versa,* since it is more difficult for a company to find a suitable niche for an outsider with no previous experience of manufacturing or marketing its product. Other activities are likely to be more practicable; of these, merchant banking would seem the most advantageous to both sides.

For a major power with a large Diplomatic Service, training must be envisaged for the top levels as well as for the lower, and it must be increasingly allied to inter-Service liaison. Many countries, even small ones, have long had military Staff Colleges. Only in the United States, with the establishment of the Foreign Service Institute, are there indications of the beginnings of a similar system for diplomacy. In particular the State Department runs the 'Senior Seminar in Foreign Policy'. This is attended by twenty-five senior officers, 60 per cent of whom come from the United States Foreign Service; to permit cross-fertilization the rest are from other government agencies. This course, which lasts one year, is presided over by USFS officers of wide experience and ambassadorial rank.

The setting up of a Diplomatic Staff College in Britain was recommended by Sir Harold Nicolson as long ago as 1934.[32] He repeated the suggestion in 1939, showing prescience when he remarked: 'Such is human frailty that it may be years before this essential reform has been achieved.'[33] Plowden did not feel able to make a definite recommendation, but the Report granted that a Staff College may become desirable when the unified Service has been in existence for some time.[34] Sir George Mallaby has advocated a Civil Staff College,[35] but the problems overseas need their own separate consideration. To give the proposal a fillip, I make bold to suggest that the Foreign Office take over the Imperial Defence College, change its anachronistic name to the Diplomatic Service College,* adapt its syllabus to the needs of the Service and of the times—and invite Sir Harold Nicolson to give the inaugural address. Such a College should be attended, not only by officers of the Diplomatic Service but also by those from other government departments whose work is closely connected with foreign affairs, by selected representatives from Commonwealth countries and the United States, and by senior personnel from British commercial and financial undertakings. What is needed is the widest possible interchange of ideas, and this should not be confined to foreign affairs in the sense of policy—to the art of diplomacy; it should also to some extent be concerned with the craft. To this end, a 'section' or 'term' of the Diplomatic Service College should be devoted to the work of Administrative Officers and the Inspectorate. Admirable though the efforts are to train personnel, the present methods suffer too much from 'scatter'. What Plowden has called 'Mid-career Training' should be expanded and brought under one roof and facilities offered to other departments of the government. Such a Diplomatic Service College would collaborate closely with those already existing. Each of the Armed Services has its own of long standing and there are many other organisms, governmental or private, that could contribute to a high standard of instructors and students.

These notes on training would be incomplete without mention that it has proved possible despite manifold difficulties to arrange 'Sabbatical Years' for a few senior officers. The term is in fact a misnomer, for these happy events do not occur every seven years, nor can they be made available to more than a handful. It would be more accurate to hope that they could be called 'Majority Years' granted after twenty-one years' service; and even then, alas, the privilege could not, with the present staffing of the Service, be given to all. At the moment it is hoped that it will be

* In no circumstances should the new institution be called, as a sardonic colleague once suggested—'because of the appropriateness of the initials'—the 'Centre for Higher Administrative and Organizational Studies'.

possible to grant a year's 'Sabbatical Leave' to about six officers at a time. This period is spent in attachment to a university or college, where the man can work in a relaxed atmosphere and his wife is relieved from the stress of diplomatic life. It is not always understood by those with no experience of work abroad that living and labouring among foreigners in itself imposes a certain strain, particularly as a member of the Service is moved intermittently from one country to another and each time has to readapt himself. No matter how agreeable foreigners may be, there is a limit to affection. The number of languages most people can learn to use professionally is also limited—perhaps five for the assiduous and a few more for the really gifted. A break after twenty years or more service is restorative, and therefore advisable.

This 'Sabbatical Year' is not a period of idleness, because the beneficiary is assigned a 'holiday task' connected with his regional, linguistic, functional or other personal experience and beneficial to the Service. Recent examples have been studies of political and economic developments in the Middle East and Foreign Aid problems.

While it is essential to provide initial instruction for new entrants and thereafter post-graduate courses throughout an officer's career—and, let us hope, also periods during which he can lie fallow—the real training can only be on the job. The advice given by Kolle should be treasured: 'Take snuff slowly and often, sit with your back to the light and speak the truth; the rest you will learn by observing your older colleagues.'[36] Seniors must be given time to help juniors and those responsible for postings must insert pegs into holes where they fit neatly. The selection of the right men for the Personnel and Administration Departments is vitally important. In turn again any Personnel Department must depend on careful and honest reporting by seniors on juniors. This is a grave responsibility for the reporting officer. He must try to exclude all personal prejudices and it is salutary for him to remember that he himself is to some extent on trial. Every word will be compared with previous reports by others; the writer can easily reveal himself as petulant or casual, unobservant, grudging or overgenerous. It is a job that, more than most, is worth doing well, if only because promotion depends on such reports. Confidential reports are not shown to the officers concerned, but it is a prescribed duty of the reporting officer to bring to his junior's notice any points on which he feels that performance has not been up to standard. In the French Service the reporting officer is obliged to show his junior the 'marks' he has given him, with the result that these are almost invariably set far too high—and the Ambassador writes a separate private report giving his real impressions. The United States Service has recently adopted a system similar to the French, and there seems to be a good deal of discontent about this in the Service. (See, for example, pages 37–43 in *Some Causes of Organizational Ineffectiveness Within the Department of State* by Chris Argyris, a study undertaken by the Center for International Systems Research and published by the State Department, Washington in 1967.) In the British Service all promotion and posting is in the hands of Boards at different levels in the Foreign Office. On their careful scrutiny and assessment much depends.

It must be emphasized that, whether in the Diplomatic Service or in any other enterprise, a major problem of training is not lack of organization or enthusiasm but simply manpower, and this ultimately boils down largely to money. The pressure of work is immense and there is little reason to expect it to decrease; the funds are grudgingly accorded; if all are slaving at their desks, none can be spared for training, still less for relaxation. For more years than it is agreeable to recall, the Foreign Service, as it then was, laboured under overstrain. The demands on it increased and every so often a Chancellor of the Exchequer, finding he was overdrawn at the bank, would impose a 10 per cent cut on government expenditure. It is a generally accepted principle that the poor should not be taxed at the same rate as the rich, but on these occasions this was ignored by the Treasury. Departments with a total expenditure of £10 million a year were cut at the same rate as those with expenditures of £100 or £1,000 million. This brought the Foreign Service near to disaster. It is encouraging that an independent observer has recently recorded as his view: 'The Service today is as well staffed as ever, and is recruiting an abler and more intelligent kind of Briton.'[37]

☆

To summarize, training courses are divisible into the following categories:

1. *Initial:* Introductory, general and not too detailed or lengthy.
2. *Switching:* To permit, say, an archivist to take an Administration or Consular post, by giving him the necessary grounding in his new work before he sets out.
3. *Specialization:* By language, area or function, or a combination of the three.
4. *Refresher:* World problems are continually changing and it is essential for officers to keep abreast of them.
5. *Senior:* To develop awareness of major policy and of the way it interlocks between departments; to teach officers to look upward and outward rather than downwards.
6. *Sabbatical:* To reduce tension in officers of long service who have been under strain and at the same time give them opportunity for some productive thought.

Education and the passing on of results to others should never cease, but the best training of all will be on the job. The main, indeed the only, test of training is in the results. A newly integrated Service, adopting new methods of training, must be given some years to prove itself. Argument will then still rage. Flair against expertise, which do you need most? Specialists or generalists? At least it can be said that an officer should learn to analyse statistically; scepticism is a valuable quality; detachment from personal emotion must somehow be combined with inquisitiveness; but how can these be taught in organized courses? There is no easily tailored solution. One can in fact only hope to expand latent talents—sometimes deep-lying—and 'on the job' training by a good Head of Chancery or Mission is as likely to be as effective, particularly in developing a 'feel' for diplomacy, as hours in the classroom, for which few can be spared.

No matter how well the training of the Service is conducted over the next decade, criticism will continue. To some extent it will be justified, because it is harder to modify an ancient machine than to construct a new one, but much of the comment will be subjective: 'The Consul I met at X was good, but at Y lousy.' When such remarks get back to the Personnel Department they smile a little wearily. They know, far better than the complainer, that the man at X is a potential Ambassador and that the one at Y will be lucky if he becomes a Consul-General, though he still has his value. They know, too, that no Service anywhere is staffed exclusively by geniuses—it would be a pretty uncomfortable organization if it were. The Personnel Department will wish ruefully that this was more widely recognized.

The British Diplomatic Service will envy allies with much larger establishments and will try to derive comfort from Jackson's sagacious comment: 'Understaffing can be the best staffing; if officers have more to do than they can possibly do, they are more likely to do what is important.'[38] In this respect some smaller Services, the French for instance, give an excellent example of concentrating on the essential.

3. WELFARE

The British Diplomatic Service employs a staff of 1,898 British subjects at home and 3,338 overseas.* In addition, there are in foreign posts some 8,600 locally engaged personnel, for the most part not of British nationality. Its employees are scattered over all the five continents. Antarctica is not yet included; north of the Arctic Circle, the Service has only one post—at Tromsö—though the Embassy at Reykjavik lies not far south of it.

This wide dispersion involves intricate problems in training, posting, maintaining, promoting and transferring personnel.

* Comparative figures for the United States Service are given in Appendix A.

Families for good reasons may have to be separated. In particular, the education of children according to a national standard or an international norm, is a grave anxiety for peripatetic parents. Good schooling must be found, but it may well not be available at certain posts. In some countries, such as Siam, schools where the primary teaching is in a foreign language are not permitted. This particular regulation is not directed at English, but the prohibition applies to it nevertheless. And what hope could there be of establishing a foreign school in the totalitarian countries, even if natives were barred from them? Very distant separation with all its heart-breaks may often be the only solution. The *comparatively* easy decision made in Britain that John and Joanna shall go together to kindergarten nearby, then to elementary schools X and Y, thence to secondary schools P and Q—all carefully inspected years in advance—is not always possible for members of a peregrinating Service.

The Service has always prided itself on its ability to 'make do', and at posts abroad senior members of the staff recognize their duty to help newcomers or those afflicted by misfortune. If these problems are overcome, it can only be because the Head of Mission and every member of the staff are alert and eager to help. There are, however, limits to self-help in a Service vastly augmented and much more scattered since the Second World War. This justifies the establishment of a Welfare Section in the Foreign Office itself. It is an example that other large Services could well follow. None, as far as I know, has yet done so in a comparable way, though the medical services the United States provides for its personnel overseas are excellent, and every effort is made on the spot in American Embassies.[39]

The attitude of mind of the good Welfare Officer can be expressed in one sentence: 'Human relations are more important than official regulations; the rules must be bent to fit people, because people should not be shaped to fit rules.' The diversity of the Welfare assistance provided in the British Service is wide, and I cannot do better than quote from some notes written to explain to new entrants the work of the Welfare Section.

At home, we help new entrants to the Service, particularly the very young, most of whom are not Londoners. We settle them into hostels here that are favourably known to us, try to interest them in further education, which we arrange for them if they are keen, and help them, through the Foreign Office Sports Association and its ancillary clubs, to find congenial social outlets in what can at first be a very lonely city. Aided by the Treasury Medical Service, we watch their health and advise parents if necessary; and we try to keep a fatherly eye on their careers, at least until they have successfully completed their first posting abroad. In short, but as unobstrusively as possible, we act *in loco parentis*. We also perform this role when we meet children arriving unaccompanied from posts abroad and speed them to their destinations.

We distribute complimentary tickets for concerts, operas, music recitals and art shows. . . . We brief staff on first posting abroad and keep a register of suitable hotels and other furnished accommodation in or near London. We put people in touch with County Council officials who can help with the care of elderly relatives and guide the search for schools, particularly for handicapped children.

We help people to obtain professional advice on such matters as preparation for retirement, the tragic occurrence of death in harness, and various legal or domestic problems. We support applications to charitable bodies such as the Civil Service Benevolent Fund and the Foreign Office Welfare Fund; and when it is needed we arrange free periods of convalescence.

This is adequate as a general briefing, but it does not disclose the immediacy or depth of many of the problems that have to be faced, either at home, where they are easier, or abroad, where they can be baffling as well as urgent. One of the most fruitful pleasures of the Welfare Section is grafting ideas on to receptive stock. Endeavours are made not only to talk with all junior staff before they leave for a post abroad, but to brief seniors about personnel problems. The wise Ambassador does not fail to avail himself of this facility, despite the great pressure under which he will inevitably find himself in Britain before he can set foot on ship or aircraft bound for his new Embassy.

An important aspect of Welfare work is medical and here the Treasury Medical Service comes into the picture. All officers must be medically examined; though wives and children cannot be compelled, they are strongly advised to take advantage of the free service. A booklet of 'Medical Hints' is also available to all going overseas. Abroad the picture is more complicated. The Service is exposed to foreign conditions in very small units and without the 'tail' of doctors, nurses, hospitals that an army, for instance, carries with it. It has been maintained with much justification that the Service needs a 'family doctor', such as anyone can have in Britain. He should be familiar, by previous examination and by carefully maintained files, with the medical background of his patients and, like the 'Flying Doctors' of the Australian Outback, he must be prepared to visit remote stations. He will have to combine sympathy with much scientific curiosity to follow the many faceted picture of health and disease around the globe. At present one doctor tours abroad to visit posts and discuss medical problems, not only with Service personnel but with local doctors. In a surprising number of places these may be rare or downright unreliable. Weird illnesses in curious places can be intensely worrying even to the phlegmatic. Where wives or children are concerned, the solace one trustworthy doctor or a well-trained nurse can inspire is worth the whole of Harley Street. Six doctors and three nurses are maintained in particularly isolated posts overseas. The British co-operate closely with the American Foreign Service, far more richly endowed, in matters of health all over the world. Medicine is particularly important in connection with the 'Post Reports' that every Mission and most Consulates are asked to produce for the benefit of those posted to the area. These should cover all aspects of life for an expatriate, and health is one of the most important of them. American Embassies also produce such reports and there is often close collaboration between British and Americans in drafting them.

Even at home and apart from the regular medical examinations, problems occur. The failure of a recent entrant to pass the probationary period may be due to medical causes and there is an investigation. People are sometimes quite unaware of the maladies from which they suffer. In one astounding case a typist had been kept in ignorance by her parents that she was liable to epilepsy; when she ran out of pills, she went down with an attack. Abroad diseases can be mystifying and victims may have to be sent home for treatment. Unfortunately there is as yet no arrangement under which such cases, perhaps extremely urgent, can receive immediate treatment under the National Health Service. The Armed Services have their own hospitals and others, such as the Police, make standing arrangements with a London hospital. The Foreign Office should do likewise.

Regrets are not infrequently expressed that the Service has 'gone soft' and that there is too much molly-coddling; this is not a peculiarly British problem. Thayer comments on the 'ex-pioneer spirit'. 'Though they have volunteered for service abroad', he writes, 'many Americans seem to believe that their forefathers did enough roughing it in the wilderness.'[40] Similar remarks are made in a variety of languages about the decadence of the younger generation. Just listen for a moment to any grandparent in any Tibetan, Bulgarian or English village and wonder what *their* grandparents said about *them*. In the British Diplomatic Service comparison is made with the heroic days when a typist in the Foreign Office posted to Barataria was expected to make all the arrangements for her journey thither and find her own accommodation on arrival. There is no doubt that this somewhat brutal method bred a superb self-reliance. Those who entered the Service soon realized they had to be prepared to learn how to look after themselves, and this versatility stood them—and their country—in good stead throughout their careers.

Three points must however be borne in mind by critics. First, the Service itself is very much larger than before the war and must employ greater numbers of men and women with little or no previous experience of life abroad. Secondly, before the war officers were almost invariably unmarried when first posted abroad and could learn the ropes more easily. Now early marriage is much more common. A young Diplomatic Wireless Service officer, for instance, with a wife and two small children, clearly needs not only a lot of help to reach his new post, but also on arrival. Thirdly, though travel is now more rapid, life in general in many countries has undoubtedly worsened in many parts of the world since 1939. It would not be unfair to say that, owing to the obstructiveness or malevolence of the local inhabitants, conditions can often be described as unpleasant, even dangerous. It is thus reasonable that more assistance should be given to Service personnel now than a quarter of a century ago, when there was only half the number of independent countries, the names of which were widely known. Could you now instantly place on a map of the world the following capitals and name the countries: Abidjan, Bamako, Bathurst, Kinshasa, Ouagadougou, Phnom Penh, Port of Spain, Taiz, Ulan Bator, Yaoundé? And how would you get to them? Yet in all these places Britain and other major countries are represented by Missions.

The balance between trying to provide a home life abroad and training all staff and wives to accustom themselves to and benefit from a foreign environment is difficult. Initiative remains a quality to be encouraged at all costs, but the inexperienced will need help and guidance. In highly civilized countries it is wrong to impose on an Administration Officer. It is particularly outrageous if seasoned officers clamour for help; they should be able to look after themselves, and a wise Ambassador, perhaps prompted by his observant Head of Chancery, will be ready to drop like a ton of bricks on any senior who troubles the Administration Officer unnecessarily. Inexperienced juniors will need more careful handling, but it will often prove possible to jolly them into independence, which may include helping them to learn something of the local language and bringing them to see that there is nothing intrinsically laudable in insisting that life in Brussels, Bujumbura, Bogotá or Basra should be rendered indistinguishable from the daily round in Basingstoke. What an American Ambassador has called 'golden ghettos',[41] where diplomats associate only with each other in luxury envied by the natives, can be very damaging, both to the individuals and to the good name of their country.

The role of wives in welfare work is increasing, in addition to their multifarious diplomatic duties already mentioned throughout this book. In 1954 the Commonwealth Relations Office wives formed an association, known, inevitably but somewhat inelegantly, as the 'Crows'. The Foreign Office followed suit in 1960 and five years later the two bodies were happily integrated as the 'Diplomatic Service Wives Association'. Membership includes wives and women members of the Service, and also wives of Attached or Seconded Officers in Missions abroad. Wives of retired members of the Service often continue their membership. There is no subscription, but voluntary donations are invited. This organization provides a link between wives and women members of the Service in all parts of the world and opportunities for maintaining contact in London and the provinces. It is unofficial, but its sterling services have been officially recognized to the extent that its secretary is paid from public funds. She can act as an 'information point', maintain contacts and help to weave together the widely dispersed strands.

A news letter, now of imposing dimensions and full of entertaining and informative matter, is published regularly; courses and social events, often with guest speakers, are arranged; and the Association works closely with the Welfare Section, particularly in such matters as hospital visiting, meeting children, arranging accommodation and even baby-sitting. Recently a group has been formed to make contact with the wives of members of the Diplomatic Corps in London. Many of these are at first very lonely in a strange city and welcome the chance to meet British wives.

In larger Embassies or High Commissions abroad there can be similar group activity. In smaller Missions or Consulates contact

233

will be maintained with the central association, but welfare and social activities will merge indistinguishably. This is as it should be; the whole emphasis of the new Association is on informality, not regimentation. The American Service also encourages this work, hints and examples being given in TWFM.[42]

In earlier pages I have paid tribute to the devotion of wives of members of the Service. Plowden emphasized how important is their part from a private and public point of view: 'A wife has to cope with the special family problems inherent in a career of constant movement and at the same time make a contribution with her husband to the work, welfare and way of life of an overseas Mission. It is no easy task to combine these roles.'[43] The Diplomatic Service Wives Association will strengthen the hand of the womenfolk of the Service and enable them to bring intelligent and experienced influence to bear in spheres where they are more expert than the male.

VIII

RETROSPECT AND PROSPECT

I T IS more profitable to reflect on what the future holds than to consider some of the changes that have taken place since the end of the First World War, but first we should note not a change but a continuance. The administration and organization of the British Diplomatic Service is still mercifully free from political influence and private pressure. In marked contrast with many, perhaps even a majority of countries,[1] this resistance includes an absolute refusal to countenance any nepotism. If you do not believe this and consider yourself an important personage, just write a letter to the Head of the Personnel Department of the Foreign Office asking that your nephew be transferred from Peking to Paris. Such an attempt at wangling recently produced a reply from the Prime Minister himself couched in blistering terms. The Cabinet dictates policy, but leaves the machinery untouched. The corollary must be complete loyalty by the official to his Service and to his political superiors.

Another tradition of independence is still rigorously maintained. Except in very special circumstances,[2] no members of the British Diplomatic Service are eligible for the Queen's permission to accept foreign decorations—'My dogs shall only wear my collars', George III is alleged to have remarked. The United States Foreign Service has a similar ruling, but diplomats of other nationalities often jangle with foreign baubles. In this matter there is a difference between the Diplomatic Services of Britain and the United States and their Armed Services, members of the latter being able to accept and wear foreign decorations gained in war.

Two features will strike any observer of both the past and present scenes: the immense increase in the responsibilities of the Service, well set out by Strang,[3] and the heavier burden borne by every individual member. We used to think—not unreasonably —that we were subjected to high pressure, whether in the Foreign Office or abroad, and the Services of other countries felt the same. Fortunately the human frame and mind are adaptable, so the slow increase in pressure has not been too intolerable, though at times one marvels at the resilience and cheerfulness of those, junior or senior, who, the world over, shoulder the load for their parent countries. The British Service has like others perforce increased in numbers. This has inevitably to some extent weakened the close family atmosphere that was so pleasant a feature before and between the wars.

As an example I shall always recall one of my first encounters in the Foreign Office. There was raging what passed for a crisis in those days and I was at work at my desk at 2 p.m. putting a file in order, while all the others were at lunch. An older man strolled in and perched amiably on a desk. We had few thoughts about 'security' in those days, and it never occurred to me to query his presence. He asked what I was up to, gossiped of the FO's problems in easy phrases and then, remarking that I must be very busy and that he would not interrupt me, drifted out. I followed him into the corridor and watched him turn a corner. I asked a passing Office Keeper who he was. Highly scandalized by such ignorance, he replied that it was Sir Ronald Lindsay, the Head of the Service. I returned chastened to my labours. I confessed to the Head of my Department when he returned, longstriding after his hurried snack. Moley Sargent laughed and said that he had told the Permanent Under Secretary, like me also lunchless, that I was doing the urgent job and that that was Sir Ronald's way of finding out what one of the 'new boys' looked like and sizing him up.

Sir Ronald Lindsay's successor, Sir Robert (later Lord) Vansittart—'Van' to the whole Service, and it did not seem too out of place on the lips of a junior—gave more of his precious time to the staff of the Foreign Office. He had every single new entrant to lunch at least once, older colleagues were fitted in, and outsiders, sometimes of the utmost eminence, were included. Were he with us today, Van would be the first to admit that pressure on purse and time has risen to such an extent that his successors cannot hope to help and educate their juniors on such a scale. In a much larger 'family' a Permanent Under Secretary must leave to officers below him intimate knowledge of juniors, but he will still include in his necessary social round those of higher rank on whom he depends. From all this one might suppose that 'entertainment', 'social life' or even 'high life' were the aim and end of diplomats, but Van was not merely a gracious host; courageous and clear-eyed, he advised and his advice was ignored. With all the qualities unattainable to most around him or above, he never forgot the human side. If he had a failing, it was to hope that others would be as devoted, as industrious and as quick-witted. He was too honest, he lacked charity to those without patience to read his overlong, periphrastic warnings. He did not advertise because he disdained such methods. Some petty minds have been impertinent enough to reckon him a failure.

Informality continues to be the keynote of the British Service and it has been happily extended to include all ranks. It is still true than an Ambassador will be addressed, at least on duty or in public, as 'Sir' by all his staff, though his wife may well prefer to be on christian name terms with senior wives. Everyone else is likely to use christian names at all levels. This is in keeping with the spirit of the age and with the far closer contact between the Service and the outside world. The aloofness that could sometimes be discerned forty years ago has vanished for ever and there is also far greater public interest in foreign affairs and in the art of diplomacy. In Britain and other Western countries there are today many organizations, often with thriving branches in the provinces, that follow foreign policy, arrange lectures and publish periodicals. Students of foreign or defence affairs in Britain can often learn more from Chatham House, Canning

House and the Institute of Strategic Studies than they can from *Hansard,* in the United States more from the Institute for Foreign Affairs than from the *Congressional Record.*

Regrettably, however, the interest in foreign affairs is not 'popular'. The editors of any but the most serious newspapers will tell you that the foreign relations of Britain rank about lowest in interest in their pages even during the pangs of a General Election. Honest Members of Parliament will admit that in the House of Commons foreign affairs cannot compare for a moment with domestic. The people of the United Kingdom or any other country worry about immediate, palpable problems and not about events elsewhere that appear more remote than they are. Even the close connection between life at home and economic policy overseas is blurred, despite intensive efforts by successive governments to make it plain to everyone.

Any review of the past, any reflections on the future must include consideration whether an Ambassador and all the expensive paraphernalia of an Embassy are worth the money spent on them. There is little new in these enquiries. The Royal Commission of 1861, which investigated the British Diplomatic Service, enquired at length into the influence of the telegraph on diplomacy. Were Ambassadors unnecessary when such rapid communication could be made with foreign powers? An Ambassador left without instructions from his government and facing an emergency might either adopt a policy both daring and dangerous—to the point of plunging his country into war—or more likely display complete inertia. The Commission's considered answer to the question was that there still had to be someone on the spot to talk to the local government and report—and, it must be added, only a senior officer can do this. If all British Embassies were reduced to Legations or Consulates for reasons of economy, the local government would be offended and the British representatives would be able to wield no influence. Imagine the likelihood of any foreign Head of Government granting a private interview to a junior officer; yet there have been British politicians so ignorant that they have advocated such courses.

'In spite of the speed of communications, I believe our Ambassador today has more important functions than ever,' testified Averell Harriman recently.[4] Moreover communications can be cut. Many an Ambassador in a smaller post, without an independent Diplomatic Wireless Service, has had to take urgent action without long awaited instructions from home. 'We wait', said de Aquila. 'I am old, but I still find that the most grievous work I know.' Sometimes, however, direct action on the spot proves best and when the belated contrary instructions arrive after events have taken their course, they may be withdrawn, with compliments. It is not infrequent for 'civilized' powers to mock less developed countries for their chaotic government. In Britain at any rate, decision-making by the government is becoming slower. No matter how urgent the problem, more and more people have to be consulted.

Nowadays the accusation of ambassadorial dispensability is differently phrased. It is maintained that in the jet aircraft age personal intervention at the highest level can be so rapid that a Minister for Foreign Affairs can be anywhere in the world in a matter of hours. Therefore only a modest establishment is necessary to receive him, when he flies in to negotiate. Failing the Minister himself one of his political underlings will suffice.

These arguments deserve a reasoned reply. In the first place Ministers are busy men, who cannot be everywhere in the world at once, if they are to do a proper job at home. Secondly, highly qualified junior politicians are not as common as might be supposed.[5] Thirdly, continuous not merely intermittent contact is necessary at high level between the home country and foreign states. This is particularly important in closed and regimented societies such as the Communist bloc, where unceasing observation and patient negotiation are required if any progress is to be made at all to improve relations. Moreover there is the problem of 'follow-up'. If a Secretary of State flies halfway round the world to conduct some brief and important negotiations, he can rarely conclude matters. The agreements must be implemented and this may prove as difficult as the original negotiations. A high-level representative on the spot is essential to ensure continuity. Fourthly, it must be remembered that even today when special visitations are more frequent than heretofore, they arouse publicity and optimistic expectations. If, as often happens, these are not fulfilled, the shock, if only temporarily—for the memory of the public is short—is greater than if an Ambassador, working quietly with the government to which he is accredited, fails to produce a satisfactory result. It is noticeable how wary the Communists are about promoting 'top-level' talks, although they have complete control over all organs of publicity at home and can tell their public as little as they like. Finally, I will recall what I have already written in another connection: it is both wasteful and unwise to fire your big guns unless it is essential; the other side may all too soon become used to the loud detonation. Better results can be attained with less expenditure of costly ammunition. This is particularly true of the so-called 'Summits', of which Hayter has pertinently remarked: 'If there is a desire to settle, a Summit meeting is unnecessary, while it is useless if there is no such desire.'[6] He adds that high level conferences can be useful, provided too much is not expected of them, because they secure the undivided and prolonged attention of leading men. The word 'prolonged' is important, because the West is sometimes too apt to try to work to a tight timetable and can be frustrated by those whose patience is subject to less domestic pressure. An excellent example of an American negotiator in Korea being prepared to outstay the Soviet delegation is quoted by Thayer.[7]

Diplomacy by multilateral conference is now with us, probably for ever. Brief periods of similar activity followed Waterloo and the Armistice in 1918. The method has grave disadvantages, which Thayer illustrates graphically, but we must share his conclusion that 'the complexity of problems requiring specialists and the increasing need for multilateral agreements point to an increasing reliance on conference diplomacy'.[8] The United

Nations provides a standing forum and the Disarmament Commission at Geneva is becoming another permanency, from which we must hope something may yet emerge. As the aims of Western policy are the preservation of peace and aid to undeveloped countries, it is essential that there should be common meeting places and that the United Nations be strengthened and reorganized to play a more efficient part.

We are once again approaching the deeper waters of foreign policy and the arts of diplomacy. For those—and I hope they will be many—who wish to navigate these turbulent seas, Nicolson's "Terminal Essay" provides reliable sailing directions.[9] He stresses *inter alia* that diplomatists should seldom be allowed to frame policy and politicians seldom to conduct negotiation. There are valuable reflections on 'the politician as a negotiator' and on 'the dangers of professional diplomacy' (subtitled 'professionalism', 'lethargy', 'narrowness' and 'timidity'). This essay should be required reading for every new entrant into any Diplomatic Service and on the first of January each year for all Ambassadors; many Cabinets could also profit from it.

While day-to-day negotiation should normally be left to professionals, the occasional outsider can play a valuable role. It was, for instance, a stimulating pleasure to serve with Oliver Franks or David Harlech in Washington and I have already mentioned d'Abernon in Berlin; Bryce in Washington even earlier is another example of intellectual eminence and exceptional skill. On the whole, however, the British Diplomatic Service has been fortunate in not having had too many, and only the best, outsiders inserted as Heads of Mission. The old Commonwealth Service was more victimized and 30 per cent of American ambassadorial posts still go to non-professionals, which has the additional disadvantage, noted in Jackson, that 'short-term non-career Ambassadors usually have no great interest in the long-term improvement of the Foreign Service'.[10] A few will be first class by any standard, but many are mediocre,[11] as they sometimes have been in the French Service. In the German and other European Services outsiders are rarer. It is difficult to persuade

good men to join a Service so ruled that only a handful can reach
the top posts. Plowden's recommendation is: 'Appointments of
this kind can be notably successful and should continue to be
made from time to time as opportunity offers. Such appointments
should, however, be the exception rather than the rule.'[12]

In newly independent countries 'amateur diplomacy' poses a
serious problem. There may well exist an efficient Civil Service,
but unless there has been a lot of forethought and advance
training, there will be no framework of a Diplomatic Service.
Fortunately many 'new' countries realized the dangers in good
time and arranged to second suitable personnel for training
elsewhere. The Foreign Office and many British Ambassadors
have been delighted to welcome such trainees from the Commonwealth. At least one British Embassy, during the pre-Plowden
parsimony, could indeed hardly have carried on some vital
activities without their enthusiastic help. The Carnegie Endowment has done sterling work in arranging training for English
speakers in the United States and for French speakers in Geneva.

New countries should bear in mind that they get the service
they are prepared to pay for. Even a modest Embassy or High
Commission is an expensive tool; half a dozen plus some Consulates will provoke a heart attack in many a Minister of Finance. It
is therefore highly unwise in the first flush of enthusiasm to set up
representatives in many capitals. After the fall of Nkrumah, the
government of Ghana closed no less than twenty Missions abroad,
which had been costing more than the country could afford.
Quite apart from the expense, an Embassy, once established, is
difficult to withdraw. If you over-reach yourself and later find
that shortage of funds compels you to economize, you are in for
trouble, for you incur the enmity of the other country. The only
solution is *from the outset* to accredit one Ambassador to several
countries. This practice is widely followed by smaller states, e.g.
Scandinavian, and by some of the Dominions, the Diplomatic
Services of which often produce outstanding men. Britain used
this 'multiple representation' in the Baltic States before the war
and still does in Africa, where one Ambassador may be accredited

to two or three posts—a practice recommended by Plowden,[13] but far from popular in the countries concerned, which tend to feel they are being denigrated. He is normally resident at only one of them; at the others the British government is represented by a Chargé d'Affaires, except when the Ambassador visits the country. This system imposes a severe strain on Ambassadors, but they are more expendable than a Minister of Finance.

☆

There have been perhaps greater changes during the last forty years in the Commonwealth Service. The Dominions Office was separated from the Colonial Office in 1925, to deal with relations with the original independent members of the Commonwealth—Canada, Australia, New Zealand and South Africa. The name was changed to Commonwealth Relations Office in 1947 when Pakistan, India and Ceylon attained independence. Even then the family remained small and relations close. Information was supplied far more freely than to foreign countries, attempts were made to reconcile opposing attitudes inside the Commonwealth and their views were taken into account in the formulation of British policy. Consultation and co-operation were still frank and easy.

Since 1947 the Commonwealth Relations Office has been as much in a state of transition as the Foreign Office. The number of independent Commonwealth countries (the UK excepted) increased from the four of 1925 and the seven of 1947 to twenty-five in 1966. Nevertheless the Commonwealth Relations Office was still concerned to promote and develop, whereas it could be maintained that the Foreign Office was conducting foreign affairs with many more countries, it is true, but in much the same way as in the past. The CRO felt itself more intimately related to the countries it dealt with and so did the High Commission staffs on the spot—with the notable exception that they rarely learnt the local language. It is to be hoped that the Commonwealth 'family' connection will continue, but the bonds are now much looser with some of the newer independent countries and rethinking is

243

required. Sentimentality is not likely to weigh much. Reassessment should not prove difficult in Whitehall and the integration of the overseas Services into one Diplomatic Service will help.

Those fortunate to be seconded by the Diplomatic Service to a High Commission before the war noted only one major difference of practice not easy to adjust to. Before 1914 it was the general rule in the Foreign Office and Embassies abroad that important despatches and telegrams were dealt with initially by seniors, not subordinates; in even earlier days the duty of juniors was merely to copy in longhand the drafts of their superiors and file them. With a comparatively small flow of paper round the world the 1914 system worked, but it was surprising to find it still in force twenty-five years later in the Commonwealth Service. In fact it began to break down under the stress of war and I sincerely trust that it has now vanished, with all the dangers it entailed. In the first place, no senior officer, no matter how able, can keep in his head all the background of every file and impulsive drafting may lead to grave errors. Secondly, it is essential that subordinates gain early experience of dealing with important subjects and there need be no loss of speed if they are warned from above that a question is urgent. This is all part of the 'on the job' training referred to elsewhere. This matter of procedure apart, the transition from an Embassy to a High Commission was stimulating and should be even easier now in both directions.

Perhaps the most significant new factor compared with pre-war days is the much increased importance of economic and commercial work, both in the Foreign Office and abroad.[14] Economic policy and planning in the Foreign Office lie outside the strict scope of this book, but they cannot be passed over, since they exert a profound influence on the work of Missions abroad. It can be maintained that in Foreign Service posts, pre-Plowden, commercial work, i.e. largely trade promotion and economic reporting, was on the whole satisfactorily performed. The Commonwealth Service had no direct experience of this and left it to the Trade Commissioners, who were nominees of the Board of Trade. Many were highly competent, but the frequent physical and ensuing mental separation from the High Commissions was prejudicial to the common effort. Now that all three Services overseas have been integrated there will be a common improvement.

It is difficult to be so happy about the Whitehall end. The FO and CRO direct Missions abroad, deal with other economic and financial Departments in Whitehall and with commerce and industry. In the ultimate analysis a successful policy will depend on whether the Secretaries of State for Foreign Affairs and Commonwealth Relations are versed in these mysteries. At the very least they must select Ministers of State in support, who can handle economic affairs. These are the policy directors, chosen by the votes of the electorate; they are fully entitled to efficient support below them from permanent officials. Thirteen US Foreign Service Officers hold PH.D. degrees in economics and 115 M.A. degrees,[15] not a high percentage of 3,700 Officers, but American Embassies are supported by many seconded experts. I do not know how many members of the now unified British Service hold degrees in Economics and am inclined to feel that FO personnel dealing with this vitally important subject are often amateurs rather than experts. It is not, for instance, easy to find Deputy or Assistant Secretaries who are fully trained in economics and who, whether *post* or *propter hoc,* are really keen on the work. The flair that is so essential a quality in all forms of diplomacy does not suffice in economic affairs.

During recent years outstanding junior members of the Service have expressed regrets that they did not know as much of economics as they would like. The best press for what would be called in academic circles 'post-graduate' courses, to fit them for the wider field, in which they feel it essential to have as full a knowledge as of the political implications. Some of the ills of nations have been attributed to the fact that politicians could not think economically, nor economists politically. It is imperative that their servants, the members of the Diplomatic Service, should be capable of both kinds of thought, though they will bear in mind that in diplomacy politics will hold the primacy over economics—

by politics I emphatically do not mean party politics, preoccupation with which distinguishes the politician from the statesman. The connection between economic and political policy is intricate but integral: in Britain it is not only in the Foreign Office but in many other important organizations, for instance the General Council of the Trade Union Congress, that awareness of and training in economics is urgently required. There will then still remain the problem that the Board of Trade, responsible for export promotion, is now practically without staff who have any experience in foreign markets.

The proliferation of international organizations is another post-war novelty. These include not only the United Nations, but offshoots such as the World Health Organization, Food and Agricultural Organization, International Labour Office and countless others. In the modern world we are inundated by acronyms, among which even the most knowledgeable swimmers risk drowning—EEC and EFTA, OECD and IFTUC, GATT and LAFTA, UNESCO, and NATO (known in France as OTAN, though sometimes described as MERDE), OAS (two of these; the more respectable having started life as PAU and being also metamorphosed into Spanish as OEA). The list seems endless and grows annually, though some die off or change their names. The *Economist* lists thirty-two and Barnett thirty-four,[16] but there are wider discrepancies between the two lists. No wonder the Germans speak of *die Politik der Buchstaben*, alphabetical politics. A concise description of work with these organizations is given in Barnett[17] and from the British angle in Strang.[18]

The diversity of subjects with which the modern diplomat must deal has as one consequence an appalling increase in the volume of paper circulating round the world. 'Choking people to death with information is one of the oldest bureaucratic techniques known to man', quotes Jackson when discussing 'a non-stop fight against over-reporting', which swamps Washington's absorptive capacities.[19] Kelly had earlier commented: 'The most serious obstacle of all in modern States is the slowing down and choking of the machinery of government through overwork.'[20] We used to think the flood unmanageable between the wars, but now it is quadrupled.* Though staffs are much larger, the strain on senior officials is intense and many are the appeals for reduction. Plowden remarks: 'Those who initiate or call for reports must discipline themselves to ask first why a report is necessary at all. If a report is necessary, its justification should be clear to anyone who reads it.'[21] Many Missions ignore this precept and the Foreign Office is apt to flood small Embassies with unnecessary paper.

Much can be done to shorten essential reports by economical drafting—but this takes time, for it is erroneous to imagine that a concise report with no important omissions is as easy to write as a lengthy one. All important despatches from British Embassies are now prefixed by summaries. If these are well written, they are often all the busy man at the other end will require in order to form a picture. Nevertheless one of the most useful knacks of any senior officer will always remain the ability to read and assimilate fast. Really outstanding men and women need only a clear outline of facts and circumstances to absorb the main points of a complicated issue and, if the summary is not sufficiently accurate or profound, will disentangle the complexities with a minimum of penetrating questions. If I may say so, I have met few greater masters of this difficult art than HRH the Duke of Edinburgh, who despite heavy pressure on his time demonstrates in many important matters the genuine interest that permits real penetration. These qualities are not new, but they are more urgently required in the high-speed modern world, of which diplomacy is a part.

The Plowden Committee recommended the unification of the overseas Services of the Crown, but not that the same course be adopted at the centre.[22] There thus still exist in London a Foreign Office under the Secretary of State for Foreign Affairs and, housed

* Papers received in the Foreign Office in various years were as follows:

1821	6,193	1916 (War)	264,537	1944 (War)	402,400
1849	30,725	1926	145,169	1962	665,951
1913	68,119	1939	270,169	1965	779,891

Of the 1965 total nearly 200,000 papers were concerned with administrative matters.

in a separate building, a Commonwealth Relations Office under its own Minister. The vestigial Colonial Office is now to be absorbed by the Commonwealth Relations Office, but a considerable detached empire is meanwhile being hacked out in the Whitehall jungles by the Overseas Development Ministry. The Plowden Committee gave a lead by recommending the amalgamation at home of certain services, e.g. Administration and Personnel, Communications, Training etc., and admitted that 'the logic of events' pointed towards the amalgamation of the CRO and FO.[23] One can but agree. In 1782 the foreign relations of Britain were dealt with by the separate Northern and Southern Departments. It is once again time for unity and for economy of that precious commodity skilled manpower throughout the field, including Aid programmes.

There should be more public awareness that the whole effectiveness of these scattered Ministries in London could be augmented were they housed in one properly designed building in Whitehall. Like many others I should regret for sentimental, though not for artistic, reasons the disappearance of the present Foreign Office. Anyone familiar with its remoter rooms, anyone who has had to try and grope his way from Room 134 in the Great George Street building (which is inexplicably next to Room 67E), via Room 366 in what used to be the India Office, to the Commonwealth Relations Office on the other side of the quadrangle with no passage under cover, and then on again to visit eleven other departments housed in Queen Anne's Mansions, Lower Regent Street or across the Thames, will be staggered by the inefficiency, even though it maintains lightness of foot and a mile-devouring stride in all weathers. Neither sentiment, artistic sensibilities, a rooted objection to any change, nor lack of money can excuse the ramshackle and expensive expedients to which devoted staff are now reduced. *Hoc opus, hic labor est*; in this respect the Service has been too long in Avernus.

Ministers in all countries tend, not unnaturally, to be wrapped up in the affairs of state with which they must deal, and very much in the public eye. Many under such pressure forget the splendid machine beneath them, without which they could effect nothing. Briggs declares: 'No President since Theodore Roosevelt and no Secretary of State since Charles Evans Hughes has taken any sustained personal interest in the *mechanics* of our foreign operations.'[24] It is most encouraging that this statement is no longer true. In March 1966 President Johnson issued an ordinance under which the Secretary of State was instructed to review the work overseas not only of the Foreign Service, but of all the attached Agencies. Great economies in manpower and money, and increased efficiency should result, but the ordinance will need continuous and forceful follow-up at high level if it is not to sink into oblivion as many such admirable initiatives have in the past.

Britain has long been luckier. There is an example in the extraordinary main staircase hall of the Foreign Office. There the visitor will look around him with awe not unmixed with well concealed ribaldry. Facing the foot of the staircase he will note two massive marble statues of nineteenth-century Secretaries of State, whose names are helpfully inscribed on the plinths. Halfway up, where the staircase divides is an unnamed bust; judging from the warts, it depicts Cromwell. The visitor should take the left hand branch of the stairs and turn left again at the top in the gallery. Here he should avert his tactful eyes from the preposterous murals and walk towards the Secretary of State's room at the end. On the way he will pass an ill-lit bronze bust, the only piece of twentieth-century sculpture in the Foreign Office. It depicts Ernest Bevin.

Bevin may not have been a great Foreign Minister, though on his death the *Economist* could write of him that he 'had learned to combine a sense of the possible with a regard for the visionary objective'—a remarkable feat during the period of stress that characterized his tenure of office. It was, however, not for these qualities that members of the Service paid him the heartfelt compliment of subscribing to a monument to him.* Quaroni

---

* The compliment is not unique. On the ground floor, near the room of the Permanent Under Secretary, is a bust of one of his predecessors, Lord Hammond, who held that post from 1854 to 1873 and helped a budding Service through its early vicissitudes. This memorial, too, was presented by his colleagues.

quotes a conversation with him in Moscow. In referring to Soviet politicians he said: 'These people have lost all human feeling. They think only in terms of power and machines. Not one of them is interested in human beings. In the little man. At the beginning of my career I was a little man. And I told myself that I would spend my life bettering the lot of little men. It's the only thing worth doing.'[25] The British Diplomatic Service found, at the end of his life when he was worn and weary, that Ernie still cared.

IX

ENVOI

IN THE previous pages an outline has been sketched of the
mechanics of a Service that seeks to evolve purposefully. It
recently surmounted another long and dreary hill with the aid
of the Plowden Committee, whose report was cheap at the price
to the taxpayer of £13,000.* Such outside inspection, large scale
or small, will always be welcome. The fresh eye can often point
to weaknesses or extravagances that elude those closely meshed
in the machinery of any Service. It should, however, be a condition precedent that the newcomer in an unaccustomed field should
start without bias, and present a balanced report—to blacken any
organization with malice aforethought is even easier than to
whitewash it.

It has been said that the seeds of obsolescence are sown in every
organization imbued with methods rather than objectives. I have
written largely of methods in this book, for the reason that the
nuts and bolts of diplomacy are less familiar to the public than the
policies that govern them. More weight should, however, be
given to objectives and there must be the right men to plan and
attain them. 'System is obviously important. But policy is not the
product of a system. It is the product of responsible men who are
in touch with one another.'[1]

Diplomacy is a man-sized job, far removed from the legendary
handing of seedcake to duchesses and the wearing of gaudy

---

* The Foreign Office Estimates are a curious document because they contain so
much extraneous matter. In 1966, for instance, you will find a like sum devoted to
the celebration of the nine hundredth anniversary of 1066 and All That.

raiment. Among other tasks it falls to the diplomat to help to preserve peace in a distracted world. 'The pressure of one finger on an adequate lever will shake the world', wrote Rousseau. 'To uphold it requires the shoulders of Hercules.' Inspiration is certainly required of members of the Service, but they will become as familiar with perspiration. They will need balance and staying power. 'There is no standard working week for staff overseas and no overtime is payable', say the Diplomatic Service Regulations.[2] The demands are high, but so are the rewards. The small independent commands, where a junior can develop his initiative, are fewer now than in the halcyon past, but they still exist. At an early age you can be an independent Consul at X or a Head of Mission at Y. Either post will be small and undistinguished in the eyes of the world—until a catastrophe brings it suddenly into the news—but it will be yours. There is the additional attraction that a wife can help her husband directly in his job to a much greater extent than is possible in other occupations. The satisfaction of this matrimonial teamwork is immense.

Heatley has well summarized the diplomat's task:

There is no smooth and easy path for the conduct of international policy; nor for its study. The fortunes of nations should not be left to the hazards of the unforeseen. Those who are responsible for guiding relations between states need a vast equipment in knowledge and in aptitude. They must know the resources, the constitution and manner of government, the treaty obligations, the character of the dominant personalities, the national temperament and national objects, both of their own state and of its connexions—sometimes unruly and suspicious connexions—in the Family of Nations. They must well consider the relation of means to ends. Here, without any doubt, there is need of eyes for the past, the present, and the future— need of the three eyes of prudence: memory, intelligence, providence. By these Fortuna is won. Of all the regions of politics there is no other of which it is so strictly true as of the international that only the most complete knowledge and command available of all the factors should be allowed to count, whether for those who direct or for those in a succeeding age who try to judge them.[3]

The work of the diplomat is highly subjective; idealism must be combined with realism and 'feel' will often have to count for more than 'fact'. Diplomatic files abound with recommendations that conclude: 'On balance I think that . . .' such and such a course should be taken. The work is qualitative and no quantitive approach, no use of the most advanced computers, is going to help.

The diplomat has acquired a queer repute. As Thayer says:

Coddled and pampered behind this formidable barrier of international law and custom, untouchable by the police, beyond the reach of the tax collector and the customs inspector, the diplomatic corps, one might suppose, would be the world's greatest breeding ground for adult delinquents.

But he continues:

However, along with the immunities there has developed an ethic based largely on custom which more or less adequately takes the place of the laws from which diplomats are exempt.[4]

What a Diplomatic Service *cannot* afford are officers unable to measure up to these standards, this ethos. Diplomacy is a way of life, like a doctor's, a farmer's or a mariner's, with few or no set hours. The diplomat suffers the additional strain that he is closely scrutinized overseas as a representative of his country. He must remember this without priggishness and with no sense of superiority, such as might tempt him to criticize the country he is serving in—even worse run down his own. Those who are not acutely interested in other human beings and in particular those who dislike foreigners, hate travel and yearn for a well regulated life, should not apply to join any Diplomatic Service. They would be unhappy in a profession where there is a totality of work and play. Worse still, they would be a nuisance in a Service that can only profitably use men and women capable, throughout their careers, of winning a series of small but not unimportant victories over their constantly changing environment.

> Something I owe to the soil that grew—
> More to the life that fed—
> But most to Allah Who gave me two
> Separate sides to my head.
>
> I would go without shirts or shoes,
> Friends, tobacco or bread
> Sooner than for an instant lose
> Either side of my head.

Not all of us can hope to be known as the 'Friend of All the World', but many are needed in diplomacy and the world is fortunate that many come forward.

Since 1884 the telegraphic address of the Foreign Office and of all British Embassies has been 'Prodrome', which derives from the classical Greek 'forerunner'. It has been an apt address in the past; I have no doubt that it will be as fitting in the future and that collaboration with sister Services in the democracies will continue as fruitfully as heretofore.

Appendix A

DIPLOMATIC SERVICE
GRADES AND PERSONNEL

As explained in chapter VI (1), entry in the British Service is by
different methods according to the educational background and age of
candidates. There must, however, be no block to prevent those recruited
at a lower level from rising to high rank. Indeed every encouragement
to do so must be given to those of ability in the course of their careers.
The Plowden Report therefore recommended a modification of the
previous Foreign Service system[1] and this has now been adopted in
the following form:

GRADE	APPROPRIATE RANK	SALARY
1 (A)*	Ambassador or Permanent Under Secretary	£8,600
2 (A)	Ambassador or Deputy Under Secretary	£6,300
3 (A)	Ambassador, Minister or Assistant Under Secretary	£5,335
4 (A)	Counsellor or Consul-General	£3,585–£4,585
4 (E)*	Counsellor or Consul-General	£4,085
5 (A)	First Secretary or Consul	£2,335–£3,192
5 (E)	First Secretary or Consul	£2,656–£3,084
6 (E)	First Secretary or Consul	£2,062–£2,496
7 (A)	Second Secretary or Vice-Consul	£1,829–£2,240
7 (E)	Second Secretary or Vice-Consul	£1,659–£1,959
8 (A)	Third Secretary or Vice-Consul	£996–£1,659
9 (E)	Junior Attaché	£633–£1,532
10 (E)	Clerical Officer	£411–£1,077

* A = Administrative; E = Executive.

The salaries of Executive Officers differ from those of Administrative Officers in the same grade. The persistence of this highly undesirable anomaly is due to Treasury insistence on keeping salary scales in line with those of the Home Civil Service.

It will be seen that even within the Executive Grade an officer can rise to the rank of Counsellor or Consul-General. Nor is this all; a vital feature of the system is what is known as 'bridging'. Thus an officer joining the Service in Grade 10 would normally advance via Grade 9 to Grade 7 (Executive). If he then showed marked ability he could 'bridge' to Grade 7 (Administrative) and would then progress upwards in the administrative grades 5 to 1. Alternatively he could continue in the executive grades up to Grade 5 or 4, then 'bridge' to the administrative grade and thence upwards. This system ensures that no officer of high quality is prevented from reaching the most senior posts in the Service merely because he joined originally at a lower level than his contemporaries. There is no limit to the number of officers allowed to 'bridge'; this is in marked contrast with the French Diplomatic Service system, under which only two officers may 'bridge' each year.

The 'officer grades' of the United States Foreign Service are as follow, with salaries given their sterling equivalents for ease of comparison:

GRADE	APPROPRIATE RANK	SALARY
Career Ambassador (CA)	Ambassador	$27,000 (£9,643)
Career Minister (CM)	Ambassador	$26,000 (£9,285)
FSO–1	Counselor or Consul-General	$23,935–$25,890 (£8,550–£9,246)
FSO–2	First Secretary or Consul	$19,333–$23,360 (£6,905–£8,373)
FSO–3	First Secretary or Consul	$15,841–$19,141 (£5,657–£6,836)
FSO–4	Second Secretary or Consul	$12,873–$15,561 (£4,600–£5,558)
FSO–5	Second Secretary or Consul	$10,602–$12,810 (£3,786–£4,575)

FSO–6	Second Secretary or Vice-Consul	$8,843–$10,667 (£3,157–£3,810)
FSO–7	Third Secretary or Vice-Consul	$7,473–$8,879 (£2,668–£3,206)
FSO–8	Third Secretary or Vice-Consul	$6,451–$7,729 (£2,304–£2,757)

It will be seen by comparison with the British table that, while the senior American grade does not much exceed its British counterpart, the junior us grades receive much higher salaries. An American new entrant is paid, for instance, almost exactly the same salary as a British First Secretary with seven to ten years' service. These are, however, basic salaries and complaint is made in the American Service (see Appendix B) that allowances are much lower than with the British.

The Secretarial Grades of the British Diplomatic Service are designated Branch S (previously and still frequently called today Branch C), as follow:

GRADE	DUTIES	SALARY
S.1	Senior Personal Assistant	£950–£1,296
S.2	Junior Personal Assistant	£779–£1,064
S.3	Shorthand Typist	£375–£846
S.4	Audio Typist	£369–£840
S.5	Copy Typist	£341–£786

Here again 'bridging' is possible from S.4–5 to Grade 10, or S.1–3 to Grade 9 and thence upward in the executive grades, with further 'bridging' possible to the administrative grades.

The Security Guards and Messengers, previously designated Branch D, are divided into three grades from which 'bridging' is possible to Grade 9 or 10 and thence upwards. Their salaries are:

S.G.1	£847–£995
S.G.2	£783–£896
S.G.3	£670–£729

The Diplomatic Wireless Service has its own system of grading, designated T (for technical).

The widened scope of the Service has led inevitably to an increase of uk based staff. In 1929 there were 340 at home and 640 overseas. Like many statistics these are misleading except as a general impression because they do not disclose that up to the Second World War far greater use was made of 'locally engaged' staff in posts that would now be regarded as confidential. Often these were not even British subjects and, as was to be painfully discovered, the gravest risks were incurred as a result of this economy in reliable manpower. By 1938 the total had increased from 980 to 1,081; in 1947 it stood at 4,139; by 1964, as a result of parsimony that brought the Service almost to its knees, the total had been reduced, despite the ever increasing burden, to 3,521 of all ranks. In this figure alone lies a justification for the Plowden Report, which in addition wisely recommended the integration of the overseas Services, part of which had previously fallen under the Commonwealth Relations Office or Board of Trade.

Since the amalgamation the figures are no longer comparable, because High Commissions in over twenty countries have been added. They stood in 1966 at 1,848 at home and 3,338 overseas, a total of 5,186. To the home figure must be added 379 working in the Commonwealth Relations Office (prior to the absorption in August 1966 of the Colonial Office), but the Diplomatic Service Administration Office, which covers the CRO as well as the FO, is included. Administration absorbs nearly two-thirds of the home total. The grand total of 5,186 includes about 1,000 non-career, temporary officers. In addition there are some 8,600 locally engaged personnel abroad; some senior and highly prized, some subordinate in equally essential roles.

One of the main achievements of the Plowden Committee was to persuade Parliament that manpower in the previously divided Services was woefully overstrained. The Committee recommended a 10 per cent increase. It well knew that it would take years to build up the cadre. The figures given for 1966 did not therefore represent its 'ideal establishment' for the Service, but rather the starting point for a long over-due expansion of manpower, which would in turn permit rationalization and increased efficiency in a rapidly changing world. It would be vain to hope that there will not be further uninformed obstruction. Indeed, the latest attempt to impose a cut, in flat contradiction of the Plowden recommendations, may result in the reduction of certain Missions to a mere 'care and maintenance' basis.

The number of posts (Embassies, High Commissions, Delegations, Consulates etc.) staffed by the newly integrated Service in wide dispersal in all five continents is now 242—180 foreign and 62 Commonwealth. To these must be added 151 consular posts presided over by locally engaged or temporary officers; all of these have to be administered by the Foreign Office and all are important in one way or another or they would not be maintained.

About 2 per cent of taxation in Britain goes to support the entire overseas Service.

In comparison with these British figures the American establishment

is far vaster. Complete statistics are set out in Barnett.[2] The figures here
are abstracted to the nearest thousand. The Department of State
employs over 7,000 US citizens in Washington and an equal number
abroad, plus 10,000 non-citizens abroad. These figures show a 10 per
cent increase during the last ten years. In addition there are 7,000 US
citizens overseas (whom the British would describe as 'Seconded
Officers'*) from other government agencies and 17,000 non-citizens
to help them, supported at home by 16,000 working in the United
States for USIA and AID. Thus the civilian total overseas is over 14,000
US nationals and 27,000 foreigners. The *non-combatant* representation of
the United States Armed Services abroad is as imposing, 16,000
Americans and 65,000 locally engaged. The grand total was 122,808
overseas on June 30, 1964, not including the Central Intelligence
Agency, for which data are not available. This compares with a British
total overseas of some 14,000. The American figures do not include the
Area Commands—semi-military but non-combatant organizations set
up in foreign countries, often on a vast scale. These add considerably
to the indirect responsibilities of United States Missions.

The French Diplomatic Service produces the following figures:
at home 1,022; overseas 2,057. This is the total (3,079) of the French
grades A to D, roughly comparable with the British grades 1 to 10 plus
the British branch S. Some 1,300 of the French total are engaged on a
contract basis and are not regular members of the Service; they correspond with the British 'temporary officers'. No figures are readily
available for French staff locally engaged abroad. The German counterparts are: at home 1,715; overseas 2,607; German total 3,322; plus
locally engaged 1,758. In addition there are 280 officers seconded from
other ministries serving in German Missions overseas.

The pleas of European Diplomatic Services for increases in trained
staff are balanced by the eloquent, but fruitless, appeals of American
Ambassadors for reductions. Briggs is only able to record one victory
and that not due to his own efforts. On arrival in Prague in 1948 he
found an Embassy staff of eighty Americans. After months of insistence
he had only succeeded in reducing the total to seventy-eight. Then the
Czech government for its own Communist reasons declared five-sixths
of the staff *personae non gratae*. The happy Ambassador was left with
thirteen, including himself. He comments: 'It was probably the most
efficient Embassy I ever headed.'[3]

The only time that the British were grossly overstaffed was in the
lush days of the so-called Control Commission for Germany up to 1951.
Only a dozen out of the thousands were members of the Diplomatic

* The comparative British total is 148.

Service. It took relays of Foreign Service Inspectors four years to cleanse that stable and the dirt disclosed stank to high heaven. Fortunately there were some comic interludes, as when one of them, going from room to room in the British Commissioner's Office in a large city, found three clerks. On enquiry he learnt that they issued dog licences. They explained that after the war the city was over-run with starving dogs, whose numbers had to be reduced. In view of the food shortage dog-owning was discouraged by the imposition of a tax amounting to about £4 for each licence. Allied personnel were exempt and drew free dog-tags from this office. The Inspector was halfway down the corridor before it occurred to him that even so a team of three was surely lavish. He returned and asked how many licences were issued annually. The clerks totted up a total of over 2,700 dogs. As there were some 700 Allied Personnel (which was at least 650 too many), every individual must apparently own four dogs. The explanation was obvious; the spiv element was being issued with free dog-tags and selling them to Germans for less than the official fee. The Inspectors presented the Commissioner with the figures and requested solemnly that all dog-owners parade at 0930 hours next morning with their dogs. The Commissioner, a man of the highest integrity who had long protested that his office was grossly overstaffed, moved rapidly to violent action.

Appendix B

EMOLUMENTS OF MEMBERS
OF THE BRITISH
DIPLOMATIC SERVICE

The word emoluments, which is necessitated in the title of this appendix because it is the gobbledygook officially approved by the financial gnomes who control such matters, requires explanation. Etymologically it means 'what is ground out', i.e. you grind away and are paid for it; yet your earnings are ground away by taxation until little remains. In the red-tape jargon emoluments cover all varieties of official income. As far as the Diplomatic Service is concerned emoluments are divided into salary (taxable) and allowances (for the most part tax-free). Allowances are of many kinds, of which details will be found in Diplomatic Service Regulations.[4] The most important are the foreign allowances.

Salaries are set out in Appendix A, but the method of calculating foreign allowances has for long been something of a mystery even within the Service. The allowances of personnel serving in the Foreign Office are fixed according to various set scales, depending on rank, whether married or single, number of children etc. Abroad the system is much more complicated, because allowances must also vary to take account of the widely differing cost of living at different posts. This is where the Inspectorate comes in. Every post in the Service is inspected at frequent intervals and the Inspectors *inter alia* recommend the scales of allowances for each. The methods used are at first sight abstruse, though easily handled by those trained to the work. Enquiries are frequently received at the Foreign Office and at posts abroad about the British system, which seems to be widely recognized as fair both to individual members of the Service and to the taxpayer, who produces the funds.

I am immensely grateful to the Diplomatic Service Administration Office for having prepared specially a note on the methods now used. If amplification of this summary is required the DSAO will be happy to supply it.

NOTE BY THE DIPLOMATIC SERVICE ADMINISTRATION OFFICE

1. SALARY

Officers serving abroad receive the same salaries* that they would receive if they were serving in the same grade in the United Kingdom, except that for the youngest officers in the junior grades there is a 'minimum rate' of salary for service overseas. This is payable without annual increments until their own substantive salary overtakes it by the increments which they would have received had they been at home.

All Diplomatic Service officers serving abroad pay United Kingdom rates of income tax on their salaries in the same way as they would if they were serving at home. Salaries are the same for men and women officers.

2. OVERSEAS ALLOWANCES

There are four components or 'layers' which go to make up the allowance paid to members of the Diplomatic Service serving abroad. They are:

(a) *Local Allowances.* This is the basic cost of living allowance which is payable not only to Diplomatic Service officers but also to Home Civil Servants serving overseas; it therefore takes no account of representational responsibilities. It is designed simply to meet the extra cost of maintaining an appropriate non-representational standard of living at the overseas post, having regard to the climate, cost of living and the habits of the local community. It is assessed by Diplomatic Service Inspectors who visit each post and price up four separate objective budgets. The standards applied in these budgets follow a generally agreed pattern, but they are subject to local variations to reflect the local pattern of living—for example, in the employment of servants. The budgets represent the standards of living which single officers and married officers with one dependent child in Grade 5A (First Secretary) and 10 (Clerical Officer) might reasonably be expected to enjoy at the overseas post. The budget provisions reflect only normal 'home' living and cover such items as household utilities (electricity, gas, water etc.), servants (if appropriate), household

* See Appendix A.

goods, household and toilet requisites, food (including meals taken away from home), clothing, recreation, transport (including the running expenses and depreciation of a suitable car), holidays, and other miscellaneous items (e.g. insurance, postage, telephone, newspapers etc.). The standards are those derived from negotiations between the Treasury and the Staff Associations representing Home Civil staff serving overseas, who do not have representational responsibilities. Once the Inspector has completed his pricing of the 'Bottom Band' budget (i.e. that for the Grade 10 officers) he discusses his proposed pricings with members of the staff at the post and may make amendments as a result of these discussions. The totals of the four budgets once they have been priced locally represent the provisions for the four categories of staff concerned. To find the local allowance payable to these categories, from each of the total budget figures is deducted a notional salary contribution, which is found by taking in the case of the Grade 5A officer the mean of the salary scale net of income tax (which means that there are different contributions for married and single officers); and in the case of the Grade 10 officer the salary of a man halfway between the 'minimum rate' of salary and the maximum of the scale, net of income tax. An adjustment is made to this figure to allow for reasonable savings for the four categories of officer, having regard to their annual salary and their commitments as married and single men. The contributions are then deducted from the appropriate budget total, and the difference, rounded to the nearest £5, represents the local allowance for these four categories of staff.

It sometimes happens, where for instance there is little choice for Diplomatic Service officers of all grades as to where they can shop locally, and where the scope for variation in recreational expenditure is very limited, that the very much larger contribution exacted from the Grade 5A officer may result in his rate of local allowance working out at a lower figure than that of a Grade 10 officer of the same marital status. Where this happens the Grade 10 allowance is paid to all staff of that marital status at the post. Where however the Grade 5A allowance (known as the 'Top Band' allowance) is higher than the 'Bottom Band' allowance local allowances for members of intermediate grades are interpolated at equal intervals between Top Band and Bottom Band allowances in three other 'salary bands'. Thus if the Top Band allowance worked out at £1,000 p.a., while the Bottom Band allowances were £800 p.a. the allowances would be:

Top Band (Grades 5A, 5E)   £1,000 p.a.
Band 2 (Grade 6)   £950 p.a.

Band 3 (Grades 7A, 7E)	£900 p.a.
Band 4 (Grades 8 & 9)	£850 p.a.
Bottom Band (Grade 10 and equivalent)	£800 p.a.

It will be noted that an officer's net salary is wholly committed to the reasonable expenditure for which provision is made; but once the rates of allowance are agreed officers are not called upon to account for their expenditure.

(*b*) *Indirect Representational Supplement* (IRS) The next layer is payable only to those officers who are regarded as representational staff (Grade 8, Third Secretary, and above). It is not payable to more junior officers who may be officially involved in a limited amount of return hospitality, but only to those whose duties are by definition wholly representational. It consists of supplements to all those items in the basic budget where these officers' duties give rise to higher expenditure (but the actual cost of the additional and identifiable expenses of giving dinner parties or cocktail parties is provided for separately in their entertainment allowances which are described later). For instance, the standards for electricity consumption in the Top Band budget are those of a non-representational household; but an IRS might well contain additional provision under this heading to take account of the actual and necessary expenditure of an officer who must use more electricity than an officer who has no representational duties to perform and is housed accordingly. When assessing the IRS of any officer who is receiving a Bottom Band rate of allowance (because his true rate of allowance works out at less than this figure) the difference between the true rate of allowance and the Bottom Band is taken into account, and only the balance needed to produce the IRS is paid to the officer.

(*c*) *Entertainment Allowance.* The third layer is the entertainment allowance. This is the readily identifiable part of the cost of giving entertainment at home and away from home to the people with whom Diplomatic Staff are constantly in official contact. Each officer is advised of the number of guests he may reasonably be expected to entertain to cocktails and to meals during a year, and is of course aware of the amount of his entertainment allowance. Further, he is told what is expected to be the average cost of entertaining each guest to a meal at home, to drinks at home, and to meals and drinks in restaurants, so that he can gauge the standards expected of him, although provided the Head of the Post is satisfied that he is adequately performing his representational duties he is not required to stick to the pattern suggested to him. The cost of food, drink, extra servants, and such additional items as candles, and invitation cards etc. where appropriate is included in the entertainment allowance. Officers of Grade 5A and below are required to account for this allowance and may recover from public funds only their actual expenditure within the provision authorized for them. The accounting is however spread right across their service at a post, and under-spending in their first year at the post may be carried forward to their second and subsequent years, while over-spending in one year may be adjusted later.

(d) *Diplomatic Service Allowance* (DSA). This allowance is payable to established members of the Diplomatic Service while they are serving abroad, and is calculated at 15 per cent of the gross mean salary of their scale for married officers and at $7\frac{1}{2}$ per cent of the same figure for unmarried officers. This allowance is intended to assist officers with expenditure on unforeseen contingencies during their service overseas, and on circumstances associated with the peripatetic nature of life in the Diplomatic Service.

3. SUMMARY

All Diplomatic Service officers serving abroad receive Local Allowance (provided of course that the total of the relevant budget at local prices exceeds the rate of contribution) and Diplomatic Service allowance; officers who are required to carry out representational duties also receive Indirect Representational Supplement and Entertainment Allowance.

The allowances of Counsellors (Grade 4, the next above those provided for in the salary bands) are worked out mainly as an extension of the Top Band figures, with the appropriate representational supplement and entertainment allowance added. Counsellors and officers above this grade are not called upon to account for their entertainment expenditure. Heads of Mission (Grades 1–3) and Ministers (Grade 3) who hold high appointments at very large overseas Missions have allowances (in the case of Heads of Mission the allowance is known as a *frais de représentation*) which are tailored more closely to the needs of the residence where appropriate. These officers, however, also receive the relevant rate of Diplomatic Service allowance.

4. CHILDREN'S ALLOWANCES

Provision for the first dependent child resident with an officer at his post is included in the married rate of local allowance. There is no difference in the rate of local allowance payable to married staff with or without dependent children at the post. But for the second and each subsequent dependent child (who must be under the age of nineteen and not gainfully employed in order to qualify) at the overseas post, the officer receives a supplementary allowance; this follows the United Kingdom pattern of assistance for families with two or more children. In addition, if no suitable free schooling is available at the post, the cost of local school fees may be refunded to officers serving abroad whose children are being educated locally.

There are separate arrangements for the refund, within certain limits, of boarding-school fees in respect of children under the age of nineteen who are resident in boarding school in the United Kingdom. There is also provision for a guardian allowance to be paid in respect of children who are left in the United Kingdom in the care of a guardian while they attend day school, provided both the child's parents are resident at the officer's post.

5. ACCOMMODATION

The above allowances contain no reference to rent, because an officer serving overseas is either:

(*a*) Provided officially with furnished accommodation suitable to his rank and requirements, either rented or owned by HM Government; or

(*b*) if this is not available he is refunded a sum equivalent to the expenditure which he incurs, excluding services and other tenants charges (which are provided for in the local allowance) in renting suitable furnished accommodation.

These are the working rules of the allowances system of the British Diplomatic Service, which must take account of the extreme variations produced by fluctuations in cost of living and/or exchange rates. In a country where the currency is stable and the local cost of living does not rise much (it never seems to fall anywhere in the world), allowances may remain unchanged for years. In another country with a rapidly rising cost of living allowances will have to keep pace. If the currency depreciates, the local cost of living, when converted into sterling, may fall, but perhaps only if you deal on the black market, of which the local government disapproves. The British Diplomatic Service insists that this game be played honestly; it does not enter the black market nor allow its personnel to do so. In 1965 a Grade 10 Clerical Officer in X had thus to be paid an allowance of £4,475 to permit a modest but adequate existence. Fortunately for the British taxpayer a legal free market is now in operation in this curious country and the allowance expressed in sterling has been cut to a tenth. The highest allowance now paid to a Grade 10 officer is £1,900.

In comparison with this junior officer at X, the Ambassador at Y, who is Grade 3, receives £1,706, because his post is in a capital where the cost of living and exchange rate are under efficient control. His salary after income tax has been deducted is, however, much higher (about £3,450 as compared with £665 for the Grade 10 officer). Their total net emoluments *in sterling* were therefore: Grade 10 officer at X £5,140 and Grade 3 Ambassador at Y £4,150. Yet the latter was able for this money to run an Embassy Residence in decent style and entertain large numbers of official guests; the junior officer was just able to live modestly abroad though he was receiving in sterling enough to keep a company director happy in Britain.

It is a mad world, but at least the British Diplomatic Service tries to be honest with the host countries. It would be pleasing if one could say the same of all others.

Space does not permit a comparison with the salary and allowance systems of the Diplomatic Services of other powers. In the nature of things the variety is enormous. In the United States Foreign Service initial *salaries* are much higher than the British— $6,451 for a Grade 8 officer, compared with the British scale (converted into dollars) of $2,770 rising to $3,830 after five years' service, but unlike his British colleagues, he receives no allowances when serving at home, which may include an assignment to the United Nations in New York, where representational expenses are high. FAPS 3 notes that this posting is unpopular with the American Service because of the 'devastating' expenses.[5] Moreover US allowances abroad are described as inadequate. Thayer comments: 'The American Diplomat is probably less adequately compensated than his colleagues from any other great power. The discrepancy arises not in the salary scale but in business expenses (i.e. allowances). These are a niggardly fraction of what the British, French and Soviet governments grant their representatives and far below what any private concern maintaining overseas establishments must pay to attract competent employees.'[6] He continues with examples that would alarm any thoughtful housewife accustomed to a settled life in her own country. Thayer does not, however, point to a serious weakness in the French system—allowances (as opposed to salaries) are only paid while the officer is at his post. When after three years he comes home for two to four months' leave, he must try to enjoy his holiday on a very meagre basis indeed.

The only solution is a headquarters in the home country that grasps the problem and takes immense pains to ensure that its employees overseas are as well cared for as in the home environment. There should be no undue lavishness and there must also be a standard of integrity towards the government and inhabitants of the foreign country in which the staff are serving. More harm than the inexperienced would find easy to believe can be caused by inefficiency or misbehaviour in such matters.

Appendix C

METHODS USED BY THE CIVIL
SERVICE SELECTION BOARD

I am greatly indebted to the First Commissioner of the Civil Service
Commission for permission to quote from notes drawn up by his
staff as guidance for the methods used by the Civil Service Selection
Board in testing candidates for Grade A in the Diplomatic Service and
the Administrative Class of the Home Civil Service. These methods
are not static; for up to date information, application should be made
to the Civil Service Commission, 23 Savile Row, London, W.1.
Candidates attaining a high standard in these tests pass to the Final
Selection Board, as I have described in chapter VII, and if successful
enter the Diplomatic Service as officers of Grade 8. Recruitment into
the Executive (Grade 9), Clerical (Grade 10) and Secretarial branches
of the Diplomatic Service is not covered in the following notes. The
method of selection for them is summarized in chapter VII. An outline
of American examination methods is given in FAPS 6, chapter 4. Fuller
information can be obtained from the Department of State, Washington, D.C.

☆

The permanent Directing Staff is of four only and two of them are
not fully permanent in the sense of being likely to provide continuity
over a period of years. The great bulk of the actual work of the Board
must be done by part-time assessors, of whom at present there are
some sixty, doing each year a number of Boards varying from over
twenty to three or four. For all competitions candidates are at present
tested in groups of five, for three days, with the third day for conferences and the writing of reports. Usually there are three groups
being tested concurrently—each with its own Directing Staff—but
with increasing numbers of candidates there will be often four groups

at once, adding to the constant problem of maintaining consistency of standards amongst groups and amongst intakes. For the Diplomatic Service there are three members of the Directing Staff to each group— Chairman, Observer and Psychologist. The Chairman may be a senior public servant, serving or retired, or occasionally a senior member of a university or headmaster of a school. The Observer is usually a serving officer in the Diplomatic Service. The Psychologist is of professional or equivalent status.

1. PRE-BOARD INFORMATION AVAILABLE TO THE DIRECTING STAFF

(*a*) An outline of the candidate's career, together with referees' reports covering his record at school and university, and, where appropriate, in the armed forces and civilian employment; personal references from two referees of the candidate's choice.

(*b*) The marks obtained in the written qualifying examination and the examiners' brief comments. The candidates' scripts are also reported on as a whole, as an independent check, by the Examinations Directorate in the Civil Service Commission. This 'Script Reader's Report' is of great value. The scripts themselves are available though they rarely need to be consulted. Examiners and Script Readers know of candidates only by numbers, not by names.

2. FURTHER INFORMATION

Each candidate at a Civil Service Selection Board (CSSB) completes Form A (Additional Information) in which, among other things, he gives his spare-time interests and offers two or three topics which he will be prepared to discuss at interview (these are shared between the Chairman and the Observer). Another source of information particularly, perhaps, for the Psychologist, is Form B (Supplementary Questions) in which candidates answer questions, for example, on factors that have influenced their career.

3. THE MAIN SELECTION BOARD TESTS

The tests fall into three groups:

(*i*) '*Analogous*' *and other Practical Exercises*. The analogous exercises, of which there are three, are so called because they bear some analogy to the kind of work which the successful candidate will have to do in the Public Service. They are based on a lengthy dossier describing an administrative problem which, although imaginary, has a substantial basis in fact. (This dossier, which takes some months to prepare, serves throughout a calendar year.)

In the first of these exercises, the candidates have about $2\frac{1}{4}$ hours in which to study the dossier and to write an answer (known as the Written Appreciation) to a question of policy bearing on the situation.

The second exercise is performed in the presence of the three Directing Staff. Each group of five candidates forms a committee to study a number of policy problems related to the central theme. Each candidate is allotted a problem beforehand and has about half-an-hour to decide how to tackle it. Each in turn then takes the chair for fifteen minutes to expound his problem and to guide his committee to a solution. Equally important is his role as a member of the committee, considering and discussing the problem with his fellow candidates. This Committee Exercise provides evidence of intellectual quality, practical ability and judgement, and of effectiveness in dealing with others in discussion and argument.

The third analogous exercise tests ability to draft memoranda clearly and tactfully. This drafting Exercise lasts not less than fifty minutes.

There is also a Group Discussion at which each group is asked to discuss informally among themselves one or two topics of current importance. This takes place on the first day and acts as an 'ice-breaker' as well as providing the Directing Staff with their first impression of the candidates in a group.

(*ii*) *Psychological Tests.* The tests grouped under this heading are, with one exception, cognitive tests designed to measure various aspects of intellectual ability. There are two short Intelligence Tests which provide some evidence of basic mental ability, though they assume a considerable educational sophistication and facility in language. Follow-up investigations have shown that the results of these tests have at least more relation to success on the job than have tests which are more purely tests of innate cognitive ability. There is, however, a further Intelligence Test which is not dependent on verbal skills and is also relatively unhurried; this may be used as a further check on a candidate who may not have done himself justice in the verbal Intelligence Tests. For the time being this test, in addition to the others, is given only to candidates reading scientific subjects and irrespective of their score in the ordinary Intelligence Tests. The result of such tests (as of every other single test or interview) is never of itself an indication of success or failure, but it does often help to interpret other parts of the performance—particularly with the (very few) candidates with really low scores in intelligence tests who are, on other evidence, on the borderline for acceptance.

Apart from the Intelligence Tests, there is a Statistical Inferences

Test which gives an indication of a candidate's ability to think numerically, and an exercise testing the range—but not the depth—of his
general information about current affairs, not too narrowly interpreted.

The non-cognitive test in the group is the Self-Description Test, in
which candidates are asked to write short descriptions of themselves
from a friendly and a critical point of view.

A Common Room is provided in which all candidates can relax,
and arrangements permit them to have meals together in the canteen
if they wish. There are thus opportunities to meet and, at the end of
the Board, each candidate is asked to select, by secret ballot, from his
fellows the first two he would place in order of preference as civil
servants and, separately, as holiday companions. This 'mutual ranking'
provides some evidence about the impact of each candidate upon his
contemporaries (as distinct from his impact on the Directing Staff)
and about the ability of candidates to size up their fellows. It is a
minor, but occasionally helpful part of the procedure. The reports
seek to paint a picture of the candidate, to estimate his prospects in
the public service, and to indicate the type of work he is likely to do
best. A report might thus recommend that a candidate was unlikely
to be suitable for the Diplomatic Service, but could do well in a
branch of the Home Civil Service. Preceding the reports is a summary
of the candidate's performance in the CSSB tests and exercises. This is
written by the Observer but is a Board summary. The Chairman,
before writing his reports, has those of the Observer and the Psychologist before him. He co-ordinates their views while also expressing his
own and summing up. In addition, the CSSB gives the Final Selection
Board a summary sheet (with the candidate's curriculum vitae, choice
of service and department, Written Examination marks and CSSB
mark) and the Referees' Reports.

From the CSSB over 70 per cent of candidates pass upwards for
consideration by the Final Selection Board. Over 30 per cent of the
total entry opting for the Diplomatic Service are accepted.

(iii) Interviews. Although the CSSB procedure owed its origins to the
unreliability of ordinary interviewing, the Interview remains a central
part of the procedure. In the context of so much other—and relatively
more objective—evidence, the reliability of interviews may be greater
than is normally the case. Each of a candidate's three interviews lasts
some forty minutes. The special 'fields' to be covered depend partly
on the background and experience of the assessors themselves. Too
much overlap is guarded against, but there must be some. The Observer
is mainly, though not exclusively, concerned with the quality of the

candidate's mind; the Psychologist with temperament and personality; the Chairman has a more general brief but pays special attention to how a candidate has spent his time since leaving school, to his leisure pursuits and to his reasons for seeking a career in the Public Service.

4. DIRECT STAFFING CONFERENCES
The Directing Staff exchange information and views about candidates informally at any stage, and formally at the conferences after the marking of the Written Appreciation, after the Group Discussion (when a mark based on first impressions may be revised on closer acquaintance) and after the Committee Exercise (where a separate mark is given for performance in the chair and as a member of the committee). There may be a short conference before testing proper starts to settle tactics, and a session before the last of the interviews. At the Final Conference, taking one candidate at a time, each member, in the order Observer—Psychologist—Chairman, gives a provisional mark. Each then gives his reasons for the mark. Each member is expected to give an assessment of the candidate's strengths and weaknesses, on the evidence both of performance and record, and more particularly of performance in interview. Where there is a substantial difference of opinion, further discussion takes place and the evidence is considered afresh. This may lead either to an agreed verdict or to an 'agreement to differ' which will be brought out in the reports. As a general rule there is not a wide gulf between the opinions and thus the marks of individual members. The Chairman is responsible for seeing that the Board mark represents the balance of opinion, and that non-CSSB evidence is fully considered.

5. REPORTS
Each member of the Directing Staff writes a brief report on each candidate. This produces less overlap than might be expected, since each member has his own line of approach, and the Final Conference gives him an idea of the line that his colleagues will take. The reports seek to paint a picture of the candidate, to estimate his prospects in the Public Service, and to indicate the type of work he is likely to do best. Thus, they may well recommend that a candidate is unlikely to be suitable for the Diplomatic Service, but could do well in a branch of the Home Civil Service. Preceding the reports is a summary of the candidate's performance in the CSSB tests and exercises. This is written by the Observer but is a Board summary. The Chairman, before writing his reports, has those of the Observer and Psychologist before him. He co-ordinates their views while also expressing his own and

summing up. In addition, CSSB gives the Final Selection Board a summary sheet—with the candidate's curriculum vitae, choice of Service and Department, Written Examination marks and CSSB mark—and the Referees' Reports.

From the CSSB over 70 per cent of candidates pass upwards for consideration by the Final Selection Board.

SELECT BIBLIOGRAPHY

Sources are listed in alphabetical order under the 'short titles' by which they are referred to in the text or in the References. Authors—many very valuable—writing before 1914 are not included here, but some are referred to in the text. Full bibliographical details of works not cited here can be found at their first noting in the References.

ASHTON-GWATKIN
The British Foreign Service, by Frank Ashton-Gwatkin; Syracuse University Press, New York 1950.
    The organization of the Foreign Office as it was in the immediate post-war period is included. The book is particularly valuable for the background it gives to the Eden–Bevin reforms of 1943, of which the author was one of the principal initiators. He also makes a strong plea for more efficient economic representation in the Service.

BARNETT
The Representation of the United States Abroad, edited by Vincent M. Barnett Jr; Praeger, New York and London 1965.
    A revised and up-to-date edition of the original work, first published in 1956. The whole field of United States representation abroad, including non-combatant military, is covered in depth by several specialists. It is required reading for the student of the American diplomatic organization.

BRIGGS
Farewell to Foggy Bottom, by Ellis Briggs; McKay, New York 1964.
    'Foggy Bottom' is the name given by iconoclasts in the United States Foreign Service and cognoscenti outside it to the level of

ground by the Potomac where the vast new State Department building was erected. These reflections of a recently retired American Ambassador are pungent and profound. The Foreword is by the late and greatly mourned Christian Herter, *quondam* Secretary of State. Briggs also testified before the Jackson Committee (*v. infra*).

DSR
British Diplomatic Service Regulations.
Though unclassified, these are not published by the Foreign Office. Access to them may be gained by application to the Diplomatic Service Administration Office, London. They provide much detailed information in a commendably brief form (less than 100 pages).

CMND, CMD, CD
These letters are an abbreviation of 'Command', itself the short title for official papers presented to Parliament by command of Her Majesty the Queen. The abbreviation is followed by a number. Command papers can be obtained from Her Majesty's Stationery Office, London.
CMND applies to official papers published since 1957, CMD to those published between 1919 and 1956, and CD to those before 1918.

ESTIMATES COMMITTEE
Sixth Report from the Estimates Committee, Session 1964–65: Recruitment of the Civil Service; printed for the House of Commons, August 3, 1965, HMSO London.
As this volume contains the verbatim evidence taken before the subcommittee, it is lengthy. It deals primarily with the Home Civil Service, but much in it is also applicable to methods of recruitment and selection for the Diplomatic Service. The Introduction is particularly relevant.

FAPS 1–6
Foreign Affairs Personnel Studies; Carnegie Endowment for International Peace, New York 1965–66.
All have a foreword by the late Christian Herter and a preface by Joseph E. Johnson, President of the Endowment. Each of the first five volumes has a different introduction by the general editor, Frederick Mosher.

1. *The Evolution of Personnel Systems for United States Foreign Affairs,* by Arthur Jones;
2. *Overseas Representation and Services for Federal Domestic Agencies,* by Robert Elder;

276

3. *The Development of Careers in the Foreign Service,* by John Harr;
4. *The Anatomy of the Foreign Service: A Statistical Profile,* by John Harr;
5. *Orientations and Behavioral Styles of Foreign Service Officers,* by Regis Walther;
6. *The Quest for Foreign Affairs Officers: Their Recruitment and Selection,* by Frances Fielder and Godfrey Harris.

These monographs are thorough and valuable, particularly to specialists. It is much to be hoped that the Carnegie Endowment will continue the series with comparative studies of non-American Diplomatic Services. Each Service can undoubtedly learn from others. No. 6 is not printed like the rest of the series, but made available to students in 'multilithed' form.

HAYTER
The Diplomacy of the Great Powers, by Sir William Hayter; Hamish Hamilton, London 1960; Macmillan, New York 1961.

The author, *quondam* British Ambassador in Moscow and now Warden of New College, Oxford, treats in this brief and excellent essay of the arts of diplomacy, based on his experience as a member of the British Diplomatic Service in China, the USSR and the USA, and in the Foreign Office in London. He touches only incidentally on the mechanics of diplomacy, but is invaluable—as are Nicolson and Thayer —where national divergencies are concerned.

HEATLEY
Diplomacy and the Study of International Relations, by D. P. Heatley; Oxford University Press, Oxford 1919.

Though considerably earlier in date than the other works listed in this bibliography, this scholarly study deals with the eternal verities of diplomacy and is unlikely to be surpassed. For the present purposes, the first 75 pages on Diplomacy and the Conduct of Foreign Policy are still an excellent guide.

JACKSON
The Secretary of State and the Ambassador, by Henry M. Jackson; Praeger, New York and London 1964.

Senator Jackson presides over the Senate Subcommittee on National Security Staffing and Operations. Apart from the Analysis and Findings, there are selected comments in essay form by several eminent authorities. Pages 62–88 on the American Ambassador are essential reading for those interested in any Diplomatic Service.

KELLY

The Ruling Few: The Human Background to Diplomacy, by Sir David Kelly;
Hollis and Carter, London 1952.

A book of diplomatic reminiscences, it is included here because of
the brief prologue, in which the author sets out the conclusions
reached after thirty years' service in four continents.

NICOLSON

I *Curzon: The Last Phase,* by Sir Harold Nicolson; Constable, London
1934.

This deals with Curzon's career, primarily as Secretary of State for
Foreign Affairs from 1919 to 1925. For the purposes of the present
book, the interest lies in the "Terminal Essay" added as an appendix
(pages 383–408). This sets out some of the author's ideas in regard to
foreign policy, diplomacy and the arts of negotiation. The problems
facing diplomacy have not altered to an extent that invalidates the
conclusions earlier reached by Nicolson, despite the violent progression
of the world during recent years. It is a pity that this essay is not
separately and cheaply available in the many lands where it could be
read with profit.

II *Diplomacy,* by Sir Harold Nicolson; Oxford University Press,
London and New York, 2nd edn 1950.

Another volume that is required reading. Though now out of date
as regards organization, it is admirable in its general precepts and in its
concise readability.

PLOWDEN

*Report of the Committee on Representational Services Overseas appointed by
the Prime Minister under the Chairmanship of Lord Plowden,* 1962–63;
presented to Parliament February 1964; HMSO, London 1964, Cmnd
2276.

The new charter of the integrated British Diplomatic Service. It is
essential reading and therefore frequently quoted in this book.

A similar Committee was set up in 1966 under Lord Fulton to examine
the Home Civil Service. This had been recommended by the Estimates
Committee (*v. supra*).

QUARONI

Diplomatic Bags, by Pietro Quaroni; Weidenfeld and Nicolson, London
1966.

Reminiscences of a distinguished Italian Ambassador of the personages he encountered during a long career. Like Kelly (*v. supra*) this book is included here because of the brief introduction, but the whole is valuable. To find its like in its penetrating analysis of statesmen and of national characteristics, one must go back to d'Abernon's memoirs of forty years earlier.

SATOW
Guide to Diplomatic Practice, by the late Sir Ernest Satow; edited by Sir Nevile Bland; Longmans, London and New York 1957.
The standard encyclopedia; an invaluable work of reference, recently brought up to date.

SEN
A Diplomat's Handbook of International Law and Practice, by B. Sen; Nijhoff, The Hague, 1965.
With a foreword by Sir Gerald Fitzmaurice, *quondam* Legal Adviser in the Foreign Office and now of the International Court, this book deserves a place on the shelf next to Satow. It is particularly valuable for the exposition of the views on diplomatic practice held by newer as well as old-established states.

STRANG
The Foreign Office, by Lord Strang; Allen and Unwin, London 1955; Oxford University Press, New York 1955.
This deals not only with the Foreign Office but with the work of the Service overseas. It is inevitably a little out of date since the Plowden reforms. Pages 167–81 are valuable for diplomatic practice.

THAYER
Diplomat, by Charles Thayer; Harper, New York 1959; also published in London by Michael Joseph, but now out of print. References are therefore to the pagination of the American edition.
Like Briggs (*v. supra*), this is an entertaining and percipient review by an experienced student of the foibles, strengths and weaknesses of diplomacy.

TWFM
This worked for me. . . . produced by the Department of State, Washington, D.C., 1964, with an introduction by William Crockett, Deputy Under Secretary for Administration.
An anthology of views, often conflicting, by anonymous American Ambassadors, it covers the duties, techniques and mechanics of diplomacy overseas. It is explicitly stated in the foreword that this is not a

manual, but merely an indication of how different Heads of Mission have seen and coped with their difficulties and helped their staffs in many parts of the world. The vast scale and scope of United States Embassies and Consulates is brought out. The whole creates a favourable impression of the devotion of the contributors and gives an instructive insight into American thinking.

WATT

Personalities and Politics, by D. C. Watt; Longmans, London 1965; University of Notre Dame Press, Notre Dame, Ind., 1965.

The subtitle, "Studies in the Formulation of British Foreign Policy in the Twentieth Century", indicates the matter of this outstanding book. It is largely devoted to the composition and influence of the British policy-making elite against various backgrounds. Particularly relevant are Essay 10 on entry and training and Essay 11 on security procedures. The book concludes with a comprehensive bibliography, covering works in many languages—immensely valuable to the student.

REFERENCES

For full title and publication details of abbreviated source references, see Select Bibliography.

Foreword

1. Barnett, excerpts from pp. 3–12.
2. Ashton-Gwatkin gives a concise history of the Foreign Office, pp. 8–15.
3. FAPS 3, Intro. by Frederick Mosher, pp. xviii–xix.
4. Briggs, p. 175.

I. A Dictionary with Digressions

1. See, e.g., Heatley, pp. 26, 27.
2. Strang, p. 170.
3. Ashton-Gwatkin, p. 4.
4. For a scholarly appreciation of American diplomacy, see Ilchman, W. F., *Professional Diplomacy in the United States, 1774–1939*, University of Chicago Press, Chicago 1961.
5. Thayer, pp. 64–80.
6. *Vienna Convention on Diplomatic Relations*, HMSO, London 1961.
7. Thayer, pp. 201–12.
8. Gowers, Sir Ernest, *Modern English Usage*, Oxford University Press, London and New York 1965.

II. The Head of Mission

1. See Barnett, pp. 226–51, and Jackson, esp. pp. 62–9, 142–54.
2. DSR, p. 37.
3. See, e.g., Jackson, p. 86, and Briggs, pp. 126–32, 151–2.
4. Plowden, §174.
5. Barnett, pp. 224–51.
6. *Ibid.*, p. 11.
7. Jackson, p. 21, also pp. 80–3.
8. *Ibid.*, p. 18.
9. TWFM, pp. 96–9.
10. D'Abernon, Lord, *An Ambassador for Peace*, Hodder and Stoughton, London 1929; contains extracts from his

The Head of Mission—continued

diaries that are not only valuable for the historian but reveal the diplomatic method of an expert.

11. Quaroni, p. x.
12. TWFM, pp. 15, 30.
13. Nicolson II, p. 50.
14. Nicolson I, p. 401.
15. TWFM, pp. 1–4.
16. Jackson, p. 73.
17. Barnett, p. 62.

18. Jackson, p. 74.
19. Kelly, pp. 1–2.
20. *Ibid.*, p. 129.
21. Thayer, p. 125.
22. Jackson, p. 76.
23. *Ibid.*, p. 45.
24. TWFM, pp. 77–80.
25. *Cf. ibid.*, p. 66.
26. *Ibid.*, p. 103.
27. *Ibid.*, p. 127.
28. *Ibid.*, pp. 81–4.

III. The Structure of a Mission

1. *The Chancery*

1. Strang deals with work in an Embassy, pp. 97–122.
2. Plowden, §215.
3. TWFM, pp. 33–7.
4. Mallaby, Sir George, *Unwritten Minutes,* Hutchinson, London 1965, p. 215.
5. Ashton-Gwatkin, p. 15.
6. See, e.g., TWFM, pp. 116–17.
7. FAPS 3, p. 18.
8. TWFM, p. 27.
9. Plowden, §71.
10. *Cf.* TWFM, pp. 121–4.

2. *The Commercial Section*

11. Barnett, pp. 47–74.
12. *Ibid.*, p. 228.
13. See FAPS 4, pp. 84, 85.
14. Kelly, p. 10.

3. *The Information Section*

15. Barnett, pp. 36–9, 75–128.
16. Plowden, §§260–3.
17. Thayer, pp. 195–9.
18. Barnett, p. 125; see also p. 114 for a general survey.
19. Beloff, Max, in *International Affairs,* Royal Institute of International Affairs, London, July 1965, p. 479.
20. Watt, p. 12.
21. Thayer, p. 70.
22. TWFM, p. 106; see also in general the four succeeding pages.
23. Plowden, §266.
24. *Ibid.*, §273.

4. *The Mission and Aid Projects*

25. "Overseas Development: The Work of the New Ministry", HMSO, London 1965, Cmnd 2736. (After *Craft of Diplomacy* went to press, another White Paper was published on this subject—Cmnd 3180, 1967. It is not referred to in the text.)
26. For relations between the United States Foreign Service and AID, see FAPS 2, esp. Appendix C.
27. *The Times,* April 26, 1966.
28. Levitt, Malcolm, in *Moorgate and Wall Street Review,* London

The Structure of a Mission—continued

and New York, Autumn 1966, p. 87 *ff.*

29. Thompson, Sir Robert, *Defeating Communist Insurgency,* Chatto and Windus, London 1966, p. 81.
30. See FAPS 4, p. 1.
31. *The Times,* September 16, 1966.
32. Luethy, Herbert, *Encounter,* London, December 1965; see also *The Times,* April 14, 1966: one of four articles by a special correspondent, "Economic Anarchy at All Levels".
33. Plowden, §307.
34. Jackson, p. 82.
35. Thayer, p. 183.
36. On the Peace Corps, see Barnett, pp. 67–70.
37. FAPS 6, ch. 1.
38. Briggs, p. 16.
39. Barnett, p. 137.

5. Service Attachés

40. See FAPS 2.
41. Barnett, pp. 129–83; Service

Attachés are specifically dealt with in pp. 155–60.

42. *Ibid.,* p. 159.
43. Plowden, §390.
44. *Ibid.,* §93.
45. Barnett, pp. 168–76.
46. Plowden, §394.
47. Jackson, pp. 28–9; also p. 82.
48. Plowden, §396.
49. Barnett, pp. 155, 157.
50. Plowden, §399.
51. Barnett, p. 178.
52. Zuckert, Eugene, "The Service Secretary", *Foreign Affairs,* Washington D.C., April 1966, pp. 458–79.

6. Seconded Officers

53. See Plowden, Annexe P, for useful notes on the departmental origins of Seconded Officers.
54. Barnett, p. 12.
55. Plowden, §273.
56. *Ibid.,* §61.
57. Briggs, p. 164.

IV. CONSULAR OFFICERS

1. See Strang on Consular Officers' work, pp. 123–36.
2. Plowden, §293.
3. *Ibid.,* §281.
4. See, e.g., TWFM, pp. 38–46.
5. For a brief summary of Walter

Plowden's career, see Busk, Douglas, *The Fountain of the Sun,* Max Parrish, London 1957, p. 85 *ff.*

6. *Ibid.,* p. 102.
7. Plowden, §291.

V. SECURITY

1. Watt, pp. 199–207.
2. *Security Procedure in the Public Service* (Radcliffe Report), HMSO, Cmnd 1681, London

1962.

3. *Encounter,* London, June 1953, p. 83.
4. Watt, p. 198.

VI. The Indispensable Auxiliaries

1. *The Inspectorate*

1. For comments on the work of US Foreign Service Inspection Corps, see FAPS 3, pp. 57–9.

2. *Diplomatic Messengers*

2. For fuller information, see Wheeler-Holohan, V., *The History of the King's Messengers,* Grayson and Grayson, London 1935. I have drawn on this for the years up to 1815.
3. Temperley, Harold, *The Crimea,* Longmans, London 1936, p. 476.
4. Ossendowski, Ferdinand, *Beasts, Men and Gods,* Arnold, London 1923, p. 110.
5. Linklater, Eric, *A Year of Space,* Macmillan, London 1953, p. 46.

3. *Cultural Representation*

6. Barnett, pp. 93–106.
7. Nicolson, Harold, in *British Council Report 1954–55,* published by the British Council, Davies St, London W.1; brought up to date in the *B.C. Report 1963–64,* which quotes some illuminating statements by staff abroad on the wide variety of Council work.
8. For a development of this important theme, see Busk, Douglas, *The Curse of Tongues,* Pall Mall Press, London 1965.
9. For further details of British Council libraries, see *B.C. Report 1964–65.*
10. Barnett, p. 101.
11. *Cf.* TWFM, pp. 86–95.
12. Beloff, *op. cit.*
13. Hayter, p. 51.

VII. Personnel, Recruitment and Deployment

1. *Recruitment and Selection*

1. See FAPS 4 and 6.
2. For conflicting views on selection and recruitment, see Estimates Committee *passim* and particularly the Introduction.
3. FAPS 6, chs. 2 and 3, sets out the difficulties.
4. Nicolson II, pp. 202–20.
5. FAPS 6, ch. 2 (Government Service in general), ch. 3 (Foreign Service).
6. See FAPS 6, p. 1.
7. *Ibid.,* 4 *passim.*
8. Plowden, §§344–80.
9. See FAPS 6, ch. 4.
10. Plowden, §354.
11. For quotations from earlier students of the problem, see Heatley, p. 216 *ff.*
12. Watt, p. 184.
13. Nicolson II, pp. 104–26; an essay as brief as it is valuable. For other views on the subject, see Strang, pp. 182–94, and Ashton-Gwatkin, pp. 62–65.
14. Hayter, pp. 43–5.
15. For description of these questions, see FAPS 5.
16. *Ibid.,* p. 34.
17. *Ibid.,* p. 43.
18. DSR, p. 10.
19. Plowden, §123.

Personnel, Recruitment and Deployment—continued

2. *Training*
20. Plowden, §356.
21. Estimates Committee, §758.
22. Plowden, §§401–40.
23. Watt, p. 4.
24. For a summary of the State Department's Career Development Program, see FAPS 3, pp. 79–98; and for the Promotion System, *ibid.*, pp. 55–78.
25. Jackson, pp. 54–6.
26. TWFM, pp. 47–51.
27. Busk, *Curse, op. cit.*, discusses methods of learning languages.
28. See FAPS 4, pp. 24–6.
29. Plowden, §178.
30. See Busk, *op cit.*, pp. 56–61.

31. Details of the language allowances are set out in DSR, p. 65 *ff.*
32. Nicolson I, p. 407.
33. Nicolson II, p. 225.
34. Plowden, §436.
35. *The Times,* October 24, 1966.
36. Kolle, *Betrachtungen über die Diplomatie,* cited in Heatley, p. 38.
37. Watt, p. 198.
38. Jackson, p. 82.

3. *Welfare*
39. See, e.g., TWFM, pp. 111–13.
40. Thayer, p. 117.
41. TWFM, p. 129.
42. *Ibid.,* pp. 81–94.
43. Plowden, §124.

VIII. Retrospect and Prospect

1. See Briggs, chs. 7 and 8; FAPS 3, pp. 50–1.
2. See DSR, p. 35.
3. Strang, p. 30 *ff.*
4. Jackson, p. 138.
5. See Nicolson II, Briggs and Thayer *passim.*
6. Hayter, p. 67.
7. Thayer, p. 47.
8. *Ibid.,* p. 107.
9. Nicolson I, pp. 382–408.
10. Jackson, p. 158.
11. See Nicolson I and II, also Briggs and Thayer *passim.*
12. Plowden, §380.
13. *Ibid.,* §34.
14. See Ashton-Gwatkin and Jackson *passim.*
15. FAPS 3, p. 44.
16. Barnett, p. 189.
17. *Ibid.,* pp. 184–213.
18. Strang, pp. 137–45.
19. Jackson, p. 72.
20. Kelly, p. 51
21. Plowden, p. 51.
22. For a percipient study of divided control in British foreign policy, see Watt, p. 177 *ff.*
23. Plowden, §44.
24. Briggs, p. 168
25. Quaroni, p. 142.

IX. Envoi

1. General Lauris Norstad, quoted by Jackson, p. 75.
2. DSR, p. 2
3. Heatley, pp. 48–50.

Appendices

1. Plowden, §§100–4.

2. Barnett, p. 19; see also FAPS 1, pp. 31, 50, 58, 68, 106; FAPS 2, p. 9.

3. Briggs, p. 168 *ff*.

4. DSR, pp. 48, 55, 59, 63, 86

5. FAPS 3, p. 42

6. Thayer, p. 220

INDEX